MYCENAEANS

The Mycenaean World was the world of the heroes who conquered Troy. Those heroes stood at the heart of Greek self-perception for centuries after the fall of their civilization. Since the rediscovery of the remains of the civilization of Mycenae by Heinrich Schliemann in the 1870s, knowledge of these Greeks of the bronze age has increased steadily. Stepping into the place of the collapsed civilization of Minoan Crete and the Peloponnese (the subject of Castleden's earlier bestselling study, *Minoans*), the Mycenaeans dominated mainland Greece and the Greek islands from about 1600 to 1200 BC. Their exploits became the subject of the legends that were immortalized by Homer.

In lively prose informed by the latest research, Castleden lays out the fundamental traits of Mycenaean civilization, its hierarchy, economy, religion and arts. Castleden transforms our perspective of Mycenaean religion by his reinterpretation of the familiar 'palaces' of Mycenae, Tiryns, Pylos and elsewhere, as temples. Their sea-empire and their relations with other peoples of the bronze age world, including the Hittites, the Egyptians and the Trojans, receive full attention. The causes of the end of their civilization are discussed.

The book is an indispensable starting point for the study of the Greek bronze age. Full bibliography and copious illustration support this comprehensive interpretation of a civilization whose legend still lives on.

Rodney Castleden has written over one hundred articles on history, prehistory and geography. Among his books are *The Stonehenge People*, *The Making of Stonehenge*, *The Knossos Labyrinth*, *Atlantis Destroyed* and *Minoans*.

By the same author:

Classic Landforms of the Sussex Coast
(1982; second edition 1996)

The Wilmington Giant
The quest for a lost myth (1983)

The Stonehenge People
*An exploration of life in neolithic Britain,
4700–2000 BC* (1987)

The Knossos Labyrinth
A new view of the 'Palace of Minos' at Knossos (1989)

Minoans
Life in Bronze Age Crete (1990)

Book of British Dates
*A comprehensive chronological dictionary of British dates
from prehistoric times to the present day* (1991)

Neolithic Britain
New Stone Age sites of England, Scotland and Wales (1992)

The making of Stonehenge (1993)

World History
A chronological dictionary of dates (1994)

The Cerne Giant (1996)

Knossos, Temple of the Goddess (1996)

The English Lake District (1998)

Out in the Cold
Ideas on glaciation (1998)

Atlantis destroyed (1998)

The Little Book of Kings and Queens of Britain (1999)

Ancient British Hill Figures (1999)

King Arthur
The truth behind the legend (2000)

The History of World Events (2003)

Britain 3000 BC (2003)

Infamous Murderers (2004)

Serial Killers (2004)

MYCENAEANS

Rodney Castleden

LONDON AND NEW YORK

First published 2005
by Routledge
2 Park Square, Milton Park, Abingdon, Oxon OX14 4RN

Simultaneously published in the USA and Canada
by Routledge
270 Madison Ave, New York, NY 10016

Routledge is an imprint of the Taylor & Francis Group

© 2005 Rodney Castleden

Typeset in Garamond by
Florence Production Ltd, Stoodleigh, Devon
Printed and bound in Great Britain by
MPG Books Ltd, Bodmin, Cornwall

British Library Cataloguing in Publication Data
A catalogue record for this book is available from
the British Library

Library of Congress Cataloging in Publication Data
Castleden, Rodney.
Mycenaeans / Rodney Castleden.
Includes bibliographical references and index.
1. Civilization, Mycenaean. I. Title.
DF220.5.C38 2005
938'.8-dc22   2004019550

ISBN 0–415–24923–6 (hbk)
ISBN 0–415–36336–5 (pbk)

CONTENTS

ILLUSTRATIONS

FIGURES

PLATES

ACKNOWLEDGEMENTS
AND PREFACE

I am grateful to the writers of several reviews of my earlier book, *Minoans*; their favourable comments encouraged me to think that it might be useful to follow it with a sequel about the Minoans' admirers and imitators, their heirs and successors, the Mycenaeans. The thoughts and observations of correspondents have helped to shape my thoughts about the Aegean and the likely scope of this book which, in its final form, incorporates rather more than just an account of the Mycenaeans. The three earlier books in this Aegean sequence – *The Knossos Labyrinth*, *Minoans* and *Atlantis Destroyed* – may be read on their own. Themes from the earlier books seem to reach a natural culmination in this book. One stern critic of *Minoans* accused me of trying to lure readers into reading *The Knossos Labyrinth*, as if this was a low trick. Obviously I *would* like readers to turn to the earlier books, but in terms of their main ideas the individual books are self-sufficient.

Thanks are due to my colleague, the classicist Maya Davis, for helping me to understand some points in Homer.

I have especially to thank Sinclair Hood for his patience through an amicable and constructive correspondence in arguing the traditional case for the Minoan megastructures as palaces. His arguments and examples forced me to think much harder about the evidence not just from Knossos but from the Aegean region as a whole. In the early stages of this project I was ready to reconsider – even recant – and to accept that the mainland mega-structures (though not the Cretan ones) functioned as palaces rather than temples. The evidence from the Mycenaean buildings nevertheless does not allow me to do this; it points squarely to their use as temples. The challenge from Sinclair Hood, and other scholars who have dismissed the temple interpretation, has if anything had the effect of strengthening my arguments in favour of temples. I am very aware that those arguments will have to withstand a beating from my critics.

I should like to thank John and Celia Clarke for their hospitality during my reading weeks in Oxford. I also have to thank the staff at the Sackler Library in Oxford; the Society of Authors as the Literary Representative of the Estate of Laurence Binyon for permission to quote lines from Laurence

Binyon's poem *For the Fallen (September, 1914)*; the British Museum Company for permission to develop into line drawings two photographic images in the book *Making Faces* (Prag and Neave 1997).

1

INTRODUCTION

Odysseus, Achilles, Ajax, Agamemnon, Menelaus, Helen of Troy – their names resonate through history, legend and literature like the plucked strings of an ancient lyre. When he wrote their stories in the *Iliad* and the *Odyssey*, Homer called them Achaeans, Danaans or Argives. When we write about the historical or archaeological reality that lies behind them we call them Mycenaeans – but that name is a modern invention. Some Mycenaeans, such as Agamemnon, came from the city of Mycenae and were therefore Mycenaeans in both ancient and modern senses of the word, but others came from other bronze age cities. Menelaus came from Lakedaimon in Laconia, Nestor from Pylos in Messenia and Odysseus from Polis in Ithaca.[1]

Homer, writing in the eighth century BC, left us tantalizing epic poems that provide a vivid image of bronze age Greece, the Greece of five or eight hundred years before, in a mix of bronze age proto-history and fictional embellishment that is very hard to disentangle. The ancient Greeks of the classical period were themselves divided about Homer. Some accepted the Homeric epics as history. Others distrusted them as sources. Thucydides, who cast a critical eye on any account of past ages, accepted that there had been a pan-Achaean expedition against Troy, but thought Homer had exaggerated its scale and importance. The later Greeks connected the final destruction of the Mycenaean centres with the invasion of the Dorians, a wave of imagined migrants. In Greek legend, the Dorians are described as the descendants of Heracles, and the invasion itself as 'the Return of the Heraclidae'. Hyllos, the son of Heracles, was defeated and killed in battle against Atreus, king of Mycenae; the Heraclidae were forbidden by the Delphic oracle to return to Greece for a hundred years. Modern scholars dispute this account, but the legend of the Dorian invasion played a major role in later, classical Greek consciousness. Athens represented itself as the only city to have held out against the Dorians and so to have become a stepping-stone for Ionian (pre-Dorian) migration across to Anatolia. The traditional division between the 'Dorians' of the south, such as the Spartans, and the 'Ionians' of the north, such as the Athenians, reinforced and seemed to justify on ethnic grounds the frictions that resulted in the debilitating Peloponnesian War. Ancient perceptions of the Mycenaean civilization and its aftermath were to be profound influences on later events. Although the Mycenaeans are long dead, the achievements and ideals attributed to them lived on to become vital forces in later centuries.

The Mycenaean heroes of Homer and the events surrounding them were generally accepted as historical until modern times. Ironically, it was not until the nineteenth century that scholars began to question Homer's historicity, and it became orthodox to dismiss as legend everything that might have happened before the founding of the Olympic Games in 776 BC.[2]

It was in the midst of this nineteenth-century climate of scepticism that Heinrich Schliemann set out to prove the historical accuracy of the *Iliad* by identifying the places described by Homer. His first major achievement was to uncover the site of Troy, which most scholars believe he did at Hisarlik in north-west Anatolia, though he misidentified the archaeological layer. He had the English archaeologist Frank Calvert to thank for guiding him to Hisarlik, though it was not in Schliemann's nature to express gratitude.

Schliemann next turned his attention to Mycenae, where he began work in 1876. The Lion Gate had already been exposed in 1841 and the walls of the citadel were fully visible; there was never any doubt about the identity of the site. Schliemann's excavations, or to be more precise the excavations undertaken by the young Greek archaeologist Panagiotis Stamatakis and a team of fifty-five workmen hired by Schliemann, spectacularly uncovered royal burials in an unexpected location within the walls of the citadel although, as at Troy, Schliemann once again misidentified the period; at both sites he focused on finds dating from centuries earlier than the Homeric period, which was around 1250 BC.

Schliemann followed a passage in Pausanias describing the tombs of Aegisthus and Clytemnestra as 'a little further from the wall, as they were not judged fit to be buried within, where Agamemnon lay and those who were murdered along with him'.[3] The tholos or beehive tombs were popularly named 'treasuries' and most scholars in 1868 reasoned that the kings of Mycenae would not have placed their wealth, whether in tombs or treasuries, outside the city wall; they reasoned that the existence of the treasuries outside the citadel argued for the former existence of a city wall much further out. Schliemann, who was not only an amateur but new to the subject, was unaware of the academic issues involved and therefore assumed, correctly, that Pausanias was referring to the citadel walls. Ironically, it was Schliemann's ignorance of the nineteenth-century antiquarian literature that led him to discover the shaft graves inside the citadel walls.

But he had another, altogether less inspiring, reason for digging there, which he mentioned in *Ithaca* but not in later works, and that was the deep pit that someone else had already opened there.[4] He says it was 6m deep, and there is nowhere within the citadel at Mycenae except the site of Grave

Circle A where it would be possible to dig down that far without striking bedrock. It seems likely that this was a clandestine dig by locals and that Schliemann heard rumours in Nauplion that the dig was producing gold; with characteristic deception, he preferred to emphasize his literary evidence and prove his worth as a scholar.[5] In his diary Schliemann noted that he would have to dig 'at least 30 feet to reach . . . the tombs of the heroes'. This is a figure he could not have deduced from any literary source or from the topography of the site; it suggests that someone had already dug down into Grave Circle A and reached a bronze age burial.[6] Controversy surrounded Schliemann, his discoveries and his interpretation of his discoveries both during his lifetime and subsequently.

Schliemann and other archaeologists such as Christos Tsountas provided archaeological evidence that there had been a 'Mycenaean' civilization in bronze age Greece, for which the only previous evidence had been literary. Since Schliemann's time, scholars have remained divided in their attitudes towards Homer and other ancient sources. Arthur Evans was an ambivalent admirer of Schliemann, and acquired the Cretan site of Knossos with the intention of unearthing a bronze age building that he would name 'the Palace of Minos' after the legendary king of Crete. In the process he discovered that there had been another bronze age civilization, slightly earlier than the Mycenaean civilization, the Minoan. Belief in the historicity of ancient tradition was proving very fruitful, though many scholars continued to maintain a sceptical attitude towards traditionary accounts.

After Schliemann, it seemed to some that Homer must be a rich seam of information about the Mycenaean heroes and the places where they lived – just waiting to be quarried. Yet we have to be wary of Homer as a source – he is no use, as history or proto-history, unless corroborated by archaeology, so the familiar image gained from Homer of the Mycenaean world and its denizens may need adjusting.

For instance, Homer describes a letter entrusted to a traveller, yet when the poetry was composed and orally transmitted through the Dark Ages writing was totally unknown. Homer is either completely anachronistically describing the letter-writing of his own time or recalling a much earlier time when letters were written, which takes us back to the Linear B tablets of the Mycenaean period, the Homeric heroic age.[7] The boar's tusk helmet Homer describes was unknown in the eighth century; it was a genuine bronze age artefact, described just as it would have looked in the bronze age.[8] The description of the helmet must therefore have been handed down from the bronze age. The objection that the whole of Book 10 might have been added to the *Iliad* later in antiquity goes no way at all towards explaining the presence of genuine late bronze age material. There are some inconsistencies in the references to iron. In Mycenaean Greece bronze was used for making weapons, so the mention of an iron arrowhead is an anachronism, perhaps imported into the poem by a story-teller retelling it for the thousandth time in 800 BC.[9] On the other hand, Achilles' offer of a lump of iron as a *prize* in the funeral games of Patroklos is a closer reflection of the metal's scarcity and value in the late bronze age.[10]

Other anachronisms are more elusive. Homer has been criticized for describing cremation as the standard method for disposing of the dead in the *Iliad*, but warrior aristocrats killed on campaign far from home at Troy could not have been buried in the customary way in their family chamber tombs or tholos tombs back in Greece; nor would there have been time to build such tombs in the Troad. As a matter of expediency it would have been necessary to dispose of their bodies in some other way.[11]

The accuracy of Homer's political geography is variable. The *Odyssey* treats the Hither and Further Provinces of Messenia as separate kingdoms, though we know from bronze age documents that both provinces were ruled from Pylos. The *Odyssey* also gives the River Alpheius as the northern frontier of the kingdom of Pylos, but the tablets imply that the River Nedha, 35km to the south, was the frontier. Perhaps Homer did not have first-hand knowledge of the geography of western Greece. He may not have understood the Argolid well either, since he gives Mycenae a kingdom with a coastline on the Corinthian Gulf rather than the Bay of Argos. The modern province boundary separating Argolida from Korinthia follows the main watershed, immediately to the north of Mycenae, and this mountain ridge is where I would have expected the bronze age frontier no-man's-land to have been. But this is dangerous ground – and not just because of the prowling lion of Nemea – as we cannot be absolutely sure where Mycenae's power reached and the logic of physical geography may have been overridden by some political consideration or some accident of dynastic history; in other words, we cannot tell from the archaeological evidence whether Homer was right or wrong.[12]

Archaeology has yet to tell us the origins of the Mycenaeans. We know *who* they were – the people who inhabited central and southern Greece in the sixteenth to thirteenth centuries BC – but little of where they came from. One theory is that they migrated into Greece from the area north of the Black Sea, the region that is now the Ukraine.[13] They were probably nomadic pastoralists organized at a tribal level. But beyond these points there is wide disagreement; there is no consensus as to when and how the ancestors of the Mycenaeans entered Greece. It is likely that there was no mass migration but a sporadic movement of small groups over a long period between 2200 and 1600 BC.[14] What we can be sure of is that they were a people of exceptional dynamism and enterprise who enthusiastically took over key ideas from neighbouring cultures – Egyptian, Hittite and Minoan – cross-fertilized them, and grafted them onto the proto-urban society developing at Greek mainland centres such as Lerna and Tiryns to make a dazzling and original new civilization.

For several centuries before the Mycenaean civilization emerged villages had been evolving into towns. The site of Malthi in Messenia had had five successive towns built on it by 1600 BC. The first two were unwalled and had been destroyed by 1900 BC; the next three were walled and centred on a major building that seems to have been a forerunner of the Mycenaean 'palaces'. The houses, upwards of three hundred of them, were huddled together with party walls, as at Thermi and Poliochne, showing a centralized, unified and purposeful community. It was already a genuinely urban society, one that would provide a firm foundation for the development of the Mycenaean civilization.

The achievements of this civilization are today looked back on with admiration and awe, though it was not always so. Pausanias described how its ruins had passed from general notice in the second century AD: 'Distinguished historians have explained the Egyptian pyramids in the greatest detail, and not made the slightest mention of the Treasure House of Minyas or the walls of Tiryns, which are by no means less marvellous.'[15]

2

CITIES AND KINGDOMS

'Without a geographical basis, the people, the makers of history, seem to be walking on air.'[1] The writer had France in mind, but the saying is as true of Mycenaean Greece. Understanding the well-defined physical geography of Greece helps enormously in understanding its political history. It is a country unusually sharply divided into many small physical units. In the Aegean that physical division is extreme, with water separating land areas from one another and imposing socio-political isolation. The mainland of Greece is not much less divided, with the Peloponnese very nearly severed from the rest of Greece by the ragged slash of the Gulf of Corinth, and high rugged mountain ridges enclosing and separating small fertile plains. Here too the sea separates, with deeply penetrating gulfs (the Saronic, Argolic, Laconian and Messenian Gulfs) breaking the land up even further. It seems quite natural to find that in the bronze age southern and central Greece was divided into many separate political units, each with a focus on a fertile, food-producing plain, and often with a harbour town on a bay. This is what Homer describes: a multitude of small kingdoms and principalities, each with its own towns, its own army, its own king, its own aristocracy, its own court and its own intrigues.[2] Homer says the kings owed allegiance to a High King, Agamemnon, and there is some documentary evidence from a Hittite inscription that the Hittite king (a High King ruling most of Anatolia) was ready to address a Greek king as his equal. The king of Ahhiyawa (the Hittite version of the name) is thought by many scholars to have been the king of Achaea (the classical Greek version) – and according to Homer Agamemnon was king of the Achaeans. There are hints in the *Odyssey* of special bonds tying the three southernmost kingdoms of mainland Greece, Messenia, Laconia and Argolis. Menelaus refers to 'the Argive country', by which he appears to mean these three kingdoms or possibly even the Peloponnese as a whole (including the kingdoms of Elis, Achaea and Arcadia as well); he uses the name 'Hellas' to describe northern Greece.[3]

Plate 2.1 The rugged mountain landscape of Greece. Steep slopes provided natural defence. This is the Chavos ravine, which defended the citadel of Mycenae, off the picture immediately to the left.

Figure 2.1 Location map: Mycenaean sites in Greece.

The best literary source for the political geography of the bronze age is Book 2 of the *Iliad*, which lists the contingents in the Greek combined expeditionary fleet. This Catalogue of Ships tells us not only how many ships were contributed by each kingdom, but which towns the men came from. It is still possible, even after nearly three thousand years, to identify two-thirds of the towns Homer listed. More significantly still, of those, all except Ithaca are known from archaeological evidence to have been important Mycenaean sites: even those which by Homer's time had been reduced to villages, like Mycenae, or wiped off the map altogether, like Pylos.[4] There are many problems in interpreting the Catalogue of Ships – it parades an absurdly large military force, for one thing – but it nevertheless sketches an ancient geography of the Aegean that is startlingly close to what we

8

now know from archaeological evidence to have been the heartland of the Mycenaean civilization.

As the present interglacial dawned, ten thousand years ago, Greece was deserted. It was not until after 7000 BC that farmers migrated into northern Greece from Anatolia, settling in the most fertile plains opening onto the Aegean, facing the lands they had come from. Until 3000 BC, agriculture was restricted to the most fertile floodplains. Only then, with the introduction of the plough, was it possible to advance onto steeper and stonier slopes in Thessaly and the foothills round the Plain of Argos, then, after 2000 BC, into southern Argolis and Messenia. The effect of this spread of agriculture was deforestation on a large scale. The pine forests in Messenia, in the south-west Peloponnese, were rapidly reduced. The combination of deforestation and ploughing led to accelerated soil erosion on hill slopes and accelerated rates of sedimentation in river mouths and bays. The landscape was undergoing a major transformation by 1600 BC, the time when the Mycenaean civilization was emerging.

Between 1600 and 1400 BC, in the early Mycenaean period, the pine and oak-woods in Messenia were wiped out, to be replaced by steppe and maquis vegetation, a result of deforestation and overgrazing.[5]

It was in the context of this aggressive onslaught on the Messenian landscape that the bronze age kingdom of Pylos came into being, the land of that wise King Nestor who boasted that he had as a young man been 'a sacker of towns'. But the Mycenaeans were not just sackers of cities: they sacked the countryside as well. It was the cause of their rise – and possibly one of the causes of their downfall. The large collection of archive tablets from Pylos allows us to attempt a reconstruction of Nestor's kingdom, or rather the kingdom of his successor, which ranged far beyond the neighbourhood of his fine 'palace' on the Englianos Ridge. If Nestor stood on the roof of his 'palace', he would have had a panoramic view to north, south and west, where Navarino Bay made a huge and magnificent harbour on the Adriatic coast; to the east, an imposing north–south ridge formed his horizon. It was a fine extensive view and yet the building was not easy for an enemy to spot: it was several kilometres from the coast and there were low hills concealing it from pirates. Nor was it easy for those modern pirates, the archaeologists, to find; it was not until 1939 that Carl Blegen discovered it.

The shores round Coryphasion explain Homer's characteristic epithet, 'sandy Pylos'. If any doubt remained after the uncovering of the 'stately citadel', the hundreds of tablets Blegen found in the Archive Room referred again and again to a place called *Pu-ro*, Pylos; the place really was called Pylos in the bronze age. There are other places that have been called Pylos, as Strabo was well aware – Coryphasion and Navarino among them – but he observed, 'The ancient Messenian Pylos was a city under Aigolaion, and when this city was destroyed some of its inhabitants settled on

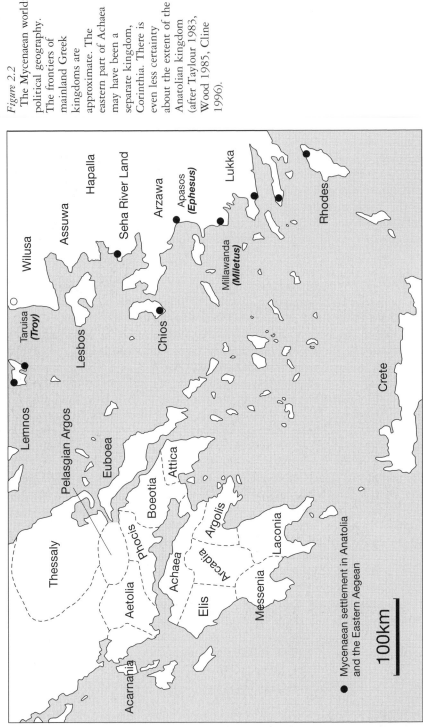

Figure 2.2
The Mycenaean world: political geography. The frontiers of mainland Greek kingdoms are approximate. The eastern part of Achaea may have been a separate kingdom, Corinthia. There is even less certainty about the extent of the Anatolian kingdom (after Taylour 1983, Wood 1985, Cline 1996).

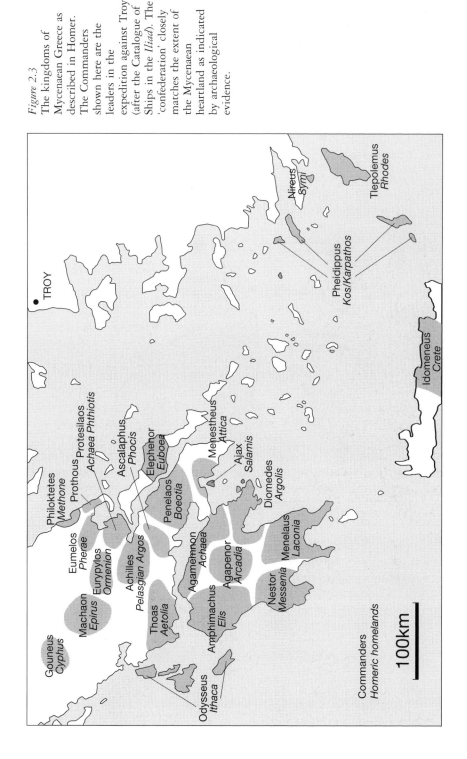

Figure 2.3
The kingdoms of Mycenaean Greece as described in Homer. The Commanders shown here are the leaders in the expedition against Troy (after the Catalogue of Ships in the *Iliad*). The 'confederation' closely matches the extent of the Mycenaean heartland as indicated by archaeological evidence.

TROY

Gouneus
Cyphus

Machaon
Epirus

Eurypylos
Ormenion

Eumelos
Pherae

Achilles
Pelasgian Argos

Philoktetes
Methone

Prothous Protesilaos
Achaea Phthiotis

Ascalaphus
Phocis

Elephenor
Euboea

Penelaos
Boeotia

Menestheus
Attica

Ajax
Salamis

Diomedes
Argolis

Agamemnon
Achaea

Menelaus
Laconia

Agapenor
Arcadia

Thoas
Aetolia

Amphimachus
Elis

Nestor
Messenia

Odysseus
Ithaca

Pheidippus
Kos/Karpathos

Nireus
Symi

Tlepolemus
Rhodes

Idomeneus
Crete

Commanders
Homeric homelands

100km

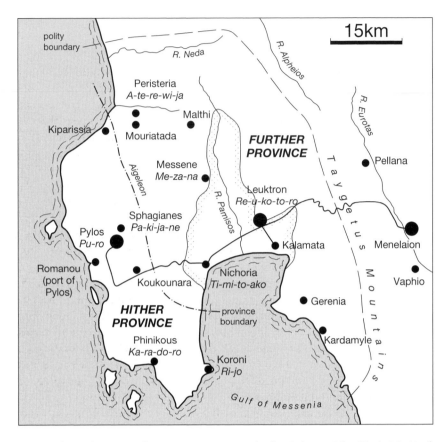

Figure 2.4 The kingdom of Messenia reconstructed (after Palmer 1961, Chadwick 1976, Bennet 1998). The small filled circles are Mycenaean settlements. The large filled circles are thought to be major centres.

Coryphasion'.[6] Strabo also quotes a Peloponnesian proverb: 'There is a Pylos before Pylos; and there is yet another Pylos.'[7] The tablets record the names of a lot of other places in the kingdom of Nestor, distinguishing those that were 'This side of Aigolaion' from those that were 'Beyond Aigolaion'. These are usually referred to by scholars as the Hither and Further Provinces, Aigolaion being both the classical and the Mycenaean name of the ridge to the east of Pylos.

Some examples include tablets Ng 319 and 332:

Ng 319
This-side-of-Aigolaion: 1,239 units of flax
and 457 units not provided.

Ng 332
Beyond-Aigolaion: [at least] 200 units of flax
and [?] units not provided.[8]

The physical geography suggests that the kingdom stretched at least as far as Kiparissia in the north, where the mountain barrier fails and a wide river valley gives access to the interior, to the Further Province. To the south there is a saddle leading east across the ridge to Nichoria; given that the peninsula extends only another 20km from that point, it is reasonable to assume that the Hither Province included the whole of the western coastal strip from Kiparissia to Methoni.[9] It is logical to assume that the Further Province had a similar north–south reach, and included the whole of the eastern slope of the peninsula, reaching the Pamisos valley and the Gulf of Messenia.

Do the tablets confirm or confound these inferences? Unfortunately there are several problems in the way. The tablets do not include maps or directions. The syllabic symbols give only approximations of words, so some of the names may be read in more than one way. It also appears that in Mycenaean times, as now, there were often several places with the same name. The situation is saved, though, by a number of favourable circumstances, among them the survival of a surprisingly large number of place names across an almost incredible time span of three-and-a-half thousand years. There is also the repetition in the tablets of a list of nine places in the Hither Province, always arranged in the same, presumably geographical, order, and a similar list of seven places in the Further Province.

The debate about the problem will doubtless continue for a long time to come, but one interpretation is as follows:

HITHER PROVINCE

Pis-wa/*Pi-jai** = Phea/Pheiai
Me-ta-pa = Metapa
Pe-to-no
Pa-ki-ja-ne = cult centre at
    or near Pylos
A-pu = Aipu/Aipeia
Ro-u-so/*E-ra-to***
A-ke-re-wa
Ka-ra-do-ro = Kharadro
    ('The Two Ravines')
Ri-jo = Cape Akritas
    (classical 'Rhion')

FURTHER PROVINCE

Ti-mi-to-a-ke-e = Nichoria
Ra-wa-ra-ti-ja/*Ra-wa-ra-to*
Sa-ma-ra
A-si-ja-ti-ja

E-ra-te-re-wa
Za-ma-e-wi-ja
E-re-i = Helos

* disputed reading of symbols   ** alternative name in tablets

Each of these districts had its own local administrator and the Provinces were themselves the responsibility of provincial governors. We even know the name of the last Governor of the Hither Province: he appears in the tablets as 'Governor Damoklos'.[10]

Other places mentioned in the tablets include *Re-u-ko-to-ro* or Leuktron (= modern Thouria) near Kalamata and *Ku-pa-ri-so* (= modern Kiparissia). Leuktron was probably the capital of the Further Province, commanding the road east to Sparta.[11] The picture as a whole is of a bronze age kingdom that incorporated the Messenian peninsula and the whole of the fertile valley of the River Pamisos, and extending as far north as Peristeria, the Tetrazi mountains or even the Alpheius valley.[12] It seems likely that the eastern boundary was the high wall of the Taygetus Mountains.

The *Iliad* to a limited extent corroborates the view of Pylos seen through the tablets. When Agamemnon tries to make restitution for his insult to Achilles, he offers seven new tripods, ten talents of gold, twenty gleaming cauldrons, ten horses, seven women skilled in handicrafts, women of Lesbos. He also offers 'cities filled with people: Cardamyle and Enope, and grassy Hira and sacred Pherae, and Antheia with its deep meadows and lovely Aipeia and vine-clad Pedasos, all near the sea in the outermost part of sandy Pylos.'[13] Strabo tells us that Pherae is on the River Nedon and 'borders on Thouria and Gerenia', by which he means that Pherae lies between Thouria and Gerenia, placing it in the east of Messenia. Modern Kalamata fits this location. Kardamili, with its fine Mycenaean acropolis, is on the coast 15km south of Kalamata. Palmer argues that Strabo's interpretation of Homer supports the idea of a kingdom of Pylos that extended right across to include the whole of the Gulf of Messenia, and this is certainly consistent with regarding the Taygetus Mountains as the likeliest frontier between bronze age Pylos and Sparta.[14] Interestingly, neither Homer nor any of his protagonists passes comment on the way that Agamemnon gives away lands that are not in his own kingdom but in Nestor's. Are we to infer from this another layer to Agamemnon's high-handedness? And are we intended to infer from Nestor's silence in the face of this affront to himself another layer in his wise counsel?

There is a reference in the *Odyssey* which suggests that the bronze age kingdom of Messenia reached right across to the eastern side of the Gulf of Messenia. Nestor is referred to repeatedly as 'the Gerenian charioteer', strongly implying that the king came from Gerenia, a town on the east coast of the Gulf.[15]

Beyond the Taygetus Mountains lay another kingdom, one about which far less is known: the kingdom of Laconia. This would later become Sparta, but the Spartans had short memories. When Herodotus visited Sparta, perhaps around 450 BC, he was able to pick up a good many tales about Cleomenes, who had been king just before the Battle of Marathon in 490, and some stories about Cleomenes' grandfather and a war with Tegea, and

Plate 2.2 The early megastructure at the hill-top Menelaion, with the Taygetus Mountains in the background.

that was about all. There was no indigenous Spartan tradition reaching back into the bronze age, in fact nothing earlier than 550 or 575 BC.[16] As yet, the capital of this shadowy bronze age kingdom remains uncertain, but it is thought that the early buildings at the Menelaion on the hill at Therapne three kilometres east-south-east of Sparta may represent remains of Laconia's bronze age political centre. An early palace-like building was raised there in about 1550 BC and rebuilt in 1400 BC, similar in plan to the Palace of Nestor at Pylos. It is the only early palace known; the others date from the thirteenth century.

The Menelaion building consisted of a big two-storey mansion with a central megaron, flanked by corridors with small rooms on either side.[17] The Vapheio tomb, a large tholos tomb with rich grave-goods, was built only 6km to the south-south-west. The tomb contained rings, gems, beads, a mirror, an ear-pick, perfume vases, a sword, nine knives and daggers, two hunting spears, axes, two alabaster vases, a Syrian axe, an iron finger-ring, an amethyst, two daggers with *niello* decoration, amber beads from the Baltic and the two famous Minoan gold cups. There can be little doubt that this was a royal burial.[18]

Homer's description of Menelaus's capital is not very helpful. He tells us that Menelaus and Helen lived no less royally than Agamemnon, and that

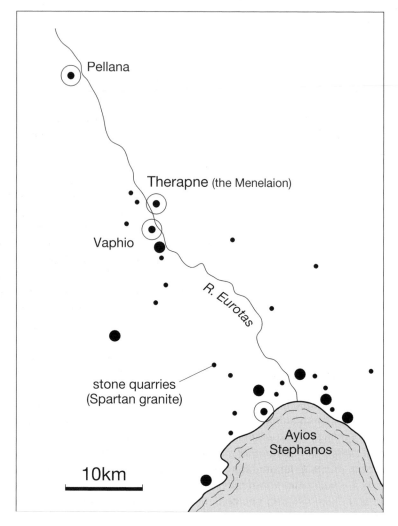

Figure 2.5 Settlement in the kingdom of Laconia. Small dots represent small settlements, large dots represent major settlements. Dots in circles represent regional centres.

their palace was at Lakedaimon, 'deep in the hills'. Given that the Eurotas plain is large and surrounded by hills and mountains, the description is not specific enough to give us the location.

An alternative site for the Palace of Menelaus has recently been uncovered by Theodore Spyropoulos at Pellana, 25km north of Sparta. The alleged palace site is close to a series of large Mycenaean chamber tombs and

Professor Spyropoulos believes that what he has found is ancient Lakedaimon, the lost Homeric capital. The principal building is 32m by 14m, apparently a palatial building on the same scale as the 'palace' at Mycenae. Associated finds date it to 1200 BC. Cyclopean walling protects it and a wide road leads up to the entrance. The nearby tombs were plundered in antiquity, but not the 'palace', which has yielded pottery, jewellery, wall paintings and many Linear B tablets.

There is a major clash of interpretation between Spyropoulos, who is convinced that Pellana was the Mycenaean capital of Laconia, and the British School at Athens, who believe that the Menelaion was the capital. The archive tablets at Pellana may help to resolve the issue.[19]

The fertile plain of the Eurotas opening onto the Gulf of Laconia looks like an obvious focus for a bronze age kingdom, while the mountain ridges to east and west make obvious boundaries. In later times this was to become Sparta, just as the bronze age kingdom of Pylos was to become Messenia. Messenia and Laconia were rival territories in the later, post-Mycenaean, period, and it is likely that they were in the Mycenaean period too.[20] Indeed both the archaeology and the legend, including the material in the *Iliad*, point to continuing friction among the Greek military city-states from the bronze age onwards. The coastline along the Laconian Gulf has changed subsequently; alluvium deposited by the River Eurotas has built the coastline out as much as 6km.

Beyond the mountains to the east lay Argolis, also with a fertile lowland, the Argive Plain, and a huge bay, the Saronic Gulf, as its focus. This was the most powerful of all the Mycenaean kingdoms.

There were other city-states north of the Gulf of Corinth: Iolkos in Thessaly, Thebes and Orchomenos in Boeotia, Athens in Attica – all centred on fertile plains and separated from one another by high ridges, all small in scale – but the greatest concentration of economic, political, military power was in the Peloponnese. Apart from Pylos, Sparta and Mycenae, the Peloponnese had at least two more kingdoms: one in the north-west corresponding to later Elis and one ranged along the southern shore of the Gulf of Corinth corresponding to later Achaea. Unfortunately very little is known of them. Arcadia has as yet not been intensively explored by archaeologists. It is assumed that, being land-locked, it must have been cut off from the mainstream of Mycenaean trading: it must have been the 'poor relation' among the Peloponnesian kingdoms. Homer implies as much when he has Agamemnon lending the Arcadians some ships to take to Troy. The kingdom of Elis to the west of Arcadia consisted of a huge plain, but it did not lend itself to early agriculture using bronze-shod ploughs. The Mycenaean settlements in Elis were mainly on the harbours of the west coast or sprinkled through the foothills along the plain's eastern edge, in much the same way that Argos, Midea and Mycenae are located on hills round the empty Plain of Argos.[21]

Plate 2.3 The southern end of the fertile basin of Arcadia. The hills in the distance marked the boundary between Arcadia and Laconia.

The precise extent of the kingdoms, other than Pylos, is uncertain, and as we have seen even with the help of all the place names in the tablets there is plenty of room for scholarly disagreement about the northward extent of the kingdom of Pylos. On the face of it, it appears peculiar for two fortified 'palace' centres to exist as close together as Mycenae and Tiryns, which are but 15km apart. Chadwick says that for strategic reasons the Argive Plain could not have been divided between them and that Tiryns must have been a dependency of Mycenae.[22] The same would have to apply to the nearby fortress of Midea. The king of Mycenae might command several 'royal' strongholds and residences, just like a medieval king. The bronze age reality may have been more complex still, as we shall see, and it may be necessary to view the relationships among power centres in a changing historical context, with large-scale shifts in the balance of power as the fortunes of ruling dynasties rose and fell. In addition to Tiryns, Mycenae and Midea there is Argos, which was an important centre before the rise of Mycenae – and after its fall.

Early neolithic pottery has been found at Mycenae, but it was a less important centre in both the neolithic and the early bronze age than Lerna, down by the sea on the Bay of Argos; even in the middle bronze age, Mycenae was less important than Lerna or Argos. The early bronze age House

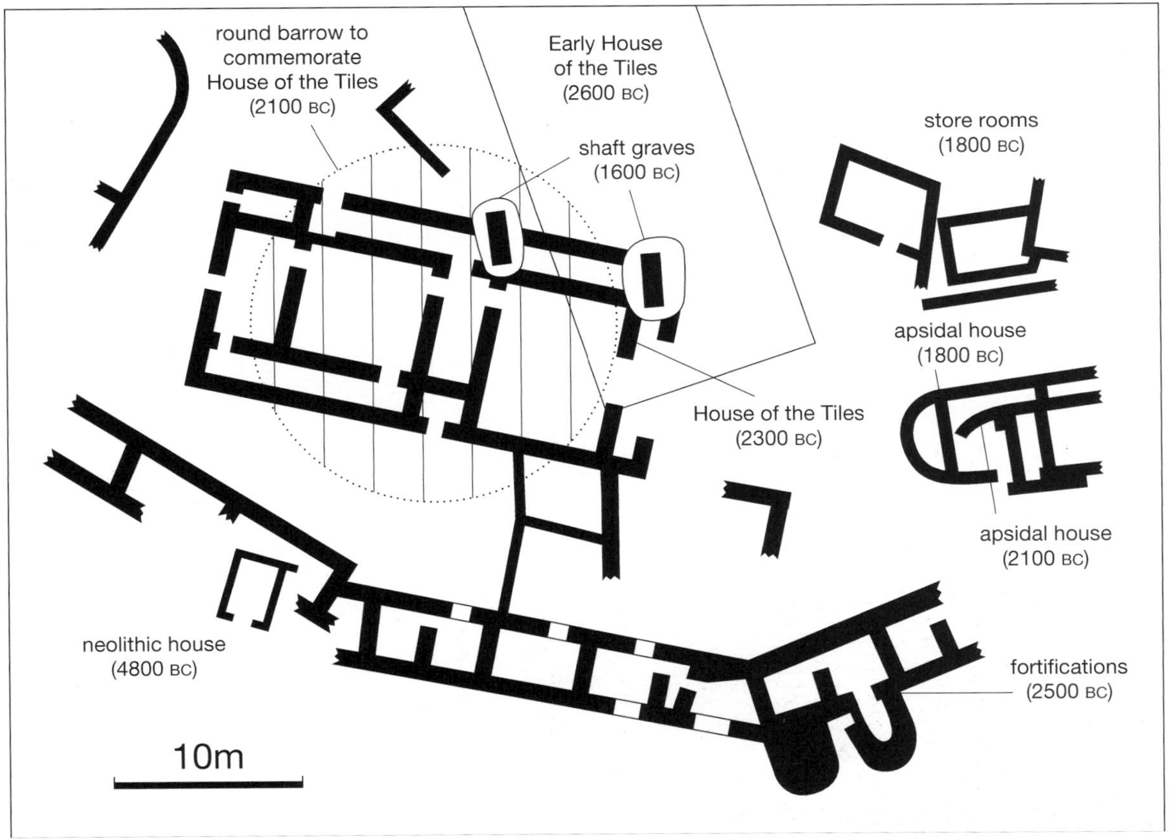

Figure 2.6
Lerna. Evolving urban architecture and evolving fortifications. The House of the Tiles was a forerunner of the later temple-palaces.

round barrow to commemorate House of the Tiles (2100 BC)

Early House of the Tiles (2600 BC)

shaft graves (1600 BC)

store rooms (1800 BC)

apsidal house (1800 BC)

apsidal house (2100 BC)

House of the Tiles (2300 BC)

fortifications (2500 BC)

neolithic house (4800 BC)

10m

of Tiles at Lerna was a well-designed, well-built and important building, with a group of sealings that show that it was involved in some administrative system. The building was encircled by a sturdy fortification made of two independent parallel walls joined every few metres by cross walls; the compartments may have been used as chambers, which would make the construction an early form of casemate architecture. Semicircular bastions were added later. Lerna's coastal site rendered it vulnerable to attack from the sea.[23] Similar fortifications were built at other sites, such as Kastri on Syros, so the ambitious walling of the later citadels had its local antecedents as well as borrowing from the fortification architecture of the Hittites.

The origins of the Mycenaean civilization are nevertheless quite obscure. There was in the early Mycenaean period, from 1600 BC onwards, a mentality that had no antecedents in Middle Helladic Greece, nor had any close correspondence with the mentality or behaviour patterns of other cultures nearby. The main characteristic of this mindset is an obsession with death, or at least with investing time and wealth in funerary rites and monuments. Many aspects of early Mycenaean culture as reflected in the shaft grave burial goods are ephemeral, and this suggests transplantation from elsewhere.[24] The period 1650–1600 BC was the most radical in Greek history in terms of the introduction of new burial customs. Until then, the main burial practice had been inhumation in single-use cist graves. In a few decades, three new forms were in use – shaft graves, tholos tombs, chamber tombs – and a completely new practice in multiple burial.

Ellen Davis described the shaft grave gold plate as almost exclusively a Mycenaean phenomenon.[25] The treatment of gold suggests limited access to gold, possibly a Minoan habit, as the Cretans had no gold of their own, or maybe a reflection of some difficulty in obtaining gold from Transylvania. The masks seem to have no antecedents and no successors, which suggests an importation of a foreign custom that did not long outlast the migration. The next and, it is believed, only other examples come from Sindos near Thessaloniki and date from the sixth century BC – and the Sindos people came from Thrace. So there is at least a possibility that some elements of the new culture were imported by migrants from the north of Greece in around 1650 BC.[26]

Some prehistorians warn that we step on quicksand as soon as we cite later documentary sources about the bronze age, but the nature of the material embedded in the writings of classical historians is such that it is at least worth hearing and evaluating. Diodorus Siculus, writing in about 50 BC, collated a huge body of folklore, legend and proto-history in his *Library of History*, among which is the dynastic legend of King Nestor. In summary, it runs as follows. Salmoneus, Nestor's great grandfather, was the son of Aeolus, the son of Hellen, the son of Deucalion. Salmoneus set out from Aeolis with a number of Aeolian followers, founding a city on the banks of the River Alpheius and naming it after himself, Salmonia. He was

Plate 2.4 A bastion in the fortification wall at the coastal settlement of Lerna.

an overbearing, impious man, hated by his subjects, and killed by Zeus with a lightning bolt. Salmoneus' daughter Tyro was first seduced by Poseidon, to whom she bore two sons, Pelias and Neleus, then married the mortal Cretheus, to whom she bore Amythaon, Pheies and Aeron. After Cretheus' death a struggle for the throne broke out between Pelias and Neleus. Pelias became king over Locris, and Neleus went on a campaign into the Peloponnese, supported by certain Achaeans, and founded the city of Pylos in Messenia, on a site given to him by the natives. Neleus, as king of Pylos, married Chloris, daughter of Amphion the Theban, and fathered twelve sons, of whom the youngest was Nestor.[27]

One characteristic of this account which makes it look like a genuine bronze age account is that the genealogy stops at Nestor. Although it would be very easy for a later prince or king to invent a genealogy reaching back to mythic heroes like Hellen and Deucalion, the later generations that would make that link are missing; what survives is just exactly what one can imagine Nestor himself telling his children about his own, and their, royal dynastic origins. Another feature that has a genuine bronze age undertone is the relaxed way in which the gods are involved in the family history – Salmoneus is struck down by Zeus, Nestor's grandfather is Poseidon – it is a piece in the same mentality as Homer. In Anatolia, gods interacted with Hittite kings of the same period in exactly the same way. King Mursilis II wrote, 'The [Weather-]god's hand smote me in a dream and the power of speech forsook me altogether.'[28] But these are digressions. The main purpose in quoting the lineage of Nestor is that it outlines a north–south migration through Greece. Aeolus is based in the south-west of central Greece; Salmoneus crosses the Gulf of Corinth and settles in Elis; Neleus moves further south still to found Pylos. Perhaps embedded in this piece of ancient family fable is enshrined the memory of a southward migration.

The beginnings of the Mycenaean civilization are to an extent rooted in the soil. The surge in the development of agriculture noted earlier certainly played a part. So also did contact with the dazzling Minoan civilization flourishing on Crete; it is plain from their artwork that the Mycenaeans were great admirers of the Minoan culture – and great plagiarizers. In the end, they even copied their ambitious trading practices and spread their own trading operation across the Aegean, effectively replacing and supplanting the Minoan civilization. The Mycenaean civilization was like a strangler fig, first harmlessly receiving help and support from its host, only to outgrow and throttle it.

At one time it was assumed that Cretans set up colonies on the Greek mainland, so strong was the similarity of cultural style, but most prehistorians now believe there was no large-scale migration of Cretans to the mainland, no military conquest and no political control over any of the mainland cities.[29]

The élite groups even in the early Mycenaean period were wealthy. The rich objects Schliemann found in the shaft graves with their military chariot scenes imply that their owners were rich, powerful and warlike. Yet at that stage the power was local. It was only later that the rulers of the Mycenaean kingdoms reached out, competed with one another, and built far-reaching economic links across the Aegean. It was between 1550 and 1400 BC that the Minoans lost their hegemony in the Aegean, shouldered aside by the Mycenaeans. Before that there had been a peaceful and fruitful co-existence between Mycenaeans and Minoans, but there was a slide into rivalry and conflict, resulting in victory for the mainland culture in around 1400 BC.[30] The fall of Knossos is usually dated to 1380 BC. Another three hundred years, and the Mycenaean civilization itself would be swept away. As Attorney-General Sir Henry Yelverton said when condemning Sir Walter Raleigh to death for no particular reason, 'He hath been a star at which the world hath gazed. But stars may fall, nay, they *must* fall.'

The kings of the Mycenaean city-states ruled from centres that at first were unremarkable. It was only in the later Mycenaean period that these centres were developed into spectacular showpieces. We have little evidence to tell us what Argos, apparently the premier settlement of the Argive Plain, looked like; it had the archaeological misfortune to continue in use as a political centre after the Mycenaean period was over. At Mycenae we have far better evidence, as the citadel site was abandoned, and at Pylos too.

The citadels themselves were the hallmark of the Mycenaean civilization. It is easy to forget that they are actually alien to Greece, that they were imported. They combine two distinctive imported architectural ideas: the Minoan temple-palace concept and the awe-inspiring Hittite fortifications. Together they made a distinctively Mycenaean citadel, the forerunner of all later European castles.

SANDY PYLOS AND MESSENIA

Homer tells us that King Nestor ruled from 'the stately citadel' built by his father King Neleus. Interestingly, the first impression given during the Pylos excavations was that the main building, presumed to be a hill-top palace, was undefended, but in the earliest phase of the late bronze age it *had* been walled, so it would certainly have been fair for Homer to describe it as a citadel. Remains of a fortification wall have been found at several points round it, notably some fifty metres to the north-east of the North-East Building, where the wall was interrupted by a towered stone-built gate. Blegen wondered if the wall had ever been complete; probably it had, but was ravaged by the combined effects of erosion and stone-robbing. One reason why the defending wall did not survive is that it was made of much smaller blocks than the great walls of Tiryns or Mycenae. Another is that the bedrock of the Pylos area is soft and marly, and good building stone is hard to come by. It is possible to get some idea of the lightweight early defences at Pylos on the north-east perimeter, where in the bronze age a sloping roadway ran down the hill, through the stone gateway and out in the direction of a conspicuous beehive tomb, Tholos Tomb IV. It looks as if the road was used, at least occasionally, as a processional way to the tomb for the dignitaries of the citadel who were privileged to bury their dead in the high-status tomb.[31] A further reason why the fortification wall has not survived is that as the kingdom of Pylos expanded the danger of attack decreased.[32] With the eastern border pushed back from the Aigolaion right across to the Taygetus Mountains, Pylos must have seemed safe, so the wall was not maintained.

Round the Pylos citadel was a substantial town. Blegen's test pits and surface finds suggested a settlement extending 50–100m out on all sides, and recent work suggests that the town was several times larger than Blegen thought.[33] In the countryside round Pylos there were evidently more settlements, one for instance at Hora, which was and is still a major route centre. There were other settlements at Volomidia, Romanou, Portes, Beylerbey, and monumental tholos tombs at Routsi, Coryphasion, Tragana, Voidokoilia and Haratsara.

The wall round the Pylian citadel marks the start of the site's domination of the kingdom some time between 1700 and 1600 BC, and probably

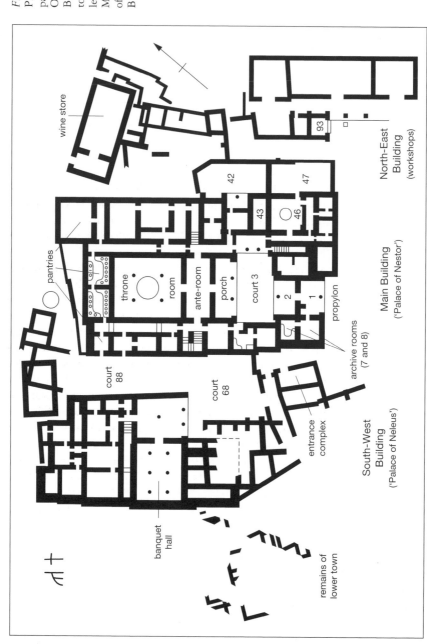

Figure 2.7
Plan of the temple-palace at Pylos. Only the Main Building is open to the public. Top left is the Mycenaean name of 'Pylos' in Linear B script.

wine store

pantries

throne room

ante-room

porch

court 3

court 88

court 68

42

43

46

47

93

2

1

propylon

archive rooms (7 and 8)

entrance complex

banquet hall

remains of lower town

South-West Building ('Palace of Neleus')

Main Building ('Palace of Nestor')

North-East Building (workshops)

marks the political unification of the area – possibly the whole of the Hither Province. The building of tholos tombs at intervals across the kingdom between 1700 and 1500 BC may reflect the determination of middle-ranking functionaries to follow the new mortuary fashion initiated by the trend-setting élite at Pylos. Pylian tholos tombs are very conspicuous features of the landscape, being built entirely above ground, very visible statements by those wishing to be seen to belong to the new élite. The outreach at this stage was already very considerable; the distinguished were buried with amber beads, exotic goods from other parts of the Greek mainland and even goods from Crete. Ambition, avarice and status-seeking were already on the map.

The settlement at Pylos was repeatedly rebuilt, on into the following period, 1400–1100 BC. The building reached a climax in the second half of the thirteenth century with the creation of the 'Palace of Nestor', replacing an earlier complex of similar character.

The building known as the Palace of Nestor was discovered by Carl Blegen in 1939. The first trench was laid out on 4 April; by 21 April he was cabling Athens: 'Found Mycenaean palace with column bases remains fresco over 50 inscribed tablets. Love, Carl.' This building, representing the hey-day of Pylos in about 1200 BC, consisted of two main structures, the two-storey Main Building near the south-western edge of the hill and the smaller South-West Building right at the edge of the steep drop. Earlier structures had stood on the site, and one of them at least had been palatial in scale and built, in 1225 BC, directly on the site of the Main Building.

The principal entrance was a canopied ceremonial porch, which had a flat corniced roof supported on a single fluted column. The cornice was surmounted by two large sphinxes facing one another; they are shown on a fresco and may have been made of stone or painted stucco.[34] This impressive porch opened onto a small asymmetrical courtyard. I emphasize this because it is a significant point of difference between the Palace of Nestor and the so-called palaces of Minoan Crete. The large Minoan buildings were temple complexes, and always had as their focus large regular rectangular courtyards designed for large-scale semi-public ceremonies.[35] The fact that the courts of the Mycenaean palaces were smaller and less regular may tell us that their function was significantly different – a point to return to later. A second porch, this time with two columns, led into the heart of the palace, the megaron. Beyond this porch was a vestibule and beyond that a large rectangular room dominated by a huge circular hearth. Above the hearth the room was open to the second storey; the four columns arranged round the hearth supported a substantial gallery. To the right of the single doorway, a throne stood against the north-east wall. Next to that was a unique feature, a straight channel in the floor connecting two round pits; it is thought this was used for pouring libations. The walls were plastered and richly painted with a variety of scenes: a lion on one side of the throne

25

Plate 2.5 The libation channel in the Throne Room at Pylos. The throne stood on the square slab in the top right-hand corner.

and a griffin on the other were the major images, but there were vignettes too, including a banquet scene and a harpist. The wall of the ante-room was decorated with a mural showing a procession of men and women leading a bull, presumably to sacrifice.

This magnificent suite with its fluted columns must have been a splendid sight when standing to its full height, every surface (wall, pillar and floor) painted in bright colours, its tall, downward-tapering pillars soaring towards a heavily timbered flat roof, and its round hearth a smouldering, crackling symbol of the life of the nation. This was the kingdom's heart and hub, the fire that warmed the king.

The Mycenaean 'palaces' seem to have been decorated with all kinds of moulded and painted features, outside as well as inside. Fresco fragments from the similar, though not identical, 'palace' at Mycenae show masonry plinths or walls painted in black and white check, wooden pillars painted red with white pillar bases and capitals. Friezes along the eaves were painted white with red discs or with running spirals. All these and a wealth of other artistic devices were borrowed from Minoan Crete. The overall effect was dazzling, a piece of great public architecture, designed for ceremony, for display, designed to impress.

26

There was a second smaller suite nearby, also centred on a room with a round hearth and a mural of a lion and a griffin. Stores near the throne room contained huge quantities of household crockery, implying large-scale entertaining. In Room 19 alone, nearly three thousand wine cups were stored. The feasting may have been purely secular – partying – but it is more likely that it had a socio-political function, like the formal banquets held at Buckingham Palace. Possibly it had a religious function, as did the sacred communion rites on Crete.[36] It has been suggested that the banqueting spilled out into the open space between the two principal buildings, Court 88.

Two small rooms at the palace entrance, Rooms 7 and 8, were used to store the archive tablets and show that the building was a focus for administration. At least thirty-three different scribes produced the tablets that were found.

A bathtub in Room 43 has been seen by some as evidence of domestic convenience, but it does not necessarily prove this; washing may be for refreshment, for cleanliness, or for spiritual cleansing in preparation for an initiation ceremony. I have suggested that the lustral areas at Knossos were used in this last way.[37] As at Knossos, there is nothing remaining of the second storey. After finding more and more evidence of religious cult use

Plate 2.6 A staircase in the temple-palace at Pylos. The masonry was fixed together with bronze dowels seated in the square sockets seen on the left and right.

on the ground floor at Knossos, Arthur Evans fell back on the missing first floor as the royal residence of the king of Knossos. At Pylos, the only evidence of the missing first floor suggests that more administration went on there; some gold and ivory objects suggest high-status occupation of some kind, but more than that cannot be deduced.

As the building aged, its function changed significantly. Much of the ground floor of the Main Building was given over to storage in the final years: storage of olive oil and perfumed oil, two of the major products of the kingdom of Pylos. In a separate building to the east, Room 99, chariots were repaired. One clay tablet (Vn 10) found there tells us simply:

Thus the woodcutters give
to the chariot workshop 50 saplings
and 50 axles.
So many saplings the Lousian fields:
100; so many saplings: 100.

A substantial part of the east side of the palace site was, at least at the end, given over to workshops.[38] These changes may be an indication of upheaval, of the Pylian authorities anticipating trouble. The same emergency can be sensed at other sites. At Tiryns and Mycenae there was frantic activity to reinforce the circuit walls. At Pylos, the old circuit walls were in ruins, and the rulers may have miscalculated when they decided not to rebuild them; as the crisis approached they decided instead to centralize important economic activities and materials.

Not far outside the town of Pylos was a cult centre, called *Pa-ki-ja-ne* in the tablets, Sphagianes in modern Greek. This seems to have been another focus for ceremonial feasting, and one of the Pylos tablets (Un 2) records the catering for a lavish feast there, apparently to celebrate a coronation:

At Sphagianes, on the occasion of the king's initiation,
the man in charge of the establishment released:
1575 litres of barley, 14.5 litres of cyperus, 8 litres of [?]
115 litres of flour, 211 litres of olives, 19 litres of [?],
    10 litres of honey,
96 litres of figs, 1 ox, 26 rams, 6 ewes, 2 billy-goats,
    2 nanny-goats,
1 fattened pig, 6 sows, 586 litres of wine, 2 pieces of [?] cloth.[39]

Behind such cryptic records we can sense complicated but long-vanished systems for assessing people for taxation, systems for collecting taxes and a well co-ordinated bureaucracy. Behind these we can detect a rigorous authoritarian control over the population as a whole. But there is also a hint of a love of ceremony and celebration.

Pylos has come to dominate the bronze age geography of Messenia, but there were over two hundred other towns and villages. We know the names of some from the Pylos tablets. Nichoria, in the north-west corner of the Messenian Gulf, went by the Mycenaean name *Ti-mi-to-a-ko*. Thouria, on rising ground just inland from the north-east corner of the Gulf, was known to the Mycenaeans as Leuktron. Both of these were in the Further Province, and Leuktron seems to have been its capital. Between the two the River Pamisos drained southwards towards the sea, crossing the broad plain that was the heartland of the Further Province. In the north, the east–west Kiparissia valley was important. For a time the town of Peristeria (*A-te-re-wi-ja*) was the main settlement in this valley, commanding an important route into the interior that was the northernmost link between Further and Hither Provinces. Later the nearby hilltop site of Mouriatadha seems to have supplanted Peristeria. Mouriatadha has the remains of a citadel walled with polygonal masonry. It also had a large megaron with four columns, a stucco floor and painted walls. Houses were grouped round the megaron.[40] Mouriatadha looks as though it functioned as a regional centre for the large area that stretched northwards from the Kiparissia valley to the Nedha valley, the likely northern frontier of the kingdom.

THE ROADS

Even the most remote parts of any of the bronze age kingdoms were probably no more than two days' walk from the capital, but reliable defence and efficient centralized government of the sort implied by the Linear B tablets will have depended on rapid communications. A highly developed, well-built road system is what we would expect, and fragments of it have survived, such as stone-built culverts over streams and larger causeways or viaducts across ravines near Mycenae. The best-known is a conspicuous and well-built viaduct about 2km south of the citadel at Mycenae, built or more likely rebuilt in about 1160 BC to carry the road from Mycenae to the Heraion over the Chavos torrent. The surviving section is 18m long, 3.8m high and 6m wide. It was the discovery of this by Captain Steffen, Schliemann's surveyor, that led on to the discovery, in 1881–82, of an entire network of roads of Mycenaean date radiating from Mycenae.[41] The hillside roads are cut-and-terraced, their outer edges often supported on roughly made cyclopean walls. Where they survive as raised, stone-built fragments, the roads are extremely well-made and trouble has been taken to make them go along the contour, skirting hills, making winding detours round the heads of ravines, avoiding steep rises and drops; they were clearly designed with minimal gradients so that they could take wheeled traffic, like carts and chariots.[42] The roads were 3.5–4m wide. Evans found similar roads in Crete.[43] The Mycenaean roads were built in as many as three layers, a foundation layer of large unworked field stones, then a 25cm thick layer of small stones and earth; spread on top of this was a surface of pebbles, earth and sand.

One road leads from the Lion Gate round the north side of the Mycenaean citadel, where ruts are visible 1.03m apart, which tells us the wheel gauge of a Mycenaean vehicle. From the sherds incorporated in it, the road passing along the southern flank of Mt Profitis Elias seems to have been built around 1250 BC. It divides in two at the foot of the mountain, one branch going round its western and northern flanks, over the main divide to Zygouries and then down to Corinth, the other running along the southern flank before turning north to reach Corinth by a more easterly route. A third road leaves Mycenae to take a north-north-easterly route towards Nemea before turning north-east to join the first Corinth road. A road south swings east to cross the Chavos ravine, heading for the Heraion and the fortress of Midea. It is assumed that another road branched off this to reach Argos, Mycenae's rival in importance and only eleven kilometres distant.[44] The remains of an old bridge built about the same time as the Lion Gate, and built of big boulders in the same cyclopean style, were found in 1962 below the south-west corner of the citadel at Mycenae. Unfortunately, the bridge was too near the mouth of the ravine, and it has been eroded out of all recognition by the force of the water; its huge blocks have been scattered along the bed of the torrent. Clues to the existence of the bridge nevertheless have survived in the sections of roadway approaching from either side. One led from the south-west to the Lion Gate. The other was the end of the road to Argos and Tiryns, which can still be followed for a short distance.[45]

Steffen assumed the roads were built with a primary military function.[46] There is no evidence that this was the case, and it would be safer to assume that a variety of traffic used the roads for trade and other everyday uses, and the way the roads zig-zag suggests that military use was not their prime function at all. No doubt warriors marched along them and noblemen drove along them in their chariots, for prestige and comfort rather than speed; it is equally probable that ordinary people used them, rather than walking through the thorny and stony scrubland of the hill country, and took their donkeys and wagons along them too.[47] Steffen's success in identifying well-planned and engineered roads radiating from Mycenae has not been matched elsewhere, even after a century-long search; it is not yet clear whether this is because the rulers at other centres did not go to the trouble of making road systems because they were less wealthy, or because their roads were not cut-and-terraced and have therefore gone unrecognized.

There were certainly some roads near Gla. One led at least 100m away from the south gate down a ramp, and another led away from the south-east gate, apparently heading for the Ptoon sanctuary, just as a road linked Mycenae to the Heraion. These roads were evidently designed to link the fortress of Gla with the reclaimed land around it. The Gla roads were wheel-rutted, like some of Mycenae's roads. Gla was almost certainly linked by roads with Orchomenos and other settlements round the lake shore; these would have been essential to carry out a major project like the draining of Lake Copais. A watchtower at Mytikas was probably used to pass signals between Kokoretsa and Vristika.[48]

Krisa, near Delphi, dominated the trade routes leading north from Kirrha into the interior. A fine stretch of roadway supported on 3m high cyclopean walls runs north-west from Krisa's badly ruined citadel's north gate, disappearing after about 500m. Another road seems to have left Krisa on the east side.[49] The protection of the trade routes was assisted by small semicircular and circular towers placed in passes in the mountains north of Amphissa. The best preserved of these is 6m in diameter, with walls standing to 2.5m.[50]

In Messenia, only one substantial 2km stretch of road has been identified, between Rizomylo and Nichoria, but it does lie on what must have been an important route linking Pylos and Kalamata.[51] No direct dating has come from the road itself, which consists of a schist gravel layer on the bare rock, but it passes tombs and settlement sites dating from 1300–1200 BC, so a Mycenaean date is likely. Near Kalamata and Giannitsa there are several sections of ancient highway scored with wheel ruts 1m apart, similar to the gauge of the wheel ruts at Mycenae.[52] At Analepsis in Arcadia there are more sections of highway with wheel ruts, heading towards Tegea and Sparta, but these have a (wider) 1.6m gauge – more likely classical, not Mycenaean.[53] Dating roads is often problematic, but the dating of the roads at Mycenae is secure; they are carried on cyclopean walling, the culverts and bridges make use of corbelled arches, and some Mycenaean potsherds were found in the road fill itself.

In Corinthia, it is now thought that the 'Isthmian Wall' was not a wall at all but a Mycenaean road built from sea to sea to join the Saronic Gulf to the Gulf of Corinth in the thirteenth century BC. Another section of highway, near Mylos Cheliotou, has been identified 4km west of Ancient Corinth; this was built in the mid-fourteenth century.[54]

In the Argolid, at least three roads led away from Tiryns. One ran east-north-east to connect the town with the dam site and may have continued to Midea. Another ran north to Prosymna and Mycenae. A third ran south to Nauplion, then east right across the peninsula to connect with Mycenaean sites near Epidaurus. The Epidaurus road is poorly preserved but several surviving bridges, like the four at Kazarma, show where the road ran: very close to the modern highway, in fact.[55]

Mycenae still stands alone as the only centre with a highly evolved, well-planned radial pattern of built roads covering the immediate hinterland. The cemeteries at Mycenae show an increase in population in the fourteenth century, whereas the built road system was developed in the thirteenth. Building the road system coincided with a phase of cultural and economic

Plate 2.7 A beautifully preserved Mycenaean bridge at Kazarma.

growth; the roads were built when the Lion Gate was built. Maybe the increase in population made it possible for the ruler of Mycenae to reorganize the economy, to attempt a more intensive exploitation of the hinterland by sending more people out to make it produce more. The roads would have made both the work and its supervision more efficient. There was a shift in the Mycenaean economy towards larger-scale agriculture, producing surpluses that could be exported. This was how Mycenae's huge balance of payments surplus was generated. The built roads reach out one or at most two hours' walk from Mycenae, probably the critical distance for effective management.[56] It may also be that the roads were pre-existing paths and that the ruler had them improved as a gesture of magnanimity towards his people – and as a display of wealth and greatness. We can see from the Lion Gate and tholos tombs that the rulers of Mycenae thought in terms of grandiose gestures of this kind.

The evidence is patchy and it may be argued that road systems only existed to tie regions economically and politically to their rulers' power bases. But it is also true that in Greece as elsewhere in Europe modern roads in many places follow, conceal and destroy earlier roads. If a bronze age Tirynthian wanted to visit Argos on the other side of the plain, the route he took would have been the one followed by the modern road, straight across flat open land. A road from Mycenae to Argos and Lerna will, equally certainly, have run along the western edge of the plain, where the present main road runs. And so on.

Jansen has argued that the road systems were exclusively intra-regional, not inter-regional, but it would be incredible if the roads leading north from Mycenae had not joined roads leading up into the mountains from Corinth and the Isthmus. It would be equally incredible if there was no road from Eleusis to Athens, and Jansen himself proposes that the route of the later Sacred Way followed the line of a bronze age road between the two centres. Evans found stretches of similar cut-and-terraced roads on Crete at intervals across the island and concluded that there was a 'great transit road' from Knossos near the north coast all the way to Kommos on the south coast, crossing the major watershed which was also the political boundary between the territories of Knossos and Phaistos,[57] although it is possible that the road was constructed after the Phaistos territory fell under the power of Knossos, in which case the 'great transit road' could still be regarded as intra-regional.

Homer gives us a vivid image of Telemachus driving in one of King Nestor's chariots with Nestor's son Pesistratus as his escort from Pylos to Sparta, to see Menelaus 'in lovely Lacedaimon'.[58] The short stretch of Mycenaean road between Rizomylo and Nichoria gives part of his route from Pylos across to the Further Province, but to the east the Taygetus Mountains

Plate 2.8 The eastern abutment of the Mycenaean bridge south of Mycenae.

posed a formidable obstacle. Were there no roads over these mountains, or were they not cut-and-terraced, or have we simply not found them yet? The easiest route across was possibly through the Leondari pass in the northeast, though it seems likely that the valley route to the east of Thouria (ancient Leuktron, the capital of the Further Province) was the main connecting road; this shorter route is likely to be the one Telemachus took to reach Sparta.[59] Homer mentions that the two-day journey was broken with a night at the house of Diocles in Pherae, modern Kalamata, not far south of Leuktron,[60] and the same route was used for the return journey, with another overnight stop at Pherae.[61] The difficult mountain roads would have been used less frequently than the lowland roads near the urban centres, but it cannot be doubted that they existed. The Greeks of Homer's time believed they existed. In the *Odyssey* Menelaus even offers to accompany Telemachus on a tour of Hellas and the land of the Argives, meaning the whole of Greece – a huge undertaking.[62] The *Odyssey* contains a recollection by later Greeks of a heroic age road system that was more effective and better integrated than the one that existed in their own day.

Chariots were doubtless used by aristocrats for transport, not least to display their rank, but they were probably rarely used in battle, except where the topography allowed. Chariots performed well on the prepared level surfaces of the roads, but would have been hopeless off-road on the rocky maquis. Homer in effect tells us that the heroes drove to battle and taunted their enemies from their chariots, but they usually fought on foot. Chariots were probably only used in close combat where armies met on flat alluvial plains, as at Troy, and even there it may sometimes have been necessary to clear the battlefield of stones, rather like preparing a pitch for a football or cricket match. Ordinary people probably used the roads as well, on foot or on donkeys, in general use as pack animals, then as in more recent times. Aristocrats owned horses, which they needed in pairs to draw their chariots.

Another form of transport was the palanquin or litter, an idea borrowed from Minoan Crete. Like the Minoan litter, the Mycenaean litter was set on four legs with a seat between the horizontal carrying poles, a closed back and a cloth cover to keep the sun off. Unlike the Minoan litter, which was flat-roofed, it had an arched roof supported on several hoops, like the wagons of the American West.[63] Litters were certainly not used by ordinary people, only by aristocrats, priests and priestesses.

Supporting his military road hypothesis, Steffen identified thirteen stone-built guardhouses at strategic points along the roads near Mycenae.[64] Some of these buildings and others identified later have turned out to be farmhouses belonging to the fourth century BC, and those of Mycenaean date do not stand next to the roads, so the links between the two are not obvious.[65] The buildings cannot be guardhouses or tollhouses, but most of them are within 4km of the citadel at Mycenae, in the same area as the built road system.

Discounting the later farmhouses, there are ten or eleven so-called block-houses in the Mycenae area.[66] One of them stood on the summit of Charvati (Mount Profitis Elias). It was first identified by Schliemann, who identified sherds of Mycenaean pottery from the site and interpreted it as a peak sanctuary.[67] Steffen preferred to see it as a signal station, seeing it as the beacon in the legend of Clytemnestra; he went on to identify a further series of look-out structures along the ridge.[68] In 1924, excavation by Wace confirmed Schliemann's and Steffen's dating. The main building, on the summit, was a small, irregularly shaped fort 20m by 15m; its surviving walls now support the platform on which the chapel stands. There were no figurines or other cult objects, so this was evidently not a peak sanctuary. The only remaining interpretation is that the building was a Mycenaean look-out. From it, sentries could observe armies approaching Mycenae from the east or north-east and signal by flag or fire to the citadel. From it, the fires of distant beacons could be seen, and it was almost certainly one of a chain of beacons transmitting key news across Greece. In Aeschylus' *Agamemnon* the last beacon fire announcing the fall of Troy is lit on this mountain top, bringing the news to Clytemnestra via a string of beacons all the way from Troy. Aeschylus' description is entirely plausible. Beacons could have taken the news by way of a series of intervisible summits from Troy to Lemnos, Mount Athos, Xiron and Dhirfis on Euboea, Parnon and Pateras in Attica and from there to Profitis Elias; the next beacon was probably on the Larissa at Argos.[69] Homer mentions that Agamemnon's eventual arrival home by sea in the Bay of Argos was observed by 'a spy in a watch-tower' posted by Aegisthus.[70]

A brazier for a beacon may have stood in the 'niche' on Voriki Diaselo. This terrace faces the citadel. Observers watching on the other side of the ridge, 100m away, would have had an excellent view of the Berbati valley, and could have used the niche to warn the citadel of danger approaching from that direction. A blockhouse on the Kalkani Hill, 1km south-west of the Mycenae citadel, had a splendid view across much of the northern Plain of Argos, and a distant view of Nauplion and Tiryns which could not be had from Mycenae itself.

Hill tops and cols were good vantage points. A few of the watch stations were on low ground, but even these had strategic value. Two were located about 100m away from bridges (the Plesia and Hagios Georgios bridges). Although they were too far back to 'defend' the bridges, they were well placed to observe any trouble there and signal it back to the citadel.

Clearly, with this series of watch stations it would not have been possible for anyone to approach Mycenae undetected.[71] With pre-arranged signals, for example raising flags of different colours, it would be possible for those in the citadel to be kept informed of everything happening within its immediate territory. The creation of a network of auxiliary posts seems

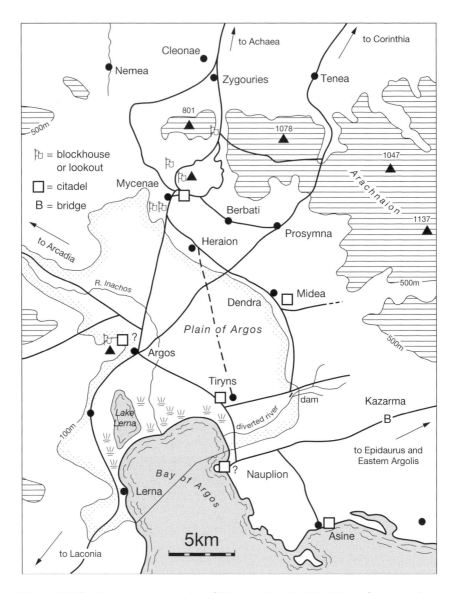

Figure 2.8 The Mycenaean geography of Western Argolis. The Plain of Argos and its surrounding mountains. Black dots are settlements, squares are citadels, flags are lookout posts, solid black lines are roads.

to have been a Mycenaean invention, devised by the increasingly wealthy and therefore increasingly vulnerable rulers of the late bronze age.

The web of roads radiating from Mycenae was almost certainly reproduced in other Mycenaean kingdoms, and in each case at the frontiers the roads picked their way over mountain passes to connect with the road systems of neighbouring states. How easy it was to travel long distances by land can only be guessed at, but Homer has Menelaus saying to Telemachus, 'It is a glorious privilege to travel far and wide in the world, but you must have a meal first.'[72] Homer implies in his reference to Telemachus' chariot journey from Pylos to Sparta that even the routes over mountains were manageable – it was the *speed* of the journey that turned it into an heroic exploit.

MYCENAE AND THE ARGOLID

Argolis was the most powerful of all the Mycenaean states, yet separated from its neighbours and defended against them in much the same way. Just as Pylos and Sparta were separated by a high ridge, the Taygetus Mountains, Sparta and Argolis were separated by the Parnon. In some ways, Argolis was a mirror image of Messenia, with its gulf, the Gulf of Argos, to the west and its mountainous peninsula to the east. But in Argolis the Hither Province must have been the Argive Plain, the location of the main cities of Argos and Mycenae, with southern Argolis taking a secondary position as the Further Province, although there are no clay tablets to confirm this. The sea bounded this great kingdom to the south and east, and it is surprising that there should be any doubt about the position of the boundary to the north. Immediately north of Mycenae a high east–west ridge makes a natural divide between Argolis and Achaea, and relatively few Mycenaean sites are found in the area; it is likely that this no man's land was the political boundary for much of the bronze age. It is only the Catalogue of Ships that throws doubt. Instead of listing Mycenae with the other Argive cities – Argos, Tiryns, Asine, Mases, Hermione, Troizen and Epidauros – Homer lists it with Corinth, Sicyon, Pellene, Cleonae and Aegion, implying that it was part of Achaea. Homer has Agamemnon remind us that his home is in Argos, yet he has the High King leading the armies of Achaea to Troy rather than those of Argolis. One possibility is that this was an expedient measure, reflecting the political tensions of the moment, rather than a long-term situation. Perhaps there was no one suitable to lead the Achaean forces; perhaps there were rival claimants for its leadership and they threatened the safety of the expedition; perhaps it was a show of solidarity with neighbours, like the provision of ships for the Arcadian troops; perhaps it had something to do with Agamemnon's wishing to give the trusted and able Diomedes a high-profile leadership role.

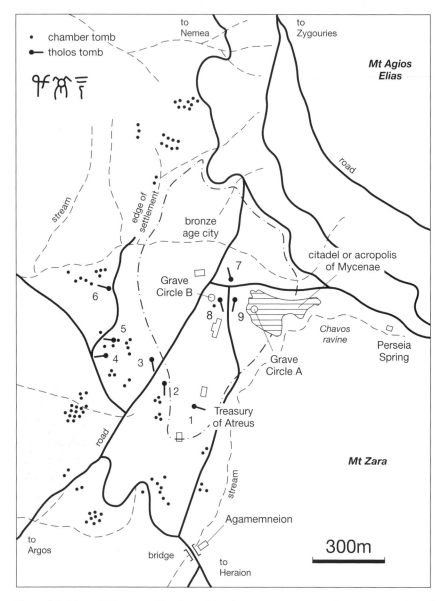

Figure 2.9 Map of Mycenae. The 'boxes' in the centre represent the scanty remains of Mycenaean houses. Note how the chamber tombs form clusters (cemeteries) outside the boundary of the bronze age city, which is shown as a dot-and-dash line. Roads are shown as solid black lines. Top left is the name 'Mycenae' in Linear B script. Tholos tombs: 1 Treasury of Atreus, 2 Panagra, 3 Epano Phournos, 4 Cyclopean Tomb, 5 Tomb of the Genii, 6 Kato Phournos, 7 Lion Tomb, 8 Tomb of Clytemnestra, 9 Tomb of Aegisthus.

The alternative, that Mycenae was an Achaean city, gives us a very strange scenario: a rich and powerful state, Argolis, with a great predatory fortress, the city of a foreign power, lurking in the hills above its plain. If so, it must have seemed to those at Argos and Tiryns as if Mycenae itself was the Lion of Nemea, the mythical gigantic lion which stalked the mountain sides between Nemea and Mycenae in ancient times, formidable in combat because invulnerable to weapons of stone, iron or bronze; only Heracles could best it. Greek legend gives Argos as the older, parent city and Mycenae as a later creation. Argos was ruled in turn by Argus, Phorbas, Triopas, Iasus, Crotopus, Gelanor, Danaus, Abas, Acrisius, Perseus, Meganthepes and Anaxagoras before being divided into three kingdoms under Alector, Bias and Melampus. It was Perseus, king of Argos, who founded Mycenae. The royal succession at Mycenae, again according to Greek legend, passed from Perseus to Electryon and then to Sthenelus, Eurystheus, Atreus, Thyestes, Agamemnon, Aegisthus, Aletis, Orestes and Tisamenus, who was the last king before the Return of the Heraclides.

Mycenae's power base seems to have been in the hills, the marginal lands, rather than in the Argive Plain. After a lull of several centuries, the Nemea valley to the north of Mycenae became densely inhabited. This expansion

Plate 2.9 The citadel at Mycenae: the view from the east. The reconstructed megaron platform can be seen jutting out top right. This is a perfect acropolis site, defended by very steep slopes on three sides.

Plate 2.10 The small coastal citadel at Asine. The entrance ramp left attackers exposed to their unshielded right. The walling to the left is Hellenistic, not Mycenaean.

of both human and agricultural resources may go some way towards explaining the increasing strength of Mycenae during the late bronze age.[73] The dynamism of the settlements across to the east, in the Berbati valley, may have had a similar effect.

The location of the Mycenaean centres is at first sight curious. They are not in the centre of fertile plains, the logical place if agricultural production was the main preoccupation. There was no Mycenaean township in the middle of the Argive Plain. The favoured sites are those with steep-sided hills, easily defended acropolis sites, and these are more often found where the hill country rises round the edge of the plain. Tiryns, like Athens, is unusual in being an acropolis site surrounded by a level plain.[74] In the Middle Helladic (2000–1600 BC) most of the Argives lived in the south, in an arc of settlements close to the Bay of Argos: Lerna, Argos, Tiryns, Asine. Of these, Lerna was the most important trading centre. As time passed, the number of settlements increased, with Midea and Berbati growing. Eventually Mycenae, well back from the sea, surpassed them all in importance – and perhaps just because it was entirely safe from attack from the sea.

The citadel of Mycenae seizes the attention of every modern visitor as an isolated fortification in a wilderness, but in its heyday it was the focus of an inhabited landscape. There was a city beside it. Only an élite group, the

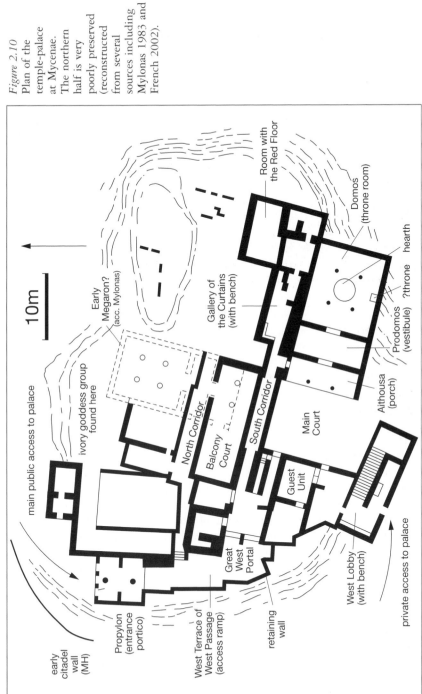

Figure 2.10 Plan of the temple-palace at Mycenae. The northern half is very poorly preserved (reconstructed from several sources including Mylonas 1983 and French 2002).

10m

main public access to palace

early citadel wall (MH)

Propylon (entrance portico)

West Terrace of West Passage (access ramp)

retaining wall

Great West Portal

West Lobby (with bench)

private access to palace

Guest Unit

Main Court

South Corridor

North Corridor

Balcony Court

ivory goddess group found here

Early Megaron? (acc. Mylonas)

Gallery of the Curtains (with bench)

Room with the Red Floor

Domos (throne room)

Prodomos (vestibule)

Aithousa (porch)

?throne

hearth

rulers, priests and priestesses and their servants, lived in the citadel. The rest of the community lived in an open and apparently informal settlement stretching away to the north, north-west and south-west. At one time it was thought that they built their houses in small distinct family groups separated by open spaces reserved for their family graves. Roads and lanes linked these neighbourhoods with each other, with the citadel, and with their farms, which straggled down towards the Argive Plain.[75] Mylonas thought Mycenae was not a city in the modern sense, but a collection of villages; he was encouraged in this because the name Mycenae, a Mycenaean survival, Mukenai, is a plural word.

The burials have been systematically explored, but the town has been relatively little studied as yet. The remains appear unexciting, as the site is badly eroded and only a few foundations seem to have survived. But recent survey work suggests that Mylonas was mistaken; the cemeteries are not associated with separate villages, but are distinct and separate from the settlement area, which formed quite a large and probably continuous area extending south-westwards along the Panagia ridge. One feature that Mycenae shares with other Mycenaean cities is that elevation is associated with status. Within the citadel, the 'palace' has deliberately been placed on the highest part of the site. The most imposing buildings in the town, outside the citadel, were built on the Panagia ridge and on its eastern slope, where they looked across the main road to Argos towards the citadel. The lower-status housing lay on the western slope of the Panagia ridge and to the north and north-west of the citadel.[76] Bronze age Mycenae begins to look more like a city, the city the goddess Hera called 'Mycenae of the broad streets'. At its southern edge, there are no signs of a fortification wall, but there was a guardhouse guarding the point where the Argos highway entered the city.

THE 'PALACE' AT MYCENAE

Building the 'palace' on the summit of the citadel, 38m above the Lion Gate, has exposed it to severe erosion, and its south-east corner long ago collapsed into the ravine. The architecture is of the same general sort as at Pylos, with a sequence of porches and small courtyards leading to an imposing megaron, a three-part rectangular building with a porch, vestibule and large room with circular hearth and four pillars.[77]

There was probably an early 'palace' on the acropolis at the time when the shaft graves of Grave Circle A were being dug for the warrior chieftains.[78] At least two building phases are evident in the surviving structure, and there seems to have been an earlier phase that pre-dated the building of the citadel wall.[79] Mylonas suggests that there was a megaron close to the summit, in the north-western area of the later 'palace'. It does seem likely that there was a focal building on the site, whether one interprets it as a residence or a temple, from the time of the shaft graves onward. To gain an impression of what the early building would have looked like, we must turn to the less spectacular site of the Menelaion, near Sparta. This was a settlement in the early Mycenaean phase, with a focal building that was not built over later, because the site was abandoned around 1350 BC. The building was about 20m square with a megaron at its centre: a large rectangular room with an ante-room and a porch. Originally the main room would have had a central hearth and a seat of honour against the wall on the right as one entered. Along each side of the megaron ran a corridor giving access to rooms beyond; behind the main room was a store room accessible from outside. Buildings like this were built at all the major centres of mainland Greece: Mycenae, Tiryns, Argos, Pylos, Athens, Thebes, Orchomenos and Iolkos.[80]

At Mycenae as at Pylos, there is a corridor along one side of the 'palace', giving access to a suite of small rooms, but unlike Pylos at Mycenae the comparable suite on the other side has gone – assuming that it once existed. A more important difference is that Mycenae's 'palace' had a second megaron, opening out of the north side of the corridor. The 'palace' remains that we now see represent a rebuilding, following large-scale levelling and terracing to create the flat surfaces needed for impressive architectural effects. It suffered badly from fire at least twice towards the end of its life. The first 'palace' is inevitably difficult to reconstruct with any confidence. There was probably a south–north oriented megaron on the summit, with a few smaller rooms ranged along its sides. It was reached by a path up the acropolis, curving round the northern, western and southern flanks of the hill; its course was formalized during the major rebuilding to make a walled and partly roofed ceremonial approach.

The second 'palace' was approached by entering the Propylon, excavated in 1959, a 7m square canopied porch with a column on each side, just like the porch at Pylos. This opened into a small courtyard open to the sky and bounded on the west by a major retaining wall forming the western boundary of the palace precinct. The floor slopes gradually up along the West Passage, a continuation of the courtyard, to the great West Portal; in front of this the West Passage made a balcony giving a magnificent view out across the Argive Plain. Only a large threshold stone remains of the West Portal, but it was probably another pillared portico. Inside it, to the east, are the remains of two passageways, one leading to the Main Court and one leading to the corridor flanking the north side of the megaron.

The Main Court measures 11.5m by 15m, larger than the court at Pylos, but only half the area of the court at Tiryns. The north wall was for hundreds of years buried beneath the foundations of a Hellenistic temple; it turns out to be 2.5m high and made of six courses of ashlars. The lower courses show signs of the two fires that brought Mycenae down. How high the south wall

Figure 2.11 Reconstruction of the temple-palace at Mycenae. The view is from west to east, with the summit complex in the foreground and the House of Columns in the background. The two entrances to the temple are bottom left and bottom right (developed from Papahatzis 1978).

of the court was is unknown, but if it was over 1.5m the superb view of the plain would have been lost, and also the relieving southerly winds that bring comfort in hot Greek summers. The court was remade, first coated with lime plaster, then later covered with a thick layer of painted stucco. Though apparently open to the sky, the courtyard was painted to simulate large multi-coloured marble tiles, yellow, blue, red, with lined textures added in black. A similar technique was used in Minoan Crete, copied on Thera – and imported to Mycenae. This painted floor did not last long as the surrounding buildings were again gutted by fire, probably generated by another earthquake.

The megaron opening from the eastern side of the court is very similar in size and design to those at Tiryns and Pylos, measuring 13m by 11.5m internally. Only the foundations survive, so the building itself must be imagined from these footings and the fragments of painted plaster found among them. The impressive portico or *aithousa*, to use its name in Homer, had a flat canopy held aloft by two big 'Minoan' tapering pillars. Round its plastered walls ran a dado with painted rosettes and triglyphs; a frieze of running spirals may have run round the wall tops. At the southern end of the portico stood two small altars and a libation bowl, underlining the cult use of the megaron. The huge doorway into the vestibule or *prodomos* was closed with heavy double wooden doors mounted on bronze-shod pivots.[81] The walls of the 4.4m deep *prodomos* were also decorated with painted plaster, while the floor was made of painted stucco, like the court outside, but bordered with one-metre slabs of gypsum, presumably imported from Crete; the great temple-palace at Knossos had both floors and wall-linings of gypsum, and was still in use in the early days of the palace at Mycenae. Another huge doorway, this time apparently closed by curtains, led into the main room, the *domos*.

The south-eastern portion of the *domos* has fallen into the Chavos ravine, but the modern reconstruction at least allows us a sense of the space. It was a fine room 13m long, 11.5m wide, paved in exactly the same way as the vestibule. Four layers of lime cement are detectable, showing that the floor was periodically remade. The fire that destroyed the building severely damaged the frescoes that lined the walls, but they evidently included scenes of warriors with their squires, horses and chariots, and their womenfolk looking on from the safety of a rocky citadel – just as described in the *Iliad*.

Plate 2.11 The Chavos ravine (left) and citadel (right and foreground). This view south from the temple-palace at Mycenae shows the citadel's spectacular defensive site.

The centrepiece of the *domos* was a huge round hearth 3.7m across –
slightly bigger than the Pylos hearth – with stylized flames painted round
its sides. Signs of fire on it are taken to indicate its use, but could as easily
be marks of the final conflagration, which left its scars on the walls outside
the megaron.[82] The four great columns round the hearth were nevertheless
sheathed in bronze, which does suggest that they needed protecting from
accidental burning from a fire that regularly burned in the hearth. It is
assumed that there was a throne on the south side, to the right on entering
the room, though there is no direct evidence of a throne here.

The pillars were 4.5m high and although it is possible it seems unlikely
there was another storey above.[83] Detailed work on the site in the 1980s
allows a confident reconstruction of a single-storey rectangular structure,
probably with an elaborately corniced flat roof and certainly with a sky-
light over the hearth to allow light in and smoke out. The discovery elsewhere on site of chimney pots opens the possibility that a chimney stood
on top of the light-well roof.[84] It may be that shutters in the clerestory
were opened or shut by servants on the roof, according to the changing
direction of the wind and the changing need for ventilation and heat conservation in the *domos*. It has been suggested that the windows at Knossos were
covered with translucent oiled parchment, so that they let in light but not
wind or dust, and it may be that this was also used on the proposed clerestory
shutters at Mycenae. At night, torches would have lit the room. Homer
describes the palace of Alcinous in Phaeacia. Odysseus notices 'golden
youths' standing 'on well built pedestals, holding lighted torches in their
hands to give light by night to the banqueters in the hall'.[85] The floor slab
immediately inside the door, on the right as you enter, is slightly raised –
just 6cm – perhaps to give a torch-bearer greater height.[86]

The gypsum flooring round the edge of the room may have been designed
to give a firm base for furniture, such as chairs. If visitors, guests, courtiers
and family were seated round the walls and circulated in that zone, the
central painted areas would receive less wear. Again, there is support in
Homer: 'When Odysseus entered the *domos* of the megaron he saw thrones
along the wall on either hand . . . and on them the leaders of the Phaeacians
were wont to sit drinking and eating.'[87]

On the western side of the Main Court was a square room (Room 52)
with probably some smaller rooms beside it. Mylonas thinks this was a
guest-house.[88] On the other hand, Homer gives no support for this. Even
princely guests in Homer are never given rooms in the palaces, nor are they
allowed, presumably out of consideration for the host's security, to sleep in
the principal room. They are always accommodated in the portico. During
their visit to Menelaus, Telemachus and Pesistratos are given beds in the
aithousa, which is explained by Homer as being 'in the forecourt of the
domos'.[89] Odysseus, visiting the palace of Alcinous, sleeps in the *aithousa*.[90]
Telemachus sleeps in the 'echoing' *aithousa* at the Palace of Nestor.[91] Given

Plate 2.12 Grand Staircase on the south side of the temple-palace at Mycenae. This is the view down onto the staircase from the temple-palace courtyard.

these very specific, repeated and consistent indications of the nature of bronze age Mycenaean hospitality, and royal hospitality at that, it is unclear why Mylonas presses for the building on the western side of the Main Court to be interpreted as a hotel.[92] It may rather be that that block was the accommodation for the king and his family.[93] Although the megaron was doubtless used for ceremonial and semi-public functions, such as entertaining visiting princes, it is unlikely to have been the everyday habitation of the king.

A South-West Grand Staircase gave access from outside the palace precinct directly into this suite, which meant that the king and his family might come and go more easily. Considerations of safety too may have dictated that a second access and exit point was worth having. We might remember here how Agamemnon's triumphant return from Troy ended in assassination in one of the chambers round the courtyard. The first flight of this staircase survives: twenty-two shallow steps of regular sandstone blocks, originally coated and smoothed up with stucco, lead up to a rectangular landing. The return flight has been destroyed. The odd orientation of the Grand Staircase shows that it was the last part of the palace to be built, not part of the original design. It may be significant that returning staircases with mezzanine landings, built within rectangular boxes of stout masonry, were a feature at Knossos and Akrotiri – and that this too was a Mycenaean borrowing from Crete.

Along the north side of the Main Court runs the wall showing signs of burning. Beside that is a corridor, apparently originally designed to lead to the small rooms (of unknown purpose) to the north of the megaron. North of the corridor is a very badly damaged area, explored to bedrock in the 1960s by George Mylonas and Leslie Shear. Scanty remains of foundations suggest the existence of a second megaron, slightly smaller than the main one, arranged to open onto the Main Court or, more likely, the corridor running alongside it. Strong evidence for this comes in the form of four large conglomerate pillar bases, which look very much like fittings for the four central pillars of a *domos*.

The area to the east of that has yet to be explored in detail. Since the other Mycenaean palaces had store rooms, this north-east quadrant may be where they lay. Alternatively, it may be the residence of the ruler. The overall picture is of an integrated and well-planned complex of buildings around 50m by 60m, substantial by Mycenaean standards. It nevertheless dwindles into insignificance once we realize that the temple at Knossos was seven times larger in area, and not the one or two storeys of Mycenae, but up to four or five.[94]

The picture changes, though, if the impressive buildings to the east of the megaron were part of the 'palace', and their architecture implies that they may have been.[95] The so-called House of Columns, which is part of this eastward extension, was evidently a high-status building, entered from the north through an imposing doorway. French comments that its layout resembles the 'palace' of Odysseus as described by Homer,[96] which may be telling us that the House of Columns is the residence of the ruler of Mycenae. The entrance passage leads to a central court 15m by 12m, colonnaded on three sides. On the north side a small megaron about 15m long by 7m wide opens onto it. This had a central hearth and a chimney. There is a corridor leading out of the south-west corner of the court on the same line as the entrance passage. The layout is a little like that of the Main Court, megaron and Guest Hostel to the west, but on a much smaller scale. If this East Wing is included in the 'palace', the area extends to one hectare, which is just over twice the size of the 'palaces' at Tiryns and Pylos, and only a little smaller than Knossos.

THE CITIES OF THE ARGIVE PLAIN

Mycenae commands an impressive view across the Argive Plain, the lowland that probably produced much of its grain, vegetables and livestock, especially horses, and must also have provided its normal route to the sea. Close to the Bay of Argos, though no longer actually on the coast, is Tiryns, a great strong-walled fortress built on a low rocky hill rising out of the flat lowland. Tiryns commanded the bay and the southern part of the plain.

Plate 2.13 The view from the citadel at Mycenae. The Treasury of Atreus can be made
out in the middle distance, just to the right of centre, and the Plain of Argos
beyond. Argos itself is marked by the two conical hills in the top left-hand
corner.

Earlier buildings stood on this crag, beginning in the neolithic, when it
would have been an island in a coastal saltmarsh.[97] As medieval strategists
in Europe were to rediscover, a swamp is the best defence, impossible to
traverse on foot, chariot or horseback, or by boat.

The visible remains are those of the final development, the thirteenth-
century fortress, the one Homer referred to as 'Tiryns of the mighty walls'.
Homer's descriptive phrase is impeccably apt. The walls of Tiryns are even
more massive than Mycenae's. All the circuit walls are very thick; at the
southern end, where attack was expected from the sea, they are thick enough
to have a suite of rooms inside them. These remarkable walls are the ones
that were the first to be described as 'Cyclopean', named after the Cyclopes
who were brought in from Anatolia by the founder of Tiryns, Proitos, who
was at war with his brother Akrisios, grandfather of Perseus, at Mycenae.
In legend, this was the first cyclopean citadel, built by Proitos using the
Cyclopes, and it seems to have been the first cyclopean citadel *in fact*, built
in around 1375 BC. In legend, the citadel at Mycenae was also built by the
Cyclopes, under the direction of Perseus, a contemporary of Meganthes,
the son of Proitos; in fact archaeology suggests that the citadel at Mycenae
was indeed built about a generation after Tiryns, around 1350 BC.[98] The
existence of the two near-contemporary but not twin fortresses at opposite
ends of the Argive Plain suggests that they may have been an expression
of rivalry between two contending powers. Probably the Argive towns were
under separate kings rather like feudal barons, with a certain amount of

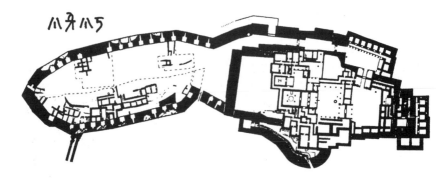

Figure 2.12 Plan of the citadel at Tiryns, showing the massive thickness of the outer fortification wall. Top left is the name 'Tiryns' in Linear B script.

freedom of action while, ultimately, owing allegiance to a High King based at Mycenae.

It would have taken five years to build the inner and outer skins of the circuit walls, before the addition of the rubble filling. The scale of work was enormous. The Tiryns walls were built after those at Mycenae, but the concept of a circuit wall had a long ancestry. At Thermi on Lesbos, five successive towns were built on the same site between 2600 and 2400 BC. Thermi was surrounded by a circuit wall and its houses were of the megaron type; the megaron too was a deep-rooted part of the Mycenaean tradition.[99] After this early phase, Thermi was abandoned for a thousand years, then briefly revived before being destroyed, apparently caught up in the Mycenaean expedition against Troy. Homer has Achilles sleeping with a woman of Lesbos, who was probably captured in the raid on Thermi. Poliochne, on the east coast of Lemnos, was another substantial bronze age town with a circuit wall, though it did not prevent Poliochne from being destroyed during another raid in 1900 BC.[100]

The entrance to the fully developed thirteenth-century citadel at Tiryns is by way of a long and intentionally tiring ramp beneath the east wall, cleverly designed so that attackers would have to file up with their unshielded right sides exposed to the defenders on the wall above. As at Mycenae, the main entrance area was carefully built of massive blocks to intimidate attackers by conveying an impression of enormous power. The ramp led to the Outer Gate, a doorless opening through the 8m thick wall, into a passage that in turn led to a massive gateway originally closed by double doors; this was the Middle Gate. The pivot holes of these doors can still be seen, and so can the slots in the huge gateposts that held the massive closing bar. Still further in is yet another gate, the Inner Gate, opening into a 25m long Outer Court. Along the eastern side of this court are casemates – seven store rooms and a service passage – built into the thickness of the

Plate 2.14 The impressive entrance passage at Tiryns, a death-trap for attackers.

wall. To the south of the larger Inner Court, the next internal feature, is a further suite of five store rooms also built into the thickness of the circuit wall. It is thought that towers rose from the south-east and south-west corners of the fortress, to ensure that nothing happening out in the Bay of Argos escaped the notice of the lord of Tiryns.

From the Inner or Great Court, visitors passed through a Propylon, like the one at Pylos, but with two columns, not one, on each side. This gave entry to a corner of another courtyard, the main feature of which was an altar with a sacrificial pit, possibly dedicated to Zeus Herkeios, God of the Fenced Court. On the north side of this court was a megaron, fitted out much like the megara at Mycenae and Pylos. It is assumed that a throne was placed against the wall to the right on entering, as at Pylos. In the centre was a large round hearth surrounded by four great columns. There are more rooms to the east of the megaron, including a second smaller megaron and two small courts. This whole suite, from the Second Propylon onwards, has the appearance of a 'palace'; it is very like the 'palace' of Nestor at Pylos, but crammed claustrophobically within the walls of the most formidable fortress imaginable.

A strong transverse wall was added to the north of the 'palace' to give it even greater protection. This incidentally created an extra court, from which a staircase descended through the west wall to make a service access;

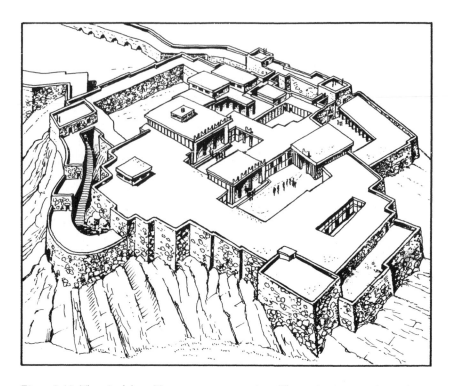

Figure 2.13 The citadel at Tiryns: a reconstruction. The main entrance is at the top
(facing towards the town and away from the coast), the postern gate bottom
left, the temple-palace at the centre.

the staircase was then seen as a weak point, and an extra loop of massively
thick circuit wall was thrown out to enclose and protect it.

Later, a much longer loop of circuit wall was thrown round the whole of
the northern end of the hill, doubling the size of the fortress. The outer
bailey this created was designed as a refuge for all the inhabitants of the
town outside the walls, and probably their livestock too. In the north-west
of the outer bailey two secret passages led down beneath the wall, so that
those trapped in the fortress could, in the event of a siege, reach the spring-
fed cisterns at the foot of the hill. The late expansion and reinforcement of
the defence works at Tiryns clearly show the apprehension and the fear of
attack that hung in the air at the end of the thirteenth century.[101]

A stream flowing towards Tiryns from the hills to the east was perceived
to be a sufficient problem by the Tirynthians that they diverted it. Work
of this kind was not usual at this period, so for the diversion to have been
considered necessary, the stream must have caused flooding in the town.
About 1km north of the modern village of Ayios Adrianos, the Tirynthians

built a dam 100m long across the stream, diverting its flow from west to south-west, well away from Tiryns.

Across the Argive Plain, on rising ground at its western edge and commanding the whole plain, stands the town of Argos. The legendary tradition of Argos as the oldest and ultimately most important Argive city in antiquity is not really borne out by the archaeological remains. It seems never to have dominated, in spite of having a perfect location and a perfectly respectable acropolis site. There are hints that Argos was subordinate, even in Homer. The Catalogue of Ships has the Argive contingent led by two descendants of kings of Argos, but they are dominated by and outshone by Diomedes, who is the son of an Aetolian exile but also totally loyal and subservient to Agamemnon. Argos was not to become the capital of Argolis until the Mycenaean period was over.

To the north-west of modern Argos are two hills. Cyclopean blocks on the Larissa hill may be the remains of a Mycenaean watchtower; probably the lower and more accessible Aspis hill would have made a more attractive site for a citadel, with its summit plateau 200m across. Many of the tombs were located on a third hill, the Deiras. The Late Mycenaean (1400–1100 BC) city below is known to have been very large with some high-status buildings, but it is by no means certain that it had a fortress.[102] Indeed, if the king at Mycenae suspected the loyalty of the king of Argos, he may have forbidden its fortification. Alternatively, the massive fortifications at Mycenae, Tiryns and Midea may have been considered sufficient defence for the Plain.[103]

Opposite Argos, dominating the eastern edge of the Argive Plain, is Midea. One of the least known Mycenaean sites, Midea was nevertheless the third fortress of the Argolid, after Mycenae and Tiryns, and built on a high conical hill about halfway between them.[104] Recent excavations confirm Midea's great importance, which might have been guessed from its massive circuit walls enclosing 24,000 square metres of acropolis and terraces – bigger than the contemporary walled city of Jericho. The south-west slope is so steep that it needs no artificial defence at all.

Midea had two gates, to east and west. The recently cleared East Gate led to an Inner Gate, a passageway between two massive walls, as at Tiryns. On the lower terrace was an important building destroyed by a great fire and probably earthquake around 1220–1200 BC, again as at Tiryns.[105] The destruction is thought to have been caused by an earthquake because the remains of a young girl were found inside a room, crushed by the collapsing building; her skull and spine were smashed by falling masonry. The West Gate was also uncovered recently. Like the Lion Gate at Mycenae it was partly defended by an extension of the fortification wall to make a bastion. Inside the West Gate was a series of workshops built on terraces parallel to the circuit wall. Fresco fragments and terracotta roof tiles hint at well-made buildings within the citadel.

Plate 2.15 The citadel wall at Midea, with the Plain of Argos top right.

Midea has yielded both ordinary household pottery and fine decorated high-status ware dating from the period 1250–1200 BC. There was also jewellery, and a large terracotta figure of a goddess very similar to the large wheel-made idols found in shrines at Mycenae and Tiryns. The admittedly fragmentary evidence points to the citadel at Midea as being similar in character to those at Mycenae and Tiryns, with a 'palace' suite, shrines, workshops, dwellings and strongly built surrounding fortifications. No doubt continuing excavation will produce more revelations in due course.

Below the citadel in the area known as Dendra was a city, evidently with a wealthy élite, as there were rich burials nearby. One fourteenth-century king of Midea was buried here in a vaulted tomb with valuable grave goods, not quite as plentiful as those found in the shaft graves at Mycenae but equally beautiful. One of the finest objects of Mycenaean craftsmanship was found here, a shallow gold cup decorated with marine motifs: dolphins, rocks and long-tentacled octopuses.[106] It was at Dendra too that the rich warrior-hero's burial was found, with a complete suit of Mycenaean bronze armour.

THE KINGDOMS OF THE NORTH

North and north-west of Argolis, as we have seen, lay the kingdom of Achaea. Its focus was the fertile lowland flanking the southern shore of the Gulf of Corinth. The Catalogue of Ships implies that its principal city was Mycenae, but for the reasons already discussed it seems more likely that one of the towns north of the divide was its capital. Corinth presents itself as a natural candidate, with its strategic location at the head of the Gulf of Corinth where roads converge to cross the isthmus, yet it is not conspicuous in Homer, and seems to have risen to prominence only in the early historic period, in the seventh or eighth centuries BC. Nevertheless, a site close to the isthmus must have commanded the road network and therefore the territory in the Mycenaean period.

Elis in the north-west Peloponnese was another kingdom. Its capital is uncertain too. The magic name of Olympia presents itself as a possible centre, but its development seems to have been entirely post-Mycenaean.[107] The Temple of Hera was very ancient and the Altis (= sacred grove) was a holy place before the temple-building started and before written records began; even so, the site does not necessarily pre-date the first millennium BC. Archaeology suggests Teikhos Dymaion, an impressive Cyclopean stronghold in the north, overlooking a fertile plain; this was ancient Dymaia.[108]

In the centre of the Peloponnese lay land-locked Arcadia, with a fertile plain perched 600m above sea level as its focus. Its main towns in the sixth century BC were Mantineia, Arcadian Orchomenos and Tegea, where only traces of the later perimeter walls remain.

The city-states of the Peloponnese were the most powerful in the Mycenaean world, but it must not be forgotten that as many kingdoms again, and of the same culture, lay to the north of the Gulf of Corinth, in the region that is now central Greece.

In the west lay the land of the Aetolians; offshore lay the island group of Zakynthos, Cephallenia and Ithaca, where, according to Homer, Odysseus was king. Later, by the fourth century BC, this would be known as Acarnania, which may or may not have been its name in Mycenaean times. The location of Odysseus' capital and palace continues to puzzle scholars, and archaeology has so far failed to resolve the matter conclusively. Homer implies that Ithaca was one of a group of four islands.[109] Zakynthos, Cephallenia and Ithaca obviously make up three of them, but where is the fourth? It could be Leucas, even though that is strictly a narrow-necked mainland peninsula. Some, following Dörpfeld's lead, have proposed that Leucas fits Homer's description of Odysseus' home better than Ithaca; Dörpfeld himself identified the remains of a building on the shore of Vlicho Bay as Odysseus' palace, but the building seems to be three hundred years too early. Ithaca does in fact answer Homer's description fairly well, and his account works well if taken literally. Telemachus may have landed at the port of Andri at the southern tip of Ithaca on his return from Pylos. The town, Odysseus' capital, was a half-day's journey from the port, so it cannot have been at Aetos, halfway along the island and only 6km away. Stavros, near the northern tip of Ithaca and 15km from Andri, is a likelier location for the stronghold of Odysseus. There is only one island that could be used to waylay the homecoming ship between Andri and the town (ancient Polis?)

and that is Daskalio, a small island immediately south-west of Stavros.[110] Stavros is on a high ridge with commanding views down into the four bays at the northern end of Ithaca: Polis Bay to the south, Afales and Frikes Bays to the north and Kioni Bay to the east. The strategic value of this easily defended site is obvious. A citadel stood there in 1200 BC and Mycenaean artefacts have been recovered, including large-handled jars for grain and oil, bronze spearheads, goblets, kylikes and spindle-whorls. Homer tells us that Odysseus was given thirteen tripod cauldrons as a parting gift by the Phaeacians of Scheria (thought by some to be Corfu), and that he took them home to Ithaca. Athene advised Odysseus to hide them 'in some corner of this sacred cave, where they may lie in safety'.[111] If Stavros was the citadel of Odysseus then Polis Bay immediately below it is likely to have been the site of his harbour town. In 1932 archaeologists working in a cave sanctuary at Polis Bay found many relics from the Mycenaean period, including a fragment of a three-legged cauldron. These bronze basins had a high value as ceremonial objects and were awarded as prizes at games; perhaps the winners were expected to donate their prizes to the gods at sanctuaries like the cave shrine. Perhaps the Mycenaean kings of Ithaca were given tripod cauldrons as gifts which they dedicated in this way, 'in some corner of this sacred cave', much as Homer describes.[112]

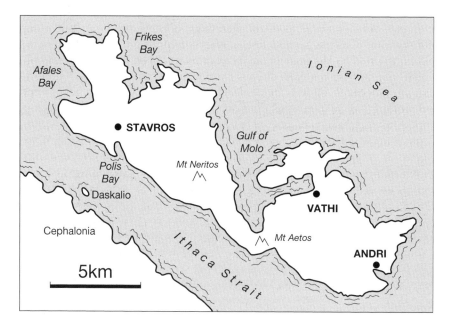

Figure 2.14 Ithaca. The citadel of Odysseus was probably at Stavros and the town below, at Polis Bay.

Figure 2.15 A procession of men and hunting dogs, with tripod-cauldrons carried as high-status offerings. Fresco from the room above Room 46 at Pylos. On the right is a reconstruction of one such bronze cauldron, found in the sacred cave at Polis – just where Odysseus left it?

In the east of central Greece lay Boeotia, a large kingdom with two coast-lines, one on the Gulf of Corinth, the other on the Gulf of Euboea. In Boeotia, Thebes was the main city. The Theban citadel, the Kadmeion, stood on rising ground in the middle of a fertile plain. The site of a great Mycenaean palatial building has been located, and along with it a miscel-laneous collection of thirty-six engraved cylinder seal-stones and nine unengraved seals. Their late bronze age Theban owner is very unlikely to have been able to read these seal-stones, so his purpose in acquiring them is obscure. Was it a Mycenaean prince who collected obscure antiquities? If so, was his interest in collecting objects from the east connected with the legendary founder of the Theban royal dynasty, Kadmos, who himself came from the Levant? Or was it instead a craftsman amassing a reservoir of exotic images to copy?[113] The answer is perhaps more prosaic, residing in the material rather than the artefact. Lapis lazuli, which came from Afghanistan, was difficult to obtain and greatly prized in the bronze age. An embassy to the king of Ugarit in the thirteenth century BC said, 'the Hittite king is very interested in lapis lazuli. If you send him some he will show you favours.' Other documents show that one mina in weight (about 500g) of lapis lazuli was considered an appropriate gift to a king to foster good relations. It must be highly significant that among the Theban seal-stones is a group from Babylon that weighs just one mina. They formed part of the temple repository of the Temple of Marduk in Babylon; Babylon was sacked by the Assyrians in about 1225 BC; presumably the Assyrian king acquired the seal-stones at that time and, perhaps shortly afterwards, sent one mina's worth of them as a gift to the Mycenaean king of Thebes. At this time the Hittites were trying to enforce a trading embargo on Assyria, and possibly on the Greeks too. This might explain why the Assyrian king was keen to forge an alliance with Greek kings who, like himself, were suffering at the hands of the Hittites.[114]

Thebes was the capital of Boeotia, but as in Argolis there were other settlements, some of them of considerable size and importance, some with their own citadels. Eutresis, eleven kilometres south-west of Thebes, had an acropolis with a Mycenaean circuit wall.

Thebes' principal neighbour and rival was the city of Orchomenos, which overlooked its own separate fertile plain. Orchomenos was a very ancient settlement dating back to around 6000 BC, when a village of round huts stood on the site. It was not until 2000 BC that the rectangular and apse-ended megaron appeared, along with wheel-made pottery; this was the early bronze age culture that Schliemann named 'Minyan', and may represent the arrival of Greek-speaking incomers. The Mycenaean civilization developed out of this, in Boeotia, without a break, but very obviously with influences from outside, especially from Minoan Crete. A fine beehive tomb survives, though with its roof collapsed; it was known in classical times as 'The Treasury of Minyas', just as the finest tomb at Mycenae was known as 'The Treasury of Atreus': in each case the tomb was named after the assumed founder of the royal dynasty.[115] The Treasury of Minyas stands just outside the jag-walled citadel of Orchomenos, much as the tholos tombs do at Mycenae, and Tholos Tomb IV at Pylos. The Orchomenos citadel stands on a low east–west ridge rising from the western end of what was a huge shallow seasonal lake fringed by swamps and level farmland – Lake Copais. The Treasury of Minyas stands just in front of its main east gate, facing the lake.

Homer describes Orchomenos as extremely rich. It was, and its wealth was founded in part on a great engineering achievement. The plain at Orchomenos was liable to floods. The River Kephissos had no surface outlet to the sea, but under summer conditions drained away to the east through a series of swallow holes in the limestone. In winter, the underground

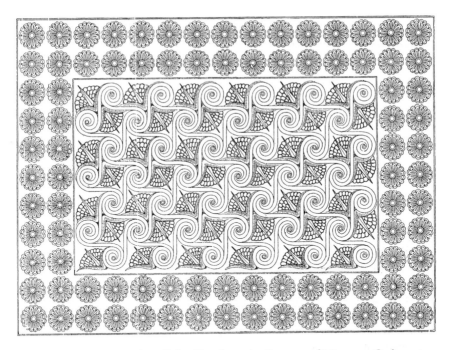

Figure 2.16 The spectacular relief ceiling from the Treasury of Minyas at Orchomenos. This illustration shows the central panel, which was surrounded by a wide border of running spirals and rosettes. Similar ceilings were moulded in plaster at Knossos, but this masterpiece was carved in *stone*. The decorated ceiling measured 2.6m by 2.7m and the design is thought to have been based on a carpet pattern. The ceiling is thought to have remained intact until 1870, when nearby villagers heard 'a great noise' as it collapsed under the weight of the overlying debris (after Schuchhardt 1891).

drainage system could not cope with the volume of rainfall, causing the water to back up and flood the plain. The inhabitants of Orchomenos worked on the swallow holes themselves, enlarging them when they could get at them in dry weather, and they also created a system of artificial channels, traces of which survive. The drainage canals were 40m wide with banks on each side. They also began a more ambitious project to tunnel through the hills to the east, though this was never finished. Lake Copais and the marshes round it were successfully drained during the Mycenaean period, creating a much larger area of fertile plain about 100m above sea level, in effect a 90km^2 polder.

The rivalry between Thebes and Orchomenos for supremacy in Mycenaean Boeotia became legendary, and the archaeology of the area supports the legend. Evidence for warfare includes the huge fortress at Gla, which was built at the eastern end of Lake Copais. This irregular, colossal, pistol-shaped

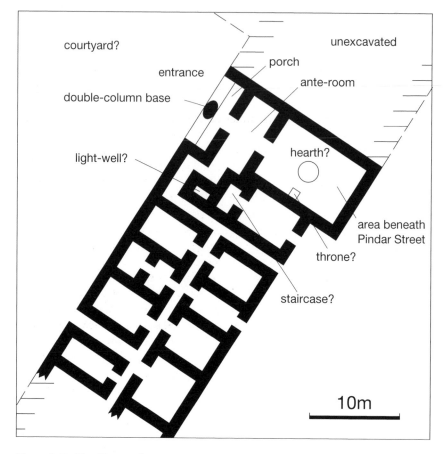

Figure 2.17 The House of Kadmos. A plan of the South Wing of the First 'Palace' at Thebes. The eastern side, which lies under a modern street, is speculative, but the megaron layout implies the presence of a hearth and a throne (after Symeonoglou 1985). The L shape is reminiscent of the 'palace' at Gla.

enclosure has massive Cyclopean circuit walls 3m thick and 3km long with four gates, enclosing a citadel seven times larger than the citadel at Mycenae. It was built two generations later than Mycenae, in around 1300 BC, and the inner and outer skins alone probably took twelve years to build.[116] The South Gate is protected, in exactly the same way as the Lion Gate at Mycenae and the West Gate at Athens, by a massive bastion projecting 11m on the right hand side. This is thought to have been the first entrance bastion the Mycenaeans built; the masons, who may have been commissioned at one site after another, went on to add them to the second building phases at Tiryns and Mycenae, and later at Athens too. The entrance bastion is thought to be a Mycenaean invention; later it was to spread to Cypriot, Anatolian and Syro-Palestinian fortresses.

The interior of the enclosure is an anticlimax, as there are few traces of settlement. Probably Gla was built as a refuge, for use in emergencies, and to defend the lake basin from interference by neighbouring Thebes. It stands on a hill at the eastern end of the Copais plain, rising seventy metres from it. Inside the South Gate, the access road wanders up the slope towards the ceremonial gate of a rectangular inner enclosure where three hypostyle halls stood, poorly floored and with ramped entrances, probably functioning as barns and fulfilling the same role as the store rooms of the Minoan temple-palaces.[117] From there the road continues north to pass through yet another gate into another enclosure. Here, on the highest point, was a substantial and very unusual L-shaped building with narrow wings, each 63m long. This has been misleadingly described as a palace, but its architecture is quite different from that of the Mycenaean 'palaces' we have seen so far, and even those who believe that the large buildings at the other sites were royal residences do not believe it here. The outer ends of each of the two wings of the building were towers, and the structure has more the design – and probably function – of a medieval castle keep. Round the keep was a sub-rectangular 'bailey' or palace yard, and next to this the larger rectangular enclosure which may have been used as a public gathering place. There were nevertheless richly decorated walls in the 'palace', with miniature fluted half-columns 8cm across not known from any other site, and sacral horns made of limestone at the corner where the two wings meet.[118]

The long citadel wall is built in a distinctive Mycenaean style, with offsets every 9 or 10m, leaving the wall projecting about 0.3m. The purpose of this carefully constructed feature has been the subject of a good deal of speculation. It may have been that adding corners made changes of direction in the wall easier when building with squared blocks. It may have been to strengthen the wall. It may have been for aesthetic effect, to create the illusion that the fortress was made in massive, block-like sections. Appearance was certainly a major consideration to the Mycenaeans. The structures inside the citadels were made in many separate blocks and breaking the circuit wall into separate blocks too would give the whole structure a unified appearance. The offsets would also have made it harder to separate the buildings inside the citadel from the circuit wall and therefore help to camouflage some of the key buildings.[119] The circuit wall at Orchomenos is built in the same style and so, significantly, is the citadel wall at Troy.

Gla is a strange place, with a large number of features not seen in any other Mycenaean citadel. It seems that Gla was an island in a marsh on the lake edge when it was built in around 1300 BC, with a defensive site not unlike that of Tiryns, which was probably separated from the Bay of Argos by a saltmarsh. The fortress of Gla was doomed to be burnt and abandoned

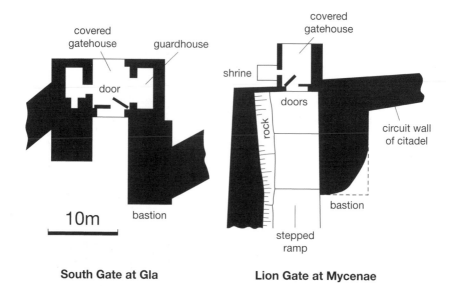

Figure 2.18 Fortified barbican gates. The projecting bastions enabled the defenders to attack enemies approaching the gate, from their unshielded right sides and from above.

within a century, just like Pylos. There is every reason to regard the Heracles adventures as pure mythology, but there is something curious about Heracles' alleged association with Boeotia. When Heracles was waging war against Orchomenos, he is said to have blocked the drainage system. It seems the outlets of the Kephissos *were* blocked, or perhaps neglected so that they became naturally choked with vegetation and silt, at about the time of the fall of Gla; the plain turned back once more into a large shallow lake.[120]

Orchomenos defended itself and its expensively drained farmland round the shores of Lake Copais with determination and spirit. A string of forts and watchtowers was built round the drained lake's former shoreline, and especially along the border with Thebes, centring on the fortress at Gla. The thirteenth-century BC fort at Krisa near Delphi may have been a dependency of Orchomenos designed to define its western frontier.[121]

Thebes too had its fortifications, including the fortress-city of Eutresis, whose circuit wall rivalled that of Gla. It looks as if by 1300 BC, Boeotia was splintering and this may be symptomatic of the general fragmentation of the Mycenaean world into mutually hostile groups. Thebes and Orchomenos were locked in a war of attrition for supremacy in central Greece; Mycenae had gained supremacy by main force (and perhaps cleverly arranged dynastic marriages) in southern Greece. Certainly we see evidence here of sophisticated city-state warfare of the same type as in the Near East, a

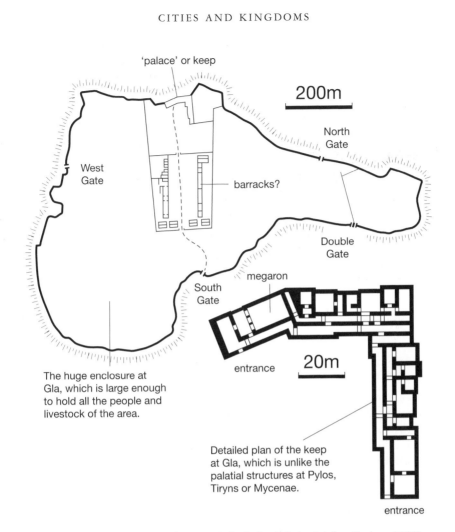

'palace' or keep

200m

North
Gate

West
Gate

barracks?

Double
Gate

megaron

South
Gate

The huge enclosure at
Gla, which is large enough
to hold all the people and
livestock of the area.

entrance

20m

Detailed plan of the keep
at Gla, which is unlike the
palatial structures at Pylos,
Tiryns or Mycenae.

entrance

Figure 2.19 Gla: the citadel (above) and the 'palace' (below) (after Taylour 1983).

civilization in which technology and wealth allowed elaborate and large-scale engineering works to be accomplished relatively quickly. Somehow – and the degree of compulsion involved cannot now be known – huge resources of labour could be mobilized for these special projects. Presumably the work was done outside the sowing and harvest seasons, although it is tempting to speculate whether the needless expenditure of resources on what was in effect an arms race may have weakened the Mycenaean civilization, and may even have precipitated its collapse.[122]

East of Boeotia, across the narrow ribbon of water where Agamemnon rallied the fleet for the Troy expedition, lay Euboea, listed as a separate

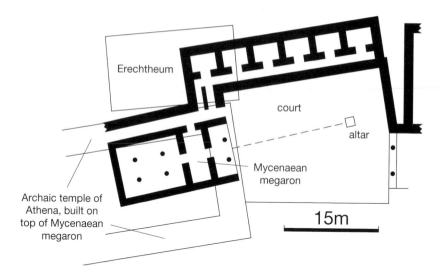

Figure 2.20 Palatial Mycenaean building on the Acropolis, Athens. This tentative plan shows how the Archaic temple of Athena may have been built to commemorate the earlier Mycenaean temple (after Holland 1924).

territory in the Catalogue of Ships under the command of Elephenor. Euboea may nevertheless have fallen under the sway of Boeotia.

To the south was the as yet insignificant city-state of Athens. The Athenian Acropolis, though repeatedly rebuilt in classical times, began as a bronze age citadel of much the same type as Mycenae, though considerably later than the first citadel at Mycenae; it was built in 1270 BC, whereas Mycenae's citadel was first walled in 1350 BC. Probably there was a palatial building on or near the summit, in the area where the Erechtheum now stands. It had an access staircase leading up from the north-west and a longer access ramp and steps leading up from the north-east. These stairways led to a series of levelled terraces with retaining walls; the largest and highest of the platforms was 100m long and 40m wide and it was probably on this that the Athenian 'palace' stood. Little of the bronze age mega-structure has survived: just two large sandstone slabs, a lot of smaller slabs and a single column base – and these were later moved.[123]

Much of the visible Athenian circuit wall is of a later date, but to the east of the classical Propylaia a segment of the Mycenaean cyclopean masonry can still be seen. Recent repair work involved taking down some of the classical revetment beside the Temple of Athena Nike, and the original bronze age masonry was found to be entombed inside. It turns out that the bastion of the West Gate was incorporated into the tower that supports the fifth-century BC temple.[124] Just like the citadels of Mycenae and Tiryns, the Athenian acropolis was strongly fortified in about 1250 BC. Just as at Mycenae and Tiryns, the Athenian citadel was extended; an extra loop of curtain wall was built out to the north-west to enclose the north-west staircase. In 1937 a secret staircase was discovered within the north circuit wall, an elaborate stairway leading down to the water table; Athens, again like Tiryns and Mycenae, had its own secret well in 1225 BC.[125]

Athenians later claimed that Athens alone never fell to invaders at the end of the bronze age, and that this was how the city became the capital of Attica, a large territory for a Greek state. Given the Athenians' hold on the presentation of the past – even from the time when Homer was first committed to writing – it must be significant that the Catalogue of Ships gives Athens a very low profile; indeed in the whole of Homer, Athens shrinks into insignificance. In Homer's time, the eighth century BC, Athens was a place of some consequence, yet not in the poem. This argues for the poems containing genuinely archaic information, having genuinely ancient roots.[126]

In Thessaly, to the north of Aetolia, Boeotia, Euboea and Athens, lay a further group of Mycenaean kingdoms of which the best-known is the easternmost, Iolkos, but the largest was Trikka, to the west. The Catalogue of Ships indicates that there were eight Mycenaean kingdoms in Thessaly. The culture of the northern kingdoms seems to have been similar to that of the southern: tholos tombs, for instance, were adopted and were in fact to continue to be built until the tenth century BC.[127] As yet, little is known of these northern kingdoms, but the overall pattern is clear. From the southern slopes of Mount Olympus south to Cape Tainaron, a tract of Greece about 400km by 200km was dominated by Mycenaean dynasts ruling upwards of twenty small kingdoms.

3

THE PEOPLE

PHYSICAL CHARACTERISTICS

Recent advances in forensic and facial reconstruction techniques allow us to know more about what people looked like in antiquity, but it is as well to recognize that the reconstruction of heads and faces from well-preserved skulls is still at an experimental stage. Highly significant details such as hair length, hairstyle, grooming, use of body paint or cosmetics still need to be added from fresco and other evidence. Skin colour cannot be deduced because of the convention, borrowed from Egypt by way of Crete, of depicting women with white skin, men with brown.

We know from their skeletons that the men were on average 1.67m tall and the women 12cm shorter, but with quite large variations from one person to another. Surprisingly, given the difference in nutrition between the bronze age and the present, modern Greeks are only half a centimetre taller than their Mycenaean predecessors.[1] The Dendra armour was tailor-made for a rather narrow-shouldered man 1.68m tall.[2] The skeletons of aristocrats in Grave Circle B show that the women were 1.58–1.61m tall and the men were 1.61–1.76m tall, around 6cm taller than commoners.[3]

Life expectancy was low. Men on average died at the age of thirty-five, women thirty, with few people reaching their fifties. Although this sounds extreme, it was the prevailing situation in Europe as a whole until relatively recent times. Medical care was poor, hygiene was poor, antibiotics were unknown; many diseases and infections were life-threatening. One aristocrat buried in Grave Circle B at Mycenae (Gamma 51) died at the age of twenty-eight, another died at thirty, while two others (Zeta 59 and Sigma 131) died at perhaps fifty or fifty-five.[4] Princes and kings probably had a better diet and better living conditions generally, given the hierarchical nature of the society, but they also had to defend their position in battle from time to time and sometimes fell victim to palace coups, as Agamemnon did. This significantly reduced their life expectancy; the average age at death of the aristocrats buried in Grave Circle B at Mycenae was thirty-six.[5] Kings could, even so, live on into their mid-fifties. It is likely that infant

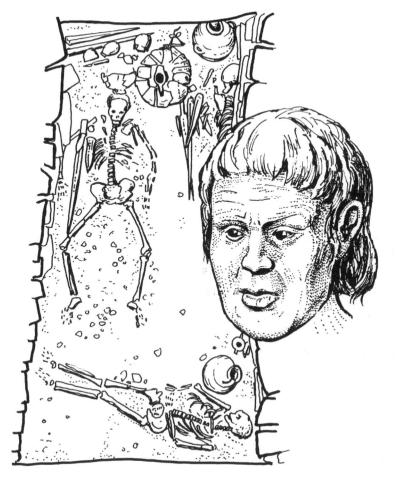

Figure 3.1 A shaft grave in Grave Circle B. Grave Gamma, one of the last in the B
   sequence, contained the remains of four aristocrats and their grave-goods.
   The reconstructed head (right) is that of the 28-year-old warrior-prince at
   the bottom (Gamma 51). He had a battle wound on his forehead and
   died as a result of a trepanning operation (developed from Prag and Neave
   1997, 131).

mortality was high and that many women died in childbirth or shortly
afterwards.[6]

The people buried in Grave Circle B had no fish in their diet, whereas
the later generations buried in Grave Circle A ate fish, meat and plants, the
men consuming more fish than the women. This implies that economy and
political geography changed through time; the early rulers of Mycenae did
not control coastal centres such as Nauplion and Tiryns, whereas the later
rulers did.[7] Lentils, peas, olives, dates, apples, pears, plums, figs, cheese and

Figure 3.2 A Mycenaean princess from the shaft graves. A reconstruction of the woman in Grave Gamma, Grave Circle B (after Prag and Neave 1997, 139). She was strongly built, quite tall and in her mid-thirties when she died. Physical similarities suggest she was a blood relation of the men who were buried with her in Grave Gamma. Modern forensic science has confirmed what was long suspected – that it was a family vault.

onions formed part of the diet, as well as bread, cakes and porridge. It may be that meat was eaten rarely by ordinary people.[8]

The Linear B tablets give no direct information on population, but a certain amount of indirect information. If 750 female slaves with as many children were being kept at Pylos, the town must have had a population of at least 2,500, and may have been much larger than that. The tablets list the names of many places; if some of these were towns and some were villages and hamlets, with an average population of 250 each, the kingdom of Pylos must have had a population of around fifty thousand.[9] The population of Mycenaean Greece as a whole may therefore have been as great as five hundred thousand.

Schliemann discovered a series of fine gold funerary masks in the shaft graves at Mycenae. There has been much discussion as to whether the images are really portraits, and if so how accurate the likenesses might be. Prag and Neave selected the largest and artistically finest of the masks and hoped to reconstruct the face from the skull, which is kept in the National Museum in Athens along with the other human remains from the shaft graves. Unfortunately they found that the bones were too fragmentary and had become too mixed up for any reliable reconstruction to be possible. The face below the mask found on the best-preserved of the bodies may eventually be reconstructed – although it is too early to have been Agamemnon's.[10] The skulls from Grave Circle B were excavated more recently (1952–4) and stored in Nauplion Museum. Four of these were complete enough for an attempt at reconstruction. Sigma 131 was a massively built 55-year-old man with a round head, a high straight forehead, rather close-set eyes, a large nose and a prominent mouth. His muscle attachments showed a powerful neck and a strong square jaw. Three teeth were diseased, with a large abscess on an upper incisor – quite a good record for a man of his age. He had some health problems, including arthritis of the spine, osteoporosis and several gallstones; the arthritis, toothache and gallstones would have kept him in fairly continuous pain.

Zeta 59 was also a big man, tall, broad-shouldered and thick-boned, also with an arthritic spine. The left shoulder blade showed pseudo-arthritis as a result of some over-use, possibly carrying a heavy shield. During his duel with Hector, Ajax felt that 'his left shoulder was weary, as steadfastly he held up his glittering shield'.[11] Zeta 59's head was strikingly large and his face long and horse-like, with a high, narrow nose and small mouth. Depressions in the skull were the result of blows inflicted by a right-handed opponent. He was 1.75m tall.[12]

One of the younger occupants of Grave Circle B was a 28-year-old, who had died immediately after trepanning. This horrific operation, in which a disc of bone is sawn out of the skull, has a long history reaching back to the neolithic. It was recommended in around 400 BC as a technique for relieving head injuries. A similar trepanning operation is known to have been performed at Lerna in the Mycenaean period; the patient at Lerna survived at least until the end of the operation, though perhaps not much longer than that.[13]

Gamma 55 was another big man, 1.76m tall, and around thirty-three at the time of his death. He had big strong bones, strong neck muscles and nearly perfect teeth. When his face was reconstructed from his skull, it bore no resemblance to the face on the gold mask that covered it, proving conclusively – and rather disappointingly – that the gold masks were not intended to be likenesses.[14] Homer tells us that Agamemnon stood out from his fellow kings like a bull in a herd of cattle, 'with head and eyes like Zeus the Thunderer, with a waist like the War-god's, and a breast like Poseidon's . . . Zeus made the son of Atreus stand out from the crowd and eclipse his fellow kings'.[15] There is no reason to see any of these individuals in Grave

Circle B as Agamemnon, but from the circumstances of their burial they will have belonged to the same élite group, and from their physique they may even have been distantly related to him.

The only woman from Grave Circle B to be examined was Gamma 58, who had a badly damaged skull. She was perhaps thirty-five years old when she died, with arthritis in her spine and hands.

CLOTHING AND JEWELLERY

The ordinary working dress for men was the loincloth or short kilt, made either of wool or of linen; cotton was not yet in use. The two garments were closely related and had been in use since neolithic times.[16] The loincloth consisted of a length of cloth passed between the legs, pulled up front and back and held in place by a second length of cloth tied round the waist; the ends of the first piece of cloth hung down front and back. If these ends were 30 or 40cm long and pulled out sideways along the belt, they created a simple kilt. The loincloth on its own was probably worn by men undertaking hard physical work in the heat of summer. The more formal style of dress consisted of a simple belted tunic with short sleeves, narrow waist and full but short skirt; a loincloth was worn under the skirt. A kilt could also be a wrap-round garment, tied round the waist in the same way as the flounced skirt worn by women on special occasions.

Often men went barefoot, but they are also shown wearing greaves on their shins. These were probably ordinarily made of leather, though the fact that they are often painted white on the frescoes is a puzzle; it does suggest the possibility that aristocrats at least had greaves made of polished metal. They extended up to cover the kneecaps like cricket pads and were tied on, with leather laces wrapped round three or four times, just below the knee and again just above the ankle. The loose ends of the laces were allowed to hang free. A curving line shown on several fresco images suggests that each greave might have been made as a flat sheet of soft leather with a curving outer edge. The sheet would have been wrapped round the leg so that the curving edge was on the outside, where it could not snag the greave on the other leg and trip the wearer. Certainly by the end of the Mycenaean period greaves were being made of metal; some finely made bronze greaves have been found. Warriors are invariably shown wearing greaves. Grooms wear only tunics, whereas warriors wear greaves and helmets. As military accoutrements, these items are probably better left to be described separately.

Some warriors, presumably higher-status warriors, wear kilts with chequered braid and a fringe round the hem.[17] A painted papyrus from El Amarna (Egypt) shows an Egyptian view of what are recognizably Mycenaean warriors. They wear helmets apparently made of boars' tusks. Some of them

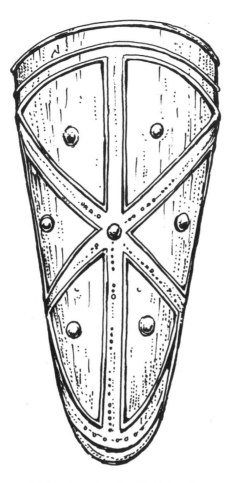

Figure 3.3 Bronze greave 25.6cm long found at Kallithea. It was made in about 1160
BC (after Papadopoulos 1979).

are bare-chested, but others wear short, rib-length capes of mottled brown
and black oxhide which hang down front and back to the same level. The
function of this cape is unclear: perhaps to reduce sunburn, or to indicate
rank, or to reduce chafing if shouldering loads. The El Amarna warriors
wear white loincloths and short kilts.[18]

The bard wore an ankle-length robe, the lower part of which was flounced
and pleated like a woman's dress. Perhaps bards were regarded as 'womanly',
rather like the cross-dressing Minoan priests. The Mycenaean bard also
wore a short cape, which hung to his chest.[19]

The clothes were treated with oil to give them a sheen. For a long
time it was thought that Homer's description of oiled cloth was a poetic

Figure 3.4 A Mycenaean soldier in action, from a fresco on the wall of the large porch
to the banquet hall in the South-West Building at Pylos. The original image
is 28cm high.

exaggeration, but Mycenaean cloth was indeed oiled.[20] Some of the cloth
was exceptionally elaborate in terms of finish. Mycenaean ambassadors are
shown on Egyptian monuments bringing tribute consisting of lengths of
elaborately ornamented cloth not available in Egypt.[21] It was the 'finishers'
who added much of the decorative detail, including coloured beads, cut-out
gold attachments and sequins sewn onto the cloth at intervals. Hems were
sometimes fitted with cylinders of thin gold plate, perforated for sewing.
Probably as many as six hundred women all over the kingdom of Pylos were
involved in textile production. The tablets refer to *te-pa*, which seem to be
heavy rugs; the word is similar to the later Greek word for carpet, *tapes*,
and the *te-pa* contains an enormous weight of wool.

One garment given special prominence in the ivory group is the shawl
which the two women are sharing. It is elaborately textured, with a tasselled
edge. It is very like the splendid cloak worn by Athena, 'the unfading everlasting aegis, from which a hundred golden tassels flutter, all beautifully
made, each worth a hundred head of cattle'.[22] The two priestesses or
goddesses seem to be wearing this sacred aegis.

The style of dress for women was originally dictated by Minoan fashion, and it is astonishing that once introduced in around 1550 BC it remained unchanged for three hundred years. The costume of the goddess in Shaft Grave III (sixteenth century BC) is recognizably the same as that of the woman on the ivory handle from the Tomb of Clytemnestra (thirteenth century BC). Several fresco images show the typically Minoan flounced dress, but perhaps the best evidence comes from the finely detailed ivory group from Mycenae, just mentioned in connection with the tasselled cloak. The tight short-sleeved bodice or bolero was made of eight separate pieces of cloth sewn together. It was drawn back at the top to expose the breasts, but sewn together below to support them. The hems and seams were edged with coloured braid, partly for decorative effect, partly to strengthen the seams. Special teams of women workers wove this braid, the 'makers of head-bands'. The skirt was a wrap-round skirt, tied with a cord belt round the waist. Some small cone-shaped objects may have been dress weights to hold down the skirt hem.[23] The foundation of the skirt was a plain trapezium of backing material. Horizontal bands of differently coloured and patterned material were sewn onto this from the bottom up, overlapping like roof tiles. Each band was sewn on along its upper edge only. Some of these were pleated by folding, then sewing down the pleats and washing, followed by unpicking the stitches; this made permanent pleats.[24] The overall effect of this full-bodied garment was extremely rich, and was no doubt very pleasing to the eye when its wearer danced or even walked along the city streets.

Everyday wear for women consisted of a long plain frock with a belt worn high under the breasts. A shawl or jacket might be worn over this, and the 'Sunday-best' flounced skirt was a wrap-round over-garment tied on round the waist.

Hairstyle was probably in the main dictated by social status, and that in turn was in part dictated by age. Very young children probably had their heads shaved, as shown in the Theran frescoes. Only when they reached puberty were they allowed to grow a single lock. Later the hair was allowed to grow out but in a range of specific styles prescribed by social standing.[25] The main evidence for this comes from sixteenth-century Thera, but there is evidence that something similar was happening on mainland Greece. The two women in the ivory group from Mycenae have very different hairstyles. One has her hair growing down her back, carefully waved and ending in a point. The other has her hair very short with a single long tress carried over the top of her head; according to the pecking order apparent in the Thera frescoes, this would make the long-haired woman the older woman, the short-haired the younger. Perhaps they are mother and daughter.[26] Homer describes the Greeks as long-haired, and this is shown in some artwork; there are gold and *niello* heads of bearded men with long hair, growing thick right down to the nape.[27] At the same time, there are other images on frescoes and pottery showing men with short hair, and it may be

Figure 3.5 Priestess carrying a vase as an offering. This fragment of a wall painting from Pylos (in debris on north-west slope of hill) shows the embroidered strips that were sewn on to strengthen and decorate the bodice seams. Note that the breast is bared, which (as in Minoan Crete) was probably only done for religious ceremonies (after Piet de Jong's reconstruction in Lang 1969).

that only the aristocracy wore their hair long; this could have been an exotic and exclusive fashion imported from Minoan Crete, where men wore their hair very long indeed. But the artwork images show no consistency. There are images of hunting in which some men have long hair, some short. Some men wore a full beard with moustache, others a beard and no moustache, while some were clean-shaven. It is hard to tell whether these variations indicate differences in social status, occupation or just personal taste.

Aristocrats wore considerable amounts of jewellery, though probably not as much as the rich burials might lead us to think. Women wore beads of gold, coloured opaque glass, amethyst, carnelian and amber, sometimes in two, three or four strands separated by spacer-beads. At first (in the sixteenth century) there were heavy and elaborate gold earrings,[28] but later (in the fourteenth and thirteenth centuries) simpler, less showy gold rosettes and rings. The early period, the period of the shaft graves, was a time of ostentation, when men were decked out with gold armlets and women with gold tiaras, though probably only in death. Almost certainly the early Mycenaeans were copying elaborate funerary practices from Egypt and the Levant, just as they were copying their dress from the Minoans.[29] The thin plate jewellery was made on steatite moulds like the one found in the Citadel House at Mycenae,[30] and then sewn onto a fabric backing.

It is thought that the diadems, which consisted of a cross band and as many as seven triangular fillets, were also attached to a cloth backing. Some of the rays are decorated with palm trees, and the way these are drawn suggests that the rays, which had edges stiffened with bronze wire, were intended to stand up.[31] The effect would be not unlike a child's drawing of a crown. Although the diadems seem to come out of nowhere, they may have an Early Minoan origin. Similar funerary diadems made of strips of gold sheet were made in Crete in around 2500 BC,[32] and they in turn may have been based on Syrian or Mesopotamian diadems. An elaborately decorated silver diadem from Kastri on Syros was made in around 2000 BC; fragments of similar silver diadems of similar date have been found at Zygouries near Mycenae.[33] The shaft grave diadems were therefore part of a continuing, if now barely visible, tradition. Two gold diadems were found in Early Mycenaean tombs near Pylos, another at Peristeria. Some of the shaft grave diadems have flowers attached to their upper edge, and even this detail may have been copied from Minoan originals.

The shaft grave art is flashy and impressive because it is made of gold, but it must be admitted that much of it is artistically poor. A gold ornament in the form of a crouching lion from Shaft Grave III is a very poor and amateurish copy of a (contemporary) Late Minoan original; a much higher quality Minoan example was found in a tomb at Ayia Triadha near Phaistos.

Elaborately shaped gold relief-beads were manufactured, initially by *repoussé* work using stone moulds, then by the addition of granulation, then, sometimes, by the further addition of blue enamel. They were made in around 1400 BC, to a very high standard of workmanship, and were exported all over the Mycenaean empire.[34]

A fine gold sceptre was found in a royal burial dating to around 1100 BC at Kourion in Cyprus, though it was then an antique piece made at least a century earlier. Probably of Late Mycenaean workmanship, it consists of a plain gold rod, surmounted by a granulated astragal. On top of that is a globe with two hawks perching on it. The globe and the hawks are covered by cellular pits that contain white, green and purple enamel. No doubt Mycenaean kings regularly commissioned regalia like this from their craftsmen. Homer describes Agamemnon holding a staff as the tribes muster on the beach in front of him.[35] The staff described in the *Iliad* was made by the god Hephaestus, who gave it to Zeus; then it was passed in turn to Hermes, Pelops the great charioteer, Atreus shepherd of the people and Thyestes rich in flocks. Thyestes bequeathed it to Agamemnon, to be held in token of his empire. Homer gives us an ancient concept of god-given regalia, which fits the Kourion sceptre well.

Figure 3.6 Sceptre found in a royal tomb of about 1100 BC at Kourion on Cyprus, but
of Mycenaean manufacture and made before 1200 BC. It is beautifully made
of enamelled gold and 16.5cm high, including the gold rod or handle. Two
realistically modelled hawks sit on a sphere; all three are coloured with white,
green and purple enamel.

A very heavy silver hair pin was found in Shaft Grave III, dating from
1550–1500 BC, and apparently made for funerary use only. It is decorated
with an embossed gold cut-out showing a goddess with long flowing hair,
flounced dress and her arms outstretched holding a double garland in front
of her. Rising from her head is a fantastic headdress made of two pairs of
volutes; this in turn sprouts six palm branches, loaded with fruit, three
bending low on each side of her. She must be a Minoan or Mycenaean nature
goddess; it is a wonderful image of fecundity.[36] Another gold cut-out of a
goddess, in Shaft Grave III, is by contrast rather crudely drawn and, very
unusually, completely naked. This nude goddess is surrounded by three
doves.

While only women wore earrings and hair pins, both men and women
wore broad gold armlets. At least one of these, from Shaft Grave IV, is of

such superb workmanship that it must have been imported from Minoan Crete. It is made of a clever combination of gold and silver: gold partly overlaid by silver, in turn coated with gold. It is reminiscent of the belt in the Cupbearer Fresco at Knossos. The armlet is decorated with grooves and a large rosette. Necklaces were worn by both men and women.

Men and women of high status wore big gold signet rings with oval bezels that were engraved with great skill, a craft learnt from Minoan Crete. The bezels were up to 6cm across, which if worn on the finger would render any manual work impossible, and this is just the kind of social statement prestige objects were intended to make. Blegen found a burial with one of the rings under the wrist, though, which implies that the rings were worn on a string round the wrist, like the seal-stones, and used in the same way. Some of the rings show religious ceremonies of great majesty. Others show fighting. One of the finest, the Danicourt ring, dating from 1450 BC, shows two muscular warriors standing back-to-back as they fight two lions; this is thought to be by a native Mycenaean craftsman and it sums up the Mycenaean mentality.[37]

Seals too were borrowed from Crete, and they made their first appearance on the mainland at the time of the shaft graves, when three were included in the burials in Grave Circle B. At first the seals were made of very hard stone such as amethyst and haematite, but later the softer steatite was preferred, because of the ease with which it could be worked. These seals seem to have had talismanic value, but they were also practical solutions

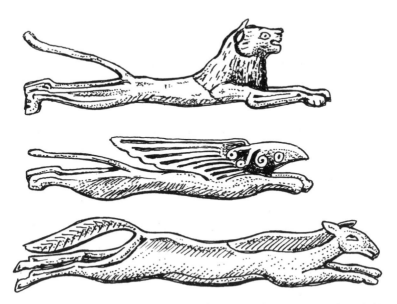

Figure 3.7 Lion, griffin, horse. Gold inlays of galloping beasts on swords and daggers from Shaft Graves IV and V, and made about 1500 BC.

to the age-old problem of security and privacy. A piece of string could be tied across the mouth of a storage jar or round the neck of a bag. A lump of soft clay was squeezed round the string and impressed with the seal. The container could not be opened without the string being cut or the seal broken; either way, the owner would know his property had been tampered with. The seals were worn on a string round the wrist.

The seals buried with the kings in the shaft graves show the gap between the civilized Minoan world and the still-barbarous mainland. At Mycenae they were included as exotica. The bearded male head on a disc of amethyst was at one time believed to be a portrait of a Mycenaean king, but the disc is of a type common in Crete – and a comparable bearded face appears on a seal at Knossos at about the same time. It is clearly an import. Eight more seals were found in Grave Circle A. The scenes of hunting and fighting are presumed to reflect the Mycenaean aristocrats' preoccupations, but similar images are to be found on Minoan seals and all of the shaft grave seals were found with women, so perhaps we should not read too much into the imagery.[38]

A distinctive decorative technique was the use of *niello*. The Lion Dagger is the best known example of this; a broad bronze blade is inlaid with gold and silver cut-outs, using a mixture of silver, copper, lead and sulphur (*niello*) as an adhesive to hold the cut-outs in place. The technique involves applying the *niello* as a powder, then heating it; it solidifies round the cut-outs as it cools. Used earlier in Byblos, the technique was probably imported direct from Syria. There is no evidence that the technique was ever used on Crete, which is surprising, and it may be that the Mycenaeans actually imported some Syrian craftsmen to make these fine weapons. The earlier compositions, like the ones on the Lion Dagger are full of movement and vitality, which suggests a Minoan influence. The compositions on the later daggers, such as the one with three lions and the one with three leopards from Pylos, are more static, and have a distinctively Mycenaean formality about them.[39]

THE NATURE OF MYCENAEAN SOCIETY

Mycenaean society was highly structured with a king or *wanax* (*wa-na-ka*), a title found in Homer as well as the tablets, at its head. Second in power and status to the king was the leader of the people or *lawagetas* (*ra-wa-ke-ta*). It is not at all certain what this role entailed but, since in Homer *lawos* has the meaning 'body of warriors, people arrayed for battle, war-host', the *lawagetas* may have been the commander-in-chief of the army. His high status was reflected in his land holding; he held an estate one-third the size of the king's.[40] The king had his principal estate or *temenos* at Sphagianes, where he was closely associated with the goddess Potnia.[41] The *lawagetas* had his principal estate at Tinos, where he was associated with the god

Hippos. This is closely echoed in Nausicaa's conversation with Odysseus in the *Odyssey*; 'You will find a lovely poplar grove of Athena near the road. In it a spring flows and about it a meadow. There is the temenos of my father [King Alkinoos of Scheria] and his fruitful orchard.'[42]

For the sake of personal safety, but no less to create a powerful mystique, the king and his family lived sequestered in the citadel. He was rarely seen by the general populace, perhaps only glimpsed during formal processions and religious festivals or when going off in great style in his chariot to lead his warriors to war. Doubtless these infrequent sightings would have been great moments in the life of the community.[43] The king had divine ancestry and a special bond with a particular deity. In Anatolia, Mursilis II had a special bond with the Sun Goddess, Muwatallis II with the Storm God of Lightning. Later Greek legends imply that the Mycenaean kings in a similar way interwove their own destinies with those of the gods. There is no evidence whatever that the Mycenaean kings were high priests, any more than Minoan kings were.

The priests were a separate and identifiable group within Mycenaean society. They were paid for their work and they were also land-owners. Some of them, though not all, were described as *i-je-ro-wo-ko*, 'those who make the sacrifices'. They evidently had high status, like the priesthood on Crete, where priestesses were carried about in litters and were entitled to special seats at public festivals. Mycenaean priestesses had their own slave women.

The king was surrounded by an élite group of followers or *hequetai* (*e-qe-ta*). These men were the equivalent of the dukes and barons of the medieval European courts, ready to do battle on the king's behalf and when off-duty functioning as his friends and table-companions. The Latin word *comes*, with the same meaning, became the English word 'count'.[44] According to Homer, the *hequetai* as well as their kings received personal allocations of land called 'cuts' (*temenos*), and this is borne out by the Pylian tablets. Their high status is shown by their land holdings and their ownership of slaves. They were the chariot-borne warrior-aristocrat class.

The people we call scribes were based in the palaces and recorded the flow of produce and objects through the palaces, but they were really far more than scribes: they were administrators and formed part of the palace élite.[45] In Anatolia it was much the same; the Hittite Chief of Scribes ranked next in importance after the king, queen and crown prince. Scribes were able to achieve exalted status. The fact that they often travelled with their tablets to read them to foreign potentates and then write down their replies meant that they wielded great power and were trusted diplomats and negotiators. The folding wooden tablet found in the Ulu Burun shipwreck, with its ivory hinges and traces of wax coating, was a notebook or letter. Homer has Bellerophon taking a wooden tablet of this kind to Lycia. Bronze hinges have been found at Pylos, suggesting that the scribes there were using similar notebooks.[46]

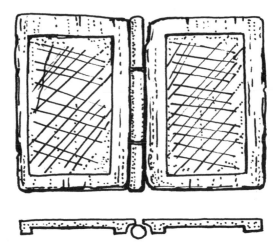

Figure 3.8 The wooden 'book' from the Ulu Burun wreck: elevation and section. It is 9.2cm high, with inner faces recessed and scored to take a layer of wax. The hinge is made of wooden dowels inside ivory cylinders.

The *damos* consisted of the people or free citizens, and the word could be used for the common people or for the land they held, a little like the use of the word 'village'. The *damos* was independent of the palace, had its own organization and spokesmen, who represented the people's interests. The *damos* contributed offerings to Poseidon (Un 718), owned land and was ready to assert its land rights (Ep 704). The *damos* appeared in the company of Echelawon (possibly the name of the king) and the *lawagetas* on the occasion of the great *dosmos* presented to Poseidon (Un 718). The *doeroi* were servants, serfs or bondsmen, who could be bought and sold. In later times there was a group of second-class citizens called the *perioikoi*, 'the dwellers round about',[47] and these may have existed in Mycenaean times too, the inhabitants of outlying rural areas.

The workforce for public projects like road and citadel building was probably drawn from the *damos* and *perioikoi*, who may have been under an obligation to do public service and were conscripted for specific tasks. In contemporary Egypt, people were released from their ordinary work when the Nile floods made agriculture impossible, and it was this seasonal availability of labour that made pyramid building possible;[48] there may have been a similar seasonality in public works in Greece. Some of the projects must have involved large numbers of people. The lintel over the doorway of the Treasury of Atreus weighs 120 tons, which would have needed perhaps two hundred people to transport it on a sledge on the flat; it seems likely that oxen would have been used for this task. The average cyclopean block could have been drawn on a sledge by fourteen oxen. It has been calculated that building the circuit walls of Gla would have taken sixteen years, but there is no way of knowing how long any of the tasks took because the tablets do not tell us how many people were involved at a time, how long the working day was, or for how many weeks in the year the work went on. Documents from ancient Egypt have shown that the Egyptians worked under very good conditions with well-organized catering, regularly taking time off to sort out domestic problems or even to celebrate birthdays. All things considered, it seems likely that the great citadels took decades to build, and the work in progress was probably in itself intended as a conspicuous show of strength on the part of the rulers.

Presumably there were reserved occupations, and if so perfume-making was probably one. The names of some of the perfume makers in Messenia are known: Kokalos, Eumedes, Philaos and Thyestes.

Pylos, the kingdom for which we have most information about political structure, was divided into sixteen administrative districts, each run by a curator (ko-re-te) with a deputy or procurator (pro-ko-re-te) to assist him. These men had other titles and therefore other duties; for instance, Klumenes was curator of Iterewa, and also commander of one section of the coastguard.[49] One of these additional titles was key-bearer (klawiphoros), which was some sort of religious function. In classical Greece this role became known by the title key-holder (kleidoukhos) and was by then a synonym for priestess. In addition, the kingdom of Pylos was divided into two administrative halves, the Further Province to the east of the mountains and the Hither Province to the west, each with its own governor and deputy governor or superintendent. Te-po-se-u was Governor of the Further Province at the time of the fall of Pylos; he oversaw the curators of seven districts. Damoklos was Governor of the Hither Province; he presumably oversaw the work of the nine curators in his province. The governors themselves appear to have been overseen by a chief palace administrator or lord high steward by the name of Alxoitas (A-ko-so-ta).[50]

The telestai (te-re-ta), or 'men of the obligation', may have been important state officials and land-owners who ran the local affairs of the damos. The telestai each had land holdings similar to those of the lawagetas.[51] It is also possible that the telestai were priests; there were at least fourteen of them at Sphagianes, which is known to have been a religious cult centre. Even if they were priests they were also men of property, who held their lands in return for some service.

A Council of Elders or Geronsia (ke-ro-si-ja) also existed.[52] It is not clear what powers or responsibilities this body had, but it may have had an advisory role, or functioned as a court of appeal, or been an emergency government-in-waiting. The fourth-century BC historian Ephoros describes ancient Crete as having a body of Gerontes, who functioned as senators and acted as counsellors in affairs of the greatest importance.[53]

81

The complex social structure as outlined here is further complicated by some fundamental ambiguities. Some land was held in the name of the god, and at Pylos taxes were levied for Poseidon. Some scholars have suggested that when the word 'king' occurs in the tablets it refers not to an earthly king but to Poseidon.[54] Homer uses the word *basileus* to describe a lesser figure than the king, a kind of sub-king or chief. There were several *basilees* in Ithaca, where Odysseus was king.[55] Alkinoos mentions twelve *basilees* among his own people.[56] Interestingly, the Mycenaeans used *guasileus* (*qa-si-re-u*) (the Mycenaean form of *basileus*) to indicate a much less important role, such a chief blacksmith.[57] But the alternative term, *wanax*, did not necessarily mean the earthly king. A series of Pylian tablets recording quantities of perfumed oil distributed to various deities includes an entry for the king; presumably the human ruler of Pylos was not meant.[58] This has serious implications for our interpretation of Mycenaean society. The large estates belonging to 'the king' might, for example, then belong to a powerful priesthood; the *lawagetas* might then become the mortal leader of his people, a kind of president. On balance, given the nature of the age and the existence of kings in comparable contemporary cultures in Anatolia and Egypt, it seems likely that there were earthly kings.

The king or *wanax* is referred to in the tablets, though rarely by name. Both Ventris and Chadwick suggested that a man called Echelawon had a high enough status to have been king. He had forty men serving as rowers in the fleet and owned a huge estate three times the size of 'the king's' *temenos*, planted with over a thousand vines and as many fig trees. John Bennet has proved that the two-page list where Echelawon seems to take the place of the king is actually a single list, and Palmer argues that this shows that the king has already been mentioned; Echelawon must be a different individual.[59] But if 'the king' in this list means the god Poseidon, it still remains a possibility that Echelawon is the earthly king. Homer refers to the god Apollo as 'King Apollo'.[60] Tablet Na 334 reads,

wa-na-ka e-ke
pi-ka-no e-re-u-te-ra SA 20,

which seems to tell us that the king's name was Pikana.[61] Pikana? Echelawon? Poseidon? Really, some new evidence is needed before this complex and important issue can be resolved.

The *lawagetas* at Pylos was called Wedaneus. Other named individuals are mentioned in the Pylian archives, many of them early Greek names: Alexandra, Theodora, Eumenes, Amphimedes. Some personal names are descriptive, like Glaukos (grey-eyed), Ekhinos (sea-urchin) and Ploutinus (rich). Others are occupational, like Poimen (shepherd) and Khalkeus (smith).[62] One man at Pylos was called Tulisios, which seems to tell us he came from the Cretan town of Tylissos. Most intriguing of all is the fact that many of the people have names that appear in Homer. A junior officer at Pylos is called Orestes, and there were other Pylians called Achilles, Hector and Tros (the name of the mythical founder of Troy). It seems that Homer was giving his heroes genuinely Mycenaean names.[63] The Damoklos who was one of the two governors of the kingdom of Pylos may have been the son of Damokles, in which case his full name would have been Damokleweios, son of Damokles. Damoklos looks like a contraction, like Patroklos (Patroclus) in Homer.[64]

The groups of women mentioned in the tablets are evidently slaves. They are mentioned as having children, but where are their men? The women are engaged in humble trades as bath attendants, corn-grinders, bread-makers, flax-workers, spinners. Some of them are listed as belonging to a place, and the place names are significant. One group came from the island of Kythera. Another came from *A-swi-ja* (Asia), the region of Anatolia referred to in the Hittite tablets as Assuwa and later to be known as Lydia. The women of Miletus came from the Mycenaean colony of Miletus on the west coast of Anatolia. Another group came from Knidos, 100km to the north of Miletus. Yet another group came from Lemnos, a large island in the north-east Aegean. The women of Zephyros probably came from Halikarnossos, whose old name was Zephyria. Palmer warns that some place-names are duplicated, reminding us that Miletus occurs in Crete as well as Anatolia.[65] The conclusion is nevertheless almost inescapable. These women were captured outside Messenia, many of them from the western Anatolia coast, rounded up and transported from Mycenaean trading posts back to mainland Greece. One possibility is that the men were killed to pre-empt any possible slave revolt, but the women and children were kept together, probably to keep them happy and make them more effective as work teams;[66] keeping language groups together would also have made it easier to communicate with them. Another possibility is that the men were taken and deployed elsewhere, perhaps building the massive fortifications at Tiryns or Mycenae.

Hittite sources show that by 1250 BC large numbers of people from western Anatolia were living in Greece. Hattusilis III wrote a letter to a king of Ahhiyawa complaining of the resettlement in Ahhiyawa of seven thousand of his western Anatolian subjects from the Lukka Lands. In view of the chronic underpopulation of Anatolia he might well complain about these large-scale abductions. The Mycenaean tablets confirm that western Anatolia was a region from which the Mycenaeans were taking people for, among other activities, textile-making. If the same region was supplying men for wall-building at Mycenae and Tiryns, refortified at just this time, it would fit neatly with Strabo's story that the walls of Tiryns were built by giants from Lycia; the Lycia of Strabo's time was the Lukka Lands of the late bronze age.[67]

The distinctive, full-blown Mycenaean society we have been looking at developed out of a still-fluid tribal society dominated by chieftains, the Early

Mycenae of the shaft graves. This Early Mycenaean society looks rather more like the warrior chief-oriented society described by Homer. Then the mainland Greeks adopted some of the forms and some of the substance of Minoan 'palatial' society, importing ideas from the east.[68] From 1600 BC onwards, social stratification developed in parallel with the architecture. The early chief's house, such as the ten-metre-long megaron at Eutresis, was the central building. By 1400 BC the chief's house had evolved into a major focus; by 1270–1200 BC this had evolved into the final phase, an imposing building of great splendour.[69] Mycenaean society had become highly developed, more like that of one of the Near Eastern civilizations than the warrior chief-centred society we hear about in Homer. The society that archaeology reveals is based not on temperamental warrior chiefs and their squabbles but on detailed information-gathering by a hierarchy of meticulous officials; it looks as if it was the administrators who were the important people, not the aristocrats, but the key administrative posts were probably occupied by aristocrats, so the contrast may not have been so extreme.

There were warriors, who can be seen painted in the murals and on kraters, and they were captained by *moiroqqas* (*mo-ro-qa*), the officers who commanded military units.

There was a distinct pecking order within this highly structured society, but it was not overwhelmingly oppressive. Even ordinary people had considerable freedom of action. They also had the freedom to bring formal complaints against their betters.[70] Protests by the *damos* on behalf of specific individuals are recorded in the Pylos tablets. One text (Eb 297) reads: 'The priestess declares that the god has a large religious holding [*e-to-ni-jo*], but the ktoina-holder [the *ktoina* is a religious land holding] says that she has leases of civic land.' A second text (Ep 704) on the same issue shows the priestess's complaint being taken up by the *damos* and is worth quoting in full:

> The priestess Eritha holds a leased plot of civic land from the damos,
> so much seed – 38.4 litres of wheat.
> The barley-women hold a leased plot of civic land from the damos,
> so much seed – 182.4 litres of wheat.
> The priestess Eritha holds a leased plot and claims to hold a freehold [?]
> for the god, but the damos says
> she holds a leased plot of civic land, so much seed – 374.4 litres of wheat.
> The key-bearer Karpathia has two public leased plots;
> being obligated with two to perform [a service?] she does not perform,
> so much seed – ? litres of wheat.

The priestess Eritha leases a small plot of land in her own right. The plot mentioned later is ten times larger. She claims it has a special status because it is 'for the god', but the *damos* is unimpressed by her claim, interpreting it as an ordinary land holding. The reason for complaining then becomes clear. In return for the benefits they derive from leased land, leaseholders are expected to perform some service for the *damos*. The key-bearer Karpathia has such a share but is failing to fulfil her obligation.[71] It is highly significant that the two land-holders here who are causing trouble are not only women but priestesses; this confirms that priestesses were significant, high-status figures in Mycenaean society, just as in Minoan society. They seem to be behaving in a high-handed way. It also confirms that the *damos* is a force to reckon with. This is not the Greece of Homer, where Odysseus beats a man of the *damos* for having the effrontery to speak in the assembly.[72]

Mycenaean society was finely structured and stratified, in many ways like the hierarchical societies of Egypt and the Near East. What is odd is the near-complete anonymity of the kings and other leaders. References to named personages who seem to be kings or other dignitaries are sparing. Odder still is the absence of any royal portraits; perhaps this custom of anonymity was borrowed from the Minoans, whose kings were nameless and faceless.

LANGUAGE – LINEAR B

The Mycenaeans are famous for being literate. A small minority of them at least could read and write a syllabic script, known to archaeologists as Linear B. It had eighty-nine different signs. Arthur Evans discovered the first clay tablets with Minoan 'hieroglyphics' at Knossos and published a selection of them in *The Palace of Minos*, though not enough to allow anyone else the chance of deciphering them; he clung to the hope that he could do that himself. They were not published until 1952, eleven years after Evans's death, although Evans had compiled them as early as 1911 – an unfortunate delay of forty years. In 1939, Carl Blegen struck the Archive Room at Pylos with his first trench, and found the first of a huge cache of Mycenaean Linear B tablets just 30cm under the surface.

Some signs represent bare vowels (a, e, i, o, u), others vowels with consonants (such as pa, pe, pi, po, pu). About half of the Linear B signs have equivalents in the earlier but still unidentified Linear A, so it is assumed that Linear B was developed from the older script so that a different language, a non-Minoan language, could be written down. The signs were simply made by drawing with a pointed stylus on a tablet of soft clay, which was usually small enough to hold in one hand while writing with the other. The scribes did not write with a perfect copybook hand but, much as we

Plate 3.1 The archive rooms at Pylos, where the Linear B tablets were found.

do today, with a great deal of individual variation in the way the signs were shaped. The signs were written in horizontal lines from left to right, just as we still do in the West today; we know this because the lines are all left-justified. The signs were also divided into groups by using a short upright bar just above the lines, which suggested from early in the decipherment process that the sign-groups might be separate words.

Decipherment started with the numbers. Most of the tablets record numerals and there are examples of sums to verify the system. Units are represented by short upright bars, tens by horizontal bars, hundreds by circles, thousands by circles with four rays. Preceding the numerals are pictograms, pictorial signs that represent men, women, horses, chariots, wheels, jars, cups, baths. Some of the pictograms are simply cartoon images of the things they stand for. The pictogram for jar is a two-handled jar. A cup is a cup. Some pictograms go a little further. There is a pictogram for a sheep which is a sheep's head with a single descending vertical line – in effect a sheep's head on a stick. If the scribe wanted to specify that the sheep was a ram he added two short cross strokes to the vertical line, if a ewe he added a second vertical line. He followed the same procedure with goats and pigs.

An early barrier to decipherment was the general belief that the Linear B language was not Greek but a Minoan language, though there were some, thinking along different lines, who cleverly saw the prevalence of Greek

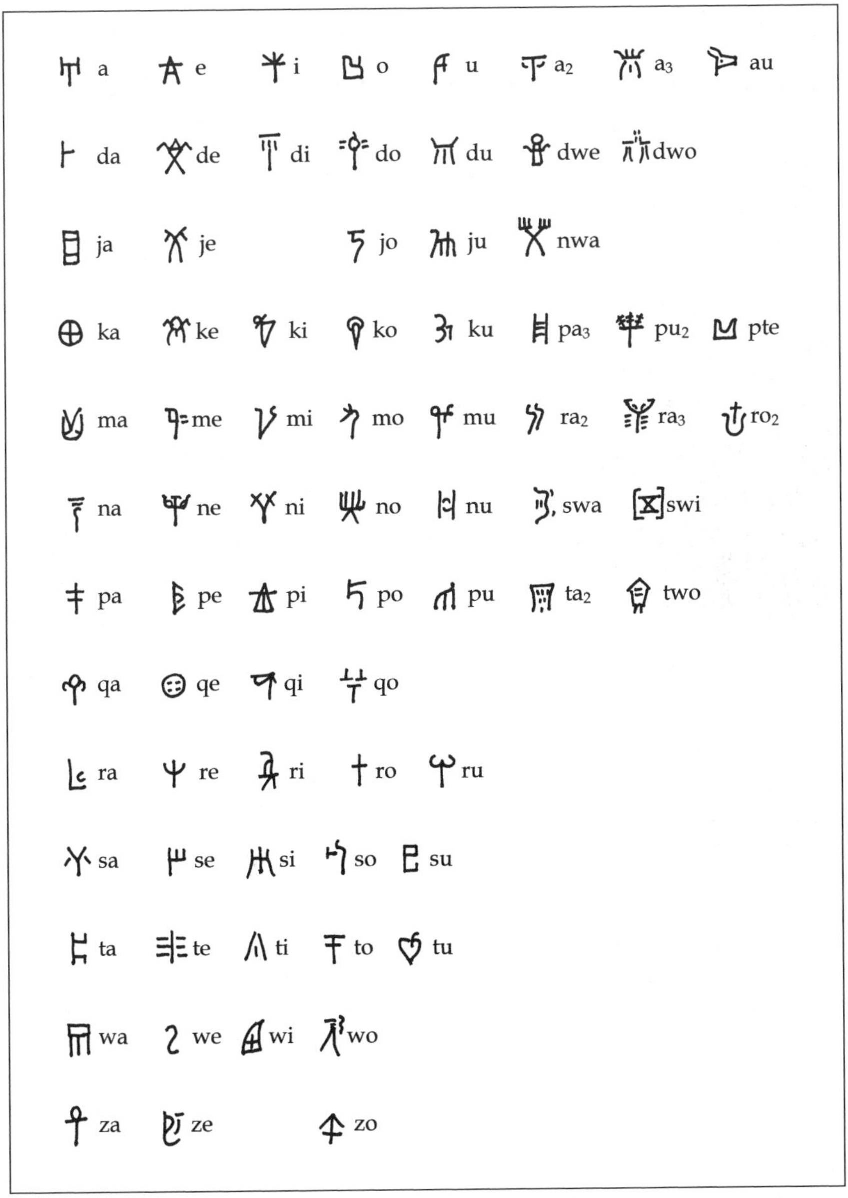

Figure 3.9 The Linear B syllabary. The basic signs are on the left, the first five columns. The optional signs are on the right, the last three columns (after Chadwick 1987).

personal names in Homer as an indication that the Mycenaean world Homer portrayed was also Greek-speaking.

Michael Ventris guessed that some words on the Cretan tablets might be names of Cretan towns. *Ko-no-so* might be Knossos, *A-mi-ni-so* Amnisos, *Tu-ri-so* Tylissos. Testing the hypothesis that the language was Greek led to the emergence of more and more Greek words from the tablets. Ventris formed an alliance with the Cambridge philologist John Chadwick, who had an interest in early Greek, and together they proved to most scholars' satisfaction that the new language was an early form of Greek. The theory was vindicated when in 1953 Carl Blegen studied some newly discovered Pylian tablets. One had pictograms of three-legged cauldrons. Blegen applied the Ventris–Chadwick values to the accompanying signs and was astonished to read *ti-ri-po-de* – tripods. Some problems in translation still remain, because the Greek dialect spoken and written in Mycenaean Greece is little known. Even by the time of Homer, it had changed significantly. *Korwos* (boy) had become *kouros*, and *gwasileus* (chief) had become *basileus*. Doubtless some Mycenaean words had gone out of use by the eighth century and will have become untranslatable. One mysterious word, *ki-ta-no*, seemed to belong to this obsolete group, but an ancient Greek lexicon revealed the word *kritanos* as an alternative name for the pistachio tree, so one of the commodities listed in the archives turns out to be retrievable as pistachio nuts.

Problems arise because some of the signs can be pronounced and transliterated in more than one way. The signs *pa*, *pe*, *pi* can sound as pa, pe, pi, pha, phe, phi or ba, be, bi. Similarly, *q-* can sound as kw, as in the English word queen, khw and gw. This latitude has caused some to be sceptical about translations from Linear B, because the translator can make choices, but it is really not very different from English words ending with -ough, which can be pronounced in at least five different ways. With these pointers in mind, it is possible to construct some words in Linear B. The Mycenaean word for bronze, *khalkos*, is represented by two signs, *ka-ko*; the 'l' and the 's' are understood in Linear B. The word for tripod, *tripos*, is represented by three signs, *ti-ri-po*, in which the final 's' is again understood. Longer words are put together in the same way, so that the Mycenaean word for bath-pourers, *leweotrokhowoi*, is represented by the six signs, *re-wo-to-ro-ro-ko-wo*; 'r' can be sounded as an 'r' or an 'l'. By Homer's time, the Mycenaean word *lewotrokhowoi* had become *loutrokhooi*, still just recognizable but making some difficulties for the would-be translator.

Here, to give a flavour of the language the Mycenaeans spoke, are some of the words they used.[73]

aleiphar (ointment)
ampiphora (amphora)
an- (no-, as in 'cup with no handles')

auloi (flutes, pipes)
demnia (beds)
dleukos (new wine)
elaiwon (olive oil)

guasileus (chief)
harmo (wheel)
hateron (other, different)
hikkwia (chariot, literally
    'horse-vehicle')
hikkwoi (horses)
khalkos (bronze)
korwa (girl)
korwos (boy)
leweotrokhowoi (bath pourers)
mallos (wool)
meli (honey)
newos (new)
pharweha (cloaks)

phasgana (sword)
phuteres (planters)
quetro- (four-, as in 'four-legged
    table')
thranus (footstool)
torpedza (table)
tosos (so many, so much,
    feminine tosa)
tri- (three-, as in 'three-legged
    table')
tripos (tripod)
turoi (cheeses)
wrinos (oxhide)

Many Mycenaeans are referred to by name. In the tablets we meet men called Phegeus, Inaon and Purwos, others called Lakedanos, Leukos, Ophelanor and Kepos, and a woman called Amphidora. Thebans (te-ba-i) are mentioned, and 'Didumus the young fuller'. One tablet from Mycenae (V 659) appears to be a list allocating bedding to pairs of people; 'For Manos and Alexandros, 2; . . . for Aeneas and daughter, 2; for Philowona and female baby, 2.'[74] These are not married couples, but the implication is that regardless of relationship people, at any rate of the lower orders, routinely slept together in pairs, perhaps for warmth.

Place names are listed on the Pylos tablets and with Knossos so plainly visible as ko-no-so on the Knossian tablets scholars have made valiant attempts to identify these places, which are assumed to be in south-west Greece as they were evidently administrated from Pylos. Two particularly intriguing names are Pe-ra-a-ko-ra-i-ja and De-we-ro-a-ko-ra-i-ja. The first two syllables in each name represent prefixes, pera meaning 'beyond' and deuro meaning 'on this side of'. Removing the prefixes leaves the word a-ko-ra-i-ja, which is not unlike the modern Greek name of the spinal mountain ridge, Aigolaion. This gives us the names of the two provinces of the kingdom of Pylos, 'This-side-of-Aigolaion' and 'Beyond-Aigolaion'.[75] Some of the other place names too have remained surprisingly little changed in the last three thousand years.

The Mycenaeans spoke at least two different dialects, unrelated to the different Greek dialects of later times. One dialect was the standard form used by the Linear B scribes, which is thought to be a slightly artificial and formal version of the speech patterns used by the Mycenaean upper class. The second is a substandard dialect which sometimes surfaces in the Linear B tablets and seems to reflect the way the lower classes spoke.[76] If the second dialect seems out of place in the formal setting of the archive tablets, it is perhaps not so very unlike the British Prime Minister's tendency to use the Cockney glottal stop in an attempt to sound like a man of the people. In twenty-first-century south-east England, Estuary English, the English of the urban working class, has become the smart thing to speak. It is significant that some of the scribes at Knossos were evidently speakers of 'the King's English', the Mycenaean upper-class dialect.[77] This does not, of course, mean that they were necessarily upper-class Mycenaeans, though they may have been.

There are some dissenting voices, some scholars who remain sceptical that Linear B is Greek. One objection is that the 'spelling rules' for Linear B are so loose that a word may be transliterated in several different ways, making translation subjective. There are also substantial chunks of the archives that remain unintelligible. Exponents of Linear B as Greek respond that many Mycenaean Greek words must have gone out of use in the six hundred years following 1200 BC and that most of the problems can be explained in terms of the evolution of the Greek language.

The tablets are disappointing compared with the archives of the Near East, which include diplomatic correspondence, treaties, religious texts and even fragments of literature. On the surviving evidence, Linear B seems to have been devised solely as a means of keeping records.[78] It is possible that other documents – perhaps history and even literature – were made and written on papyrus, which would have been available from Egypt, but if so none of them have survived.

The Linear B tablets from the citadel at Mycenae, Thebes and all but five of the 1,100 tablets from Pylos date from about 1200 BC, when they were baked in (otherwise destructive) fires. The tablets from houses outside the citadel at Mycenae are older, but no more than fifty years older. The five unusual tablets from Pylos seem to be older still, but their date is unknown. The Knossos Linear B tablets are now thought to date not from the destruction in 1380 BC but later, in fact more or less contemporary with the mainland Mycenaean tablets, and some scholars believe that Linear B was a strictly thirteenth-century phenomenon. Re-dating the Knossian Linear B tablets in this way creates problems for those who want to connect the appearance of Mycenaean invaders at Knossos in 1450–1425 BC with the beginning of Linear B.

Some dispute whether Linear B is really Greek, on the grounds that many of the Mycenaean words have no cognates in later Greek; it is possible, though, as we have just seen, that such words fell into disuse some time between 1200 and 600 BC. Some Mycenaean words which appear similar to later Greek words actually mean something else; it is possible that this may be explained by the fact that Linear B developed out of Linear A, a system designed to express a different language.

Wa-na-ka is nevertheless clearly *wanax*, the Greek word for king, in both form and meaning. The Homeric words for king, *wanax* and *basileus*, are both seen in the Linear B tablets. Other archaic forms conserved by Homer are also seen in the tablets, such as the genitive singular forms -oio and -ao, and the ending -phi. The Linear B equivalent of Homer's -oio is the ending -o-jo.

Linear B was derived from the earlier non-Greek Linear A language in Crete, and then apparently adopted by mainland Greeks. This proves that there was verbal as well as cultural communication between Minoans and Mycenaeans. The Hittite archives imply spoken or written communication between Hittites and Mycenaeans. The Egyptian tomb paintings imply communication between Egyptians and Mycenaeans. The Near East increasingly looks like one world, linked by expert translators, scribes, traders and diplomats.

In classical times, land-locked Arcadia was a surviving pocket of a Greek dialect that was otherwise known only in Cyprus. This may have been the Mycenaean Greek dialect, known as Achaean, which had been wiped out right across the Aegean and in all the coastal regions of the Greek mainland.[79] Sheltered from change by their inland position, the Arcadians may have gone on speaking Mycenaean, the oldest known form of Greek, into the classical period.

TOMBS OF THE KINGS

It was the discovery of the 'grave of Agamemnon' with its gold portrait mask that enabled Heinrich Schliemann to put Mycenae and the Mycenaean civilization on the archaeological map not much more than a hundred years ago. Even if Schliemann was mistaken about what he found – not a portrait mask and not after all the grave of Agamemnon but the grave of a much earlier king – the tombs of these ancient kings have remained a legitimate focus for archaeologists. The burial practices of the Mycenaeans continue to tell us much about the nature of Mycenaean society and the way it evolved.

The earliest Mycenaean graves were simple and functional, without pretension, and virtually unchanged from those of the preceding Middle Helladic. They consisted of either a shallow pit dug into the rock, just large enough to take a folded-up body lying on its side, or a rectangular grave pit lined with stone slabs – a cist grave.

As the Mycenaean culture developed and its leaders increased in personal status from 1620 BC onwards, more elaborate graves called shaft graves were made. These were developed from the cist graves in being rectangular pits, but much deeper. Some were 4m deep. Some were small in area and intended for single burials. Others were much larger and intended as family graves. The biggest family vault was 6.5m by 4.5m. A layer of stones was spread on the floor of the pit for the body and its rich grave goods to rest on, and a low rubble wall was built along each of the long sides of the pit to support

Plate 3.2 Shaft graves at Mycenae. At the top is the bounding wall of Grave Circle A.

the edges of a timber roof. After the body was interred, the roof was built, using carefully squared timbers with copper-sheathed ends, and the shaft filled with earth. When the shaft grave was to be reopened for subsequent burials, the fill had to be dug out and the timber roof lifted out. This happened several times, and the gifts from earlier burials were deliberately smashed and either shoved to one side or unceremoniously mixed into the backfill.

At Mycenae there is a collection of fourteen of these shaft graves in Grave Circle B, just outside the citadel, dating from around 1600 BC. The six shaft graves in Grave Circle A, just inside the citadel wall, are fifty to a hundred years later and richer, reflecting the increasing wealth and ambition of the Mycenaean rulers – and a new phase in the development of the Mycenaean civilization. The graves are not just richer, they show evidence of an enormously widened horizon that stretched across the entire continent, reaching from Britain in the north-west to Syria in the east, as with the gold masks, a feature not seen before or later.[80] Ostentation on this scale suggests deliberate mimicry of Egypt, where an unmatchable standard in grandeur, wealth and ostentation had been set.[81]

The gold masks say something more about the mindset of the Mycenaeans. The use of gold masks must have made a great impact on those attending the wake and the funeral. It has recently been established, by

Figure 3.10 Gold mask from Shaft Grave IV at Mycenae (after Schuchhardt 1891).

reconstructing the faces of those buried in the graves, that the masks were in no sense portraits of the dead. To the onlookers who knew the dead person the mask would have looked alien, as if the wearer had already crossed over into the exotic world of the ancestors, already undergone a transformation. There was a huge element of theatricality in the use of masks, and it is significant that they were a major element in drama in classical Greece; they were very likely used in drama in Mycenaean Greece too.[82]

But there is some uncertainty about the scale of the richness of these graves, as Schliemann was deceitful and unscrupulous in the extreme and may have salted Graves III, IV and V with finds from elsewhere during the last week in November 1876 in order to intensify world interest in his work at Mycenae, just as he had done three years earlier with his collation of 'Priam's Treasure' at Troy. Both at Troy and at Mycenae Schliemann himself made spectacular discoveries during the final fortnight of his excavation, finding practically all the gold and silver the sites were to yield at one spot, before darting away to publish, lecture and trawl publicity. There was general bewilderment among contemporary Athenian archaeologists when Schliemann left the excavation before his workmen had finished opening the Mycenae Grave Circle, and the likeliest explanation for his departure is that Schliemann had good reason to believe that there would be no more very rich burials.[83] In fact, Stamatakis went on to open Grave VI in 1877, where he found some more gold. As for the terracotta idols, they could have been washed into the tomb from above by rain when it was partially open on 12–16 November 1876; it rained all day on the 14th.[84] Many of Schliemann's contemporaries were ready to believe that he had faked the shaft grave discoveries, because of his record of dishonesty, but the case against him is not entirely proved.

The grave circle itself is unusual, but may be related to a type of round barrow that is surrounded by stone slabs; examples have been found, widely separated, at Malthi in Messenia, Pazhok in Albania and Lake Ostrovo in Macedonia.

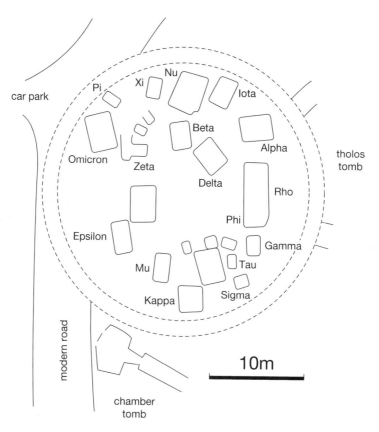

Figure 3.11 Plan of Grave Circle B at Mycenae.

The early shaft graves in Grave Circle B span the evolution of the type from simple pit graves cut in the rock to take a single burial to more elaborate multiple burials in shafts that are wall-lined and roofed. The scatter of twenty-six graves in the grave circle nevertheless looks rather disorderly; there are graves of a variety of different types, with different orientations, and no overall plan. It looks as if they are graves of several different and separate family groups. Only the bounding wall unifies them and sets them apart as belonging to an élite class. People buried in the same grave bore family resemblances and therefore probably belonged to the same family. Usually people in other graves belonged to other families, but there were some family connections, to judge from facial similarities. Gamma 51 and Zeta 59 appear to have been related. The young man, Gamma 51, died perhaps fifty years after Zeta 59, and may have been a grandson, or great-grandson of the older man. DNA studies may one day reveal more.[85]

The Grave Circle A graves overlap in time with the Grave Circle B graves, but continue for a generation longer. The cluster of six rich shaft graves was (much later, in 1250 BC) singled out for special treatment of a unique kind. It was surrounded by a carefully made double circle of stone slabs roofed with stone lintels; this replaced a much older grave circle boundary. At the same time, the land surface was built up to make a level precinct for ceremonies, with the heroes' grave stones (stelae) re-erected on the new land surface; then the entire west wall of the citadel was rebuilt further out so that the Grave Circle was inside the citadel. A new entrance, the Lion Gate, was designed to bring people into the citadel right next to the burial enclosure.[86] The scale of these great works suggests that some imaginative and powerful ruler was in charge; the timing suggests that it might have been the legendary King Agamemnon. The shaft graves belonged to an earlier age, and there may have been an oral tradition that these ancient graves, some as much as 250–300 years old, were the graves of the Perseids; perhaps Perseus himself was one of the occupants.[87] It is not known whether there was any family connection between the occupants of the shaft graves and the thirteenth-century ruler who ordered the landscaping of the royal cemetery, but it is likely that the later ruler either perceived such a connection or wanted his subjects to perceive it.[88] The grave circle project was a glorification of his dynastic past, real or imagined. King Agamemnon may have wanted to identify himself with the founder of Mycenae by identifying and glorifying Perseus' grave.[89] Certainly it looks as if the occupants of the Grave Circle A graves were the first to display their authority as rulers of Mycenae through their wealth and monuments, the first real dynasts[90]; their self-image was accepted and perpetuated by their descendants – or usurpers – over two hundred years later.

Shaft graves were not in vogue for very long, probably at most five generations: just one hundred years from around 1600 to 1500 BC. The last shaft grave at Mycenae was built in 1500 BC, though the custom of building

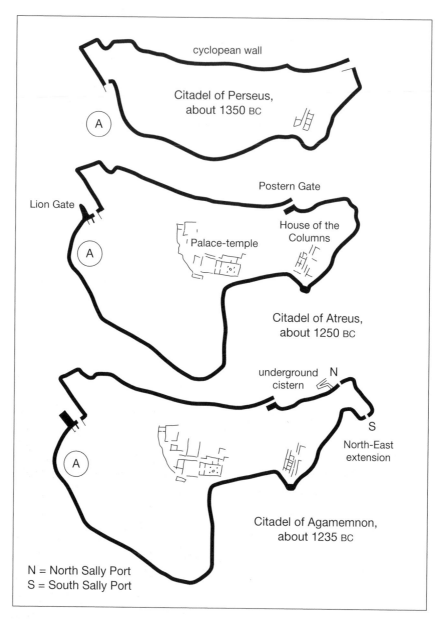

cyclopean wall

Citadel of Perseus,
about 1350 BC

A

Lion Gate

Postern Gate

House of the
Columns

Palace-temple

A

Citadel of Atreus,
about 1250 BC

underground N
cistern

S

North-East
extension

A

Citadel of Agamemnon,
about 1235 BC

N = North Sally Port
S = South Sally Port

Figure 3.12 The citadel at Mycenae. Three stages in its development (after Mylonas 1983).

shaft graves continued elsewhere for another hundred years. The rulers at Mycenae abandoned shaft graves in favour of a new and more imposing form of tomb that had been developing for some decades in Messenia, the tholos tomb, and the first tholos tomb at Mycenae, known as the Cyclopean Tomb, was made immediately after the last shaft grave, Shaft Grave I, in about 1490 BC.[91] Presumably the ruling families decided to follow the new fashion, though it involved a much larger investment in terms of time and therefore money. It took ten men ten days to dig a shaft grave, but more like a year to build a tholos tomb. A tholos tomb was very expensive, and implies an even more conspicuous display of wealth than the older tomb architecture.

The tholos tomb consisted of a beehive vault built of oversailing courses of drystone masonry. The Messenian tombs were built on level ground and had to be covered by an artificial mound or tumulus; the weight of the mound material was supposed to hold the beehive vault together. A horizontal entrance passage (dromos) went into the mound on one side, leading to an impressive stone doorway. The advantage of the new tomb design was that it was easier to clear the entrance passage and open the door to insert new burials than to dig out the shaft grave and dismantle the wooden roof. The tholos also made it possible for the officiants and mourners to accompany the dead right into the tomb, rather than observing from several metres

Plate 3.3 The heavily restored free-standing tholos tomb at Pylos.

above. After the first cluster of tholos tombs was built in Messenia, they became popular with rulers all over Greece. Over a hundred tholoi have been excavated.

Interestingly, the design is not dissimilar to that of some megalithic tombs in Spain, but the latter were at this time a thousand years old and already in a poor state; it is unlikely that they were the model for the Mycenaean tholoi. Probably the Middle Minoan round tombs were the inspiration; in this as in other ways, the Mycenaeans were copying the Minoans.[92]

The covering mounds used for the Messenian tholos tombs were not heavy enough to hold the drystone vaults in place, so they tended to collapse. The domed roofs were also visible and could be opened relatively easily by tomb robbers. It was for these reasons that, several decades later, the tholos tombs at Mycenae were built in cuttings in the sides of hills; the solid rock walls of the hill surrounding the tomb on three sides held in the lower half of the vault much more effectively. In a similar way it was found that the early dromos corridors, cut vertically into weathered rock, often collapsed into the dromos. Later dromos corridors were lined with rubble walls to revet the rock. In a final stage of development, they were lined with magnificent walls built of huge ashlar blocks and so became impressive pieces of architecture in their own right.[93] One reason for the collapse of the early tholos tombs was water penetration. Rainwater seeped between the stones, lubricating and loosening them. By the time the sequence of tholos tombs at Mycenae was built a technique had been devised to combat this; several layers of clay were laid over the beehive domes to waterproof them.

The success of the tholos tombs depended on the engineering principle of the horizontal ring, which had the equivalent strength of the arch. The overriding problem was that it needed to be complete to hold itself together. The huge door opening was a major weakness in the structure, an open wound. The problem was partly resolved by the relieving triangle, which deflected stresses diagonally outwards into the door jambs, which took an enormous amount of pressure from the rings of masonry abutting onto them.[94] The monumentality of the doorway, with its huge lintel, huge jambs and massive threshold, was not there just to impress, but to act as the lynchpin, the three-dimensional keystone of the whole structure.

The last tholos tomb in the sequence at Mycenae is thought to be the Tomb of Clytemnestra, built in about 1250 BC, and this was covered in a coat of white plaster. Lord William Taylour suggests that this very conspicuous tomb right beside the approach to the Lion Gate may have been King Agamemnon's.[95] The Mycenaean rulers wanted their graves to be highly visible: they were a major public statement about the rulers' status. The design and building of a tomb, which would have occupied several years

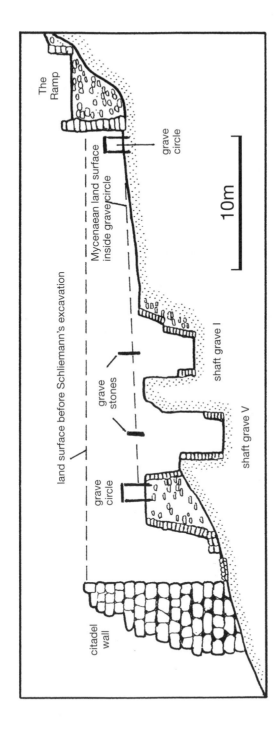

Figure 3.13 Grave Circle A at Mycenae. This section shows the relationship between the later grave circle and the earlier shaft graves. It also shows how far down Schliemann had to dig to reach the burials (after Piet de Jong).

during the lifetime of the king who commissioned it, was itself a major form of image projection.[96] This parade of status is seen in many societies, on large scales and small, from the Egyptian pyramids down to the medieval family chapels in English churches, with their conspicuously expensive alabaster statues and funerary hatchments. It is a flaunting of social superiority.

The Tomb of Clytemnestra cuts across the eastern side of Grave Circle B. This shows that by the time of this late tholos tomb, there was no memory of the occupants of the older grave circle, no need to respect them. This could be taken as confirmation that the occupants of the shaft graves in Grave Circle A were regarded as the ancestors of the Late Mycenaean kings, whereas those buried in Grave Circle B were not.

In spite of their huge size, the tholos tombs at Mycenae appear to have contained few burials. Astonishingly, each of these great monuments was for a single king and maybe his consort and a favoured child. This says much about the wealth and sense of self-worth of the later kings of Mycenae. The tombs were huge, theatrical, ostentatious. They also made spectacular settings for elaborate funerals. Priests, priestesses and mourners walked in procession up the long dromos, increasingly hemmed in by the towering walls on each side as they approached the huge doorway with its elaborately carved jambs, weighty lintel and decorated relieving triangle. The huge studded bronze doors into the underworld swung open. Inside, the dead king was laid out on a carpet under the centre of the yawning vault, torchlight glinting on the gilded bronze rosettes studding the masonry like a well-ordered firmament. The dead king in his royal robes and diadem lay surrounded by his belongings: utensils, food, wine, perfume, weapons and his great figure-of-eight shield. The funeral obsequies were chanted, animals were sacrificed, and the living retreated into the daylight. The doors were closed on death and the huge cache of wealth it was supposed to defend, for a time. Masons hastily built a rubble wall, often with an ashlar course halfway up, to cover the bronze doors, then an army of slaves moved forward to fill the dromos with rubble and earth.

Later burials in these great tombs were less dignified. If it was a sudden death in summer, the burial had to be speedy. This meant that sometimes there was not enough time to clear the dromos completely, and a ramp of earth was left up to the ashlar course. Only the upper half of the doorway was cleared and people had to scramble down ladders to get inside. The air in the tomb was foul and the remains of the last burial had to be hastily removed, usually by being buried in a pit in the floor on one side.[97]

The most impressive tholos tomb of all, not just at Mycenae, but anywhere, is the one that has been known since ancient times as the Treasury of Atreus. Built in about 1410 BC, it shows huge advances architecturally on the earlier tombs in overall size, the size of blocks used, the elaboration

Plate 3.4 The beehive vault of the Treasury of Atreus.

of the façade, the well-built enclosure wall. The façade was elaborately decorated with carved stone in various contrasting colours, including half-columns
with zig-zags, and a decorative slab, flanked by half-columns with spirals,
to fill the relieving triangle above the huge lintel. The dromos is made of
huge ashlar blocks, some large enough to be reminiscent of the great megalithic architecture of the north, like the unnecessarily large slabs of sandstone
used in the entrance passage of Maes Howe, built in Orkney in 3000 BC.
The dromos is 39m long and up to 4m high at the doorway. The vault
inside is 14.3m in diameter and 13m high. It is an awe-inspiring space to
modern visitors used to large-scale architecture; it must have been even more
awe-inspiring in the bronze age. The Treasury of Atreus, possibly the *Tomb*

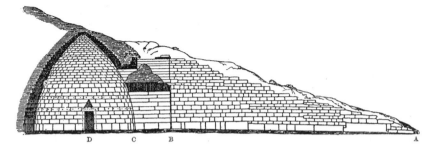

D   C   B   A

Figure 3.14 The Treasury of Atreus. A long section showing the dromos (A–B), doorway
(B–C) and entrance to side chamber (D). Notice how the dromos has become
a major architectural feature in its own right.

101

of Atreus, is the great masterpiece of Mycenaean architecture. It is a great loss that this tomb was robbed in antiquity; it would presumably have been one of the richest burials of all.

A set of thirteen tablets at Pylos records an inventory of furnishings for a major event. Michael Ventris and John Chadwick believed the event was the investiture of Damoklos, governor of the Hither Province, and the furnishings were the fittings of the suite of rooms where this investiture was to take place. Palmer believed the event was the funeral of a great subject, at which the king officiated.[98]

> Thus Pu-ke-qi-ri made inspection on the occasion when the king
>   ?buried Sigewas, son of Damokles;
> One jug decorated with Mother Goddess, bull's head and shell
>   pattern.
> One jug decorated with chariot scene and host of soldiers.
> One jug decorated with Mother Goddess, women, bull's head and
>   spiral pattern.

The list of utensils merges with a list of furniture that includes items such as 'One chair of ebony with golden birds on the back, and a footstool inlaid with ivory rosettes.' And so on, for thirteen pages. Whether this is the scene of a great funeral or an investiture really makes little difference. It shows the wealth and extravagance of the most privileged echelons of the Mycenaean aristocracy, and leaves a sense of what has been lost; where are the tables, chairs and footstools inlaid with ivory rosettes now?

The many chamber tombs built all over Mycenaean Greece – there are three hundred in the Mycenae area alone – were similar in concept to the tholos tombs, but smaller and less grandiose, and often just cut out of the living rock.[99] They developed in Messenia as the family tombs of the fairly well-off, and it was out of them that the tholos tomb evolved.[100]

In the fourteenth-century cemetery at Tanagra, the dead were buried in large clay chests, called larnakes (singular = larnax). The sides of these chests were painted with scenes of funeral rites, telling us much about the cere-monies surrounding death. There were processions of mourning women; later, in classical times, it was the role of women to perform the lament for the dead. The body was prepared by the older women of the immediate family, then laid in state the day following the death. During this viewing, or *prothesis*, grieving relatives came to terms with the death and said their farewells. Women tore their hair and scratched their faces; one picture on a larnax shows women with their hands to their heads, another movingly shows two women laying the body in the larnax. Winged figures may be the freed spirits of the dead, suggesting a belief that the soul survived

Figure 3.15 Old women of the immediate family lay a body out for viewing in a sarcophagus. This scene of *prothesis* is painted in black on a sarcophagus found
in the cemetery at Tanagra (after Immerwahr 1995).

death. A ship sets off through the underworld. Overall, we see a complex
of beliefs that looks closer to the Homeric ideal than the Egyptian.

The large numbers of ordinary people that we have for the moment
lost sight of must have been disposed of in other ways when they died. The
silent masses were not buried in tholos tombs, shaft graves or chamber
tombs, and there is no way of knowing whether they were accorded any
respect at all.[101] At least we have the tombs of the kings.

4

EVERYDAY LIFE
IN THE COUNTRYSIDE

A RURAL ECONOMY

The everyday lives of ordinary people left their traces in the archaeological record of the Greek bronze age, but for a long time they received little notice. Early treasure hunters, and even early archaeologists, had little interest in the humble evidence of domestic life and threw aside the pots, pans and tools; a lot of the evidence for the way of life of ordinary people was overlooked or even destroyed in the pursuit of treasure. Much of the information we have comes from indirect sources, images on wall paintings, pictures on vases and metalwork and ivories – and of course the Linear B tablets.

The Greek landscape was richer and more varied then than now, with coastal marshes heading the bays and extensive forests in the hill country, all teeming with wildlife. There were hares, red deer, roe deer, turtles and wild boars to be had.[1] In Messenia, the hills were richly clad in deciduous oak-woods that included several other tree species, such as Ilex oak, Austrian pine, chestnut and walnut, pistachio, carob, olive, cedar, cypress and fig.[2] Though not all of Greece was fertile, most Mycenaeans were engaged in agriculture, a highly organized activity, and most of the people lived out in the rural areas. In spite of the huge emphasis in the archaeological literature on the 'palaces', citadels and the urban development that accompanied them and clustered round them, most Mycenaeans lived out in the countryside. The towns to a great extent depended upon the tracts of countryside around them for food, labour and materials. They must have relied on them for political and even military support. In the towns there were administrators who devised elaborate systems to record some aspects of the rural economy – though not all – and it is evident from their records that the towns relied on the countryside. The tablets record deliveries of wool, for instance, implying that wool production was a major industry and a major source of wealth. Flax too was an important crop, and the tablets record huge quantities of olive oil. Many of the crops grown must have been

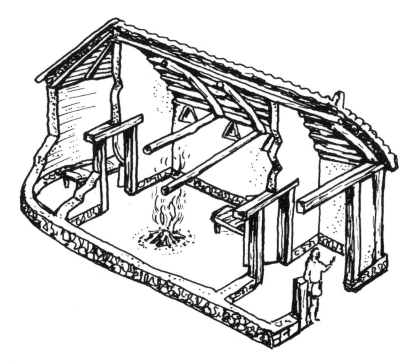

Figure 4.1 A reconstruction of one of the houses at Korakou, near Corinth, seventeenth century BC. Mudbrick walls stood on a stone rubble base. Note the distinctive apsidal form of the inner end, and the beginnings of a megaron layout (after Leacroft 1966).

consumed locally for subsistence, but by the peak of the Mycenaean period large surpluses were being produced for export.[3]

The houses people lived in were often simple rectangular structures with stone footings, mudbrick walls and ridge roofs. They had a single door at one end. A development from this was an apsidal design. This had a semicircular annex at the inner end, partitioned off to make a sleeping area. There was often an open porch at the entrance. Small triangular windows were made in the walls by inserting three slabs of stone to make an aperture not unlike the relieving triangles over the tholos tomb doorways. The ridge roofs of ordinary houses were probably covered with brushwood smeared with wet clay; it is likely that only higher-status buildings were tiled.

People lived in small hamlets and villages similar to the rural settlements of Greece a hundred years ago. Large areas of Greece must have been covered by this dispersed settlement pattern. Doubtless, as on Crete, a favoured location was in the foothills of mountains. The practice of transhumance would have been widespread, and locations midway between the high summer pastures in the mountains and the low winter pastures on the edges of the plains would be favoured.

In Achaea, this pattern emerges clearly. The population density was high in the Patras and Pharae areas. There are several fertile plains that were agricultural foci, but the late bronze age settlements were mainly on the coast or in the hill country above 200 metres, on the boundary between the summer and winter grazing. The main focus for the area was Patras harbour, which probably functioned as a Mycenaean port. Through it, the Achaeans made their trading contacts with southern Italy, Thessaly, Euboea, Argolis, Crete, Rhodes, Cyprus and Syria; the rural backwoodsmen were less cut off than might have been assumed.[4]

Cereals were the staple crops. Wheat and barley grain was measured in several units, the smallest being the cup, which was 0.6 litre.[5] The Mycenaean word and classical word for this unit was the same, *kotyle*, and it has continued in use in Arcadia, as *koutoli*, to the present day. In both Mycenaean and classical systems, four cups made a *khoinix*, but above this level the Mycenaean system diverged; the *khoinix* is ⅟₄₈ of the largest classical measure, but ⅟₆₀ of the major Mycenaean unit. It must be significant that the Mycenaean system was very similar to the one used in Mesopotamia.[6] Barley rations for workers were exactly three cups per day; wheat rations half that, presumably in recognition of the higher nutritional value of wheat. It is unclear whether other food was given to workers. The Pylian slave women were given figs as well as grain. Maybe other food was given out as well, but not recorded.[7] Meals were made more interesting by the use of spices and herbs such as coriander, cumin, fennel, sesame, mint, basil, oregano, rosemary, sage and thyme, and cooked in olive oil or safflower oil. There were also wild foods, such as almonds, cherries, plums, wild strawberries, walnuts and pistachio nuts.[8]

Wheat and barley were equally important, and cereals were evidently regarded as the foundation of the economy. When estates are mentioned, they are not described by area but according to the amount of seed needed to sow it. This continues in the Aegean to the present day; in Naxos a vineyard is measured according to quantity of seed needed if it was turned over to cereals.[9] It should be remembered that the modern plough had not been devised, and that the ard broke up but did not turn the soil; crop yields are unlikely to have been high.

Occasionally we glimpse a more intensive approach to food production. The shallow Lake Copais was drained when the citadel of Gla was built on an island above what had been shallow water and swamp. This 'improved' land was converted to farmland for cultivation and pasturage.[10] The draining of Lake Copais was a major undertaking, with the fortress of Gla only one of several structures designed and built to maintain and protect the new plain; there were look-out posts, forts and strong-points built on the hills surrounding the plain. This was a colossally ambitious scheme, grandiose in conception and execution. Gla may be seen as the headquarters of the officials responsible for managing and maintaining the agricultural system of the region.[11] When the drainage system was destroyed, the citadel of Gla was abandoned.

Olives were probably grown from very early on in the development of the culture, for there to have been surplus oil in exportable quantities by the late bronze age.[12] Olives are recorded as growing with grain. This sounds very much like a description of the interculture practised in some places in Greece today, where wheat is grown between rows of olive trees.[13] Olive trees produce a crop every other year, and all the trees in one district tend to be in phase with one another, so there are years when few olives are harvested. Fortunately, the fruit can be stored easily in jars, and the oil too keeps well, so it is unlikely that there were major shortages in antiquity.[14] Huge quantities of olive oil were produced and it must have been a major source of wealth. The simple fact that southern Greece is far more suitable climatically for olive production may explain why the Mycenaean civilization made far greater advances in the south than in the north.[15] The oil had a variety of uses, in cooking, as a dressing, as soap, as lamp oil, and as a base for manufacturing unguents.[16] Figs, which were also grown, were probably dried so that they were available as food all year round.

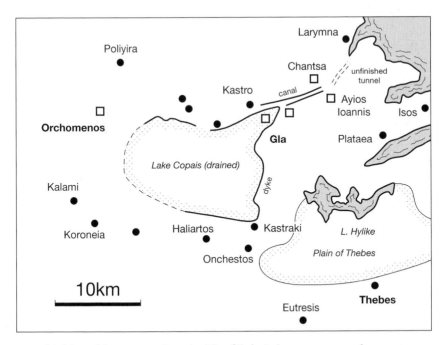

Figure 4.2 Map of bronze age Boeotia. The filled circles represent settlements; open squares represent citadels. Dotted areas are fertile plains.

Vines were also grown in the south of Greece, for wine production. Grape pips have been found at Lerna.[17] Grapes and olives were probably added to cereal production in the early bronze age to create the 'Mediterranean triad'.[18] Olives were produced to eat as fruit and for their oil. Grapes similarly were eaten as fruit, but many were pressed to make wine.

The perfume makers may also have worked out in the villages. These high-status craftsmen used a variety of rural produce to make perfumes and unguents. The tablets even tell us the ingredients:

o-do-ke a-ko-so-ta	Axotas gave to
tu-we-a a-re-pa-te (*ze-so-me*)	Thyestes, the perfume maker,
ze-so-me-no (*ko*)	the following ingredients to make perfume;
ko-ri-a2-da-na AROM	6 coriander seeds 576 litres
ku-pa-ro2 AROM 157 16	cypress seeds 576 litres 157 16 units
KAPO 2 T 5 VIN 20 ME 2 LANA 2 VIN 2	fruit – 240 litres, wine 576 litres, honey 58 litres, wool 6 kg, wine 58 litres.

Maybe the wool was used as a filter.

Some of the flax was processed to make oil. The flax fields were worked by slave women. Large quantities went to the army, so possibly linen was used for clothing issue or even sails for ships. It is not clear whether the flax was processed in the villages or in the towns, but many people were involved. There were flax carders (*pe-ki-ti-ra2*), women working with distaff (*a-re-ka-te-ja*), flax spinners (*ne-we-wi-ja*), linen weavers (*ri-ne-ja*) and seamstresses (*a-ke-ti-ja*). The only job for men in the textile industry seems to have been fulling (*ka-na-pe-wo*). At Pylos, about two hundred women are recorded as making cloth. Presumably there were proportionate numbers of women working in other centres or in the countryside round them, so there may have been over seven hundred women involved in the linen-making industry in the kingdom of Messenia.[19]

STOCK-REARING

The Mycenaeans reared livestock. Oxen are not mentioned much, but there were ninety ox-herds. We can reasonably assume that there were some oxen in each small agricultural community for ploughing. Another clue to the widespread presence of oxen is the assessment for 234 oxhides every year for the Pylos palace, which suggests that there must have been substantial herds of cattle. It should always be assumed that large quantities of food, and everything else for that matter, did not enter into the palace bureaucracy but were consumed locally. Only a limited range of produce is recorded by the administrators as coming into the palaces, and the surviving tablets cover a relatively small territory.[20] Cattle were regularly offered in sacrifices, so we should not always assume that stock were reared for economic reasons.

The same could be said of horses, which did not appear in the south of Greece until just before the emergence of the Mycenaean civilization, when their remains are found at Argissa, Lerna and Nichoria. In the Mycenaean period, horses are known only in association with the aristocracy. The first representations of horses appear on the grave stones for the shaft graves, where they are shown harnessed to chariots. Horses were indispensable for chariot teams, and they may have been reared under palace supervision for this specific purpose. Horses and chariots seem to be a distinctly Mycenaean cultural feature. Whether they were adopted from the Minoans or the Mycenaeans introduced them to Crete after the Mycenaean 'conquest', is hard to tell. Horse harness is shown in the frescoes, as is the distinctive tufting of the manes with the use of rings.[21] Homer tells us that Argos – presumably the Plain of Argos – was noted for horse-rearing and that there was 'a place called Ephyre in Argos where the horses graze'.[22] The kingdom of Elis, with its extensive plains, was also noted for horse-rearing. Then there is Diomedes' interest in the blood stock of horses. The Cadmeians loved horse-racing and one of the heroes was named 'horse-tamer'.[23] The horses of Aeneas 'are bred from the same stock as those that all-seeing Zeus gave Tros in return for his boy Ganymedes; and they were the best horses in the world. . . . If we could capture them we should cover ourselves in glory'.[24] When Paris runs through Troy on his way to battle, dressed in his splendid armour, Homer uses an extended simile vividly comparing him with a stallion breaking loose. The association between horses and the aristocracy is obvious from these vivid references. The colour of the horses seems to have been significant. White horses were preferred, presumably so that the warrior-princes would be even more visible when driving their chariots and cut even more of a dash.[25]

Horse-trading may have been the major source of wealth in Argolis. Around 1620–1600 BC, the rich royal graves of the earliest shaft graves contained the odd long sword and dagger, Minoan in style, which *may* have been imported, and amber beads which *must* have been imported. The rest is local. As the Mycenaean economy developed, more exotic goods and materials were bought – but with what? Intensifying agricultural production is possible, as the Plain of Argos is fertile, but horse-rearing is also likely, and it is after all what Homer keeps emphasizing about Argolis. There is good evidence of trade with Aegina, so it is reasonable to suppose that Aegina functioned as a transhipment point for trade with the Cyclades. If horses were traded further afield, it may be significant that horses made their first appearance in Minoan Crete in the seventeenth century BC (Middle

Minoan III or Middle Helladic), at a time when Argolis was developing from a mainly subsistence economy into a more market-oriented mixed economy.[26]

The Mycenaeans had flocks of goats, kept for their hair which was used in textiles, for their meat and for their milk, which was processed to make cheese, as it still is today.[27] The hill and mountain country of much of Greece lent itself to the rearing of goats and sheep. In a flock of sheep, rams and ewes were usually counted separately, but when grouped together only the 'ram' symbol was used, giving a false impression that there were many more rams than ewes. Wool is not mentioned in the Pylos records, probably because the spring sheep-shearing had not taken place at the time of the palace's destruction. The main sheep-rearing regions were in the north of the Hither Province, especially the Kiparissia valley, and the west side of the Pamisos valley in the Further Province. Just four men are named in connection with responsibility for wool production and it must be assumed that they are all of high rank: Wedaneus, Alxiotas, A-ke-o and Amphimedes. Wedaneus was the *lawagetas*; Alxiotas was the chief palace steward; the roles of the other two men are not known. Echelawon, who may have been the king of Pylos or at least a powerful aristocrat, had holdings of agricultural land and owned livestock, to judge from the offerings he made: cheese, bulls, sheepskins.[28] Homer's description of the shield Hephaestus made for Achilles includes scenes of everyday life, not unlike the hunting scene on the Lion Hunt Dagger; large cattle graze in the water meadows and sheep graze on upland pastures.

An elaborate system of assessment was in play calculating the quantities of wool and other agricultural produce that were due to the urban centres. Certain types of produce in particular seem to have attracted this attention, such as wool, wheat, barley and oil. These were apparently seen as taxes in kind that were due to the 'palace' centres, and sometimes expressed as offerings to gods, priests or named officials. The system appears to have acted as a kind of tithe. It is not certain whether the scribes keeping the 'palace' archives controlled all of the agricultural production, though it is likely that they concerned themselves with only a fraction of the total. The bronze age rural economy must have been primarily a subsistence economy, with village communities producing enough to sustain themselves and a small surplus; a relatively small proportion of their output would have been a surplus that would go off to the towns as offerings.

Pigs were reared in small herds, some of which were being fattened up in various districts in the Hither Province of Pylos.[29] Chadwick assumed that the lower classes only ate meat on special occasions such as sacrifices, but assumptions like this have proved to be wrong for other early societies. Certainly a major product of stock-rearing would have been leather, which had a wide range of uses from bridles and other horse harness to straps, fastenings, shoes, sandals and laces.[30]

HUNTING

Wild boar were hunted, not reared, and for a very particular reason. Between thirty and seventy-five pairs of boars' tusks were needed to make a single boars' tusk helmet, which became a major object of desire among Mycenaean officers. Once the tusk helmet became a prestige object, the cull of boars must have been relentless.

The Mycenaean aristocrats loved hunting, whether from their chariots or on foot, and often using packs of dogs.[31] The dogs are shown in frescoes, and their importance in the socio-economic web is clear from Homer. In his touching description of Odysseus' relationship with his hound Argus, we can see the special bond of sentiment that existed between the huntsman and his dog.[32] Hunting produced food, and there were plenty of wild creatures to hunt: deer, hare, duck, goose, partridge. Lion hunting was evidently a sport, and a very dangerous one too. For a long time it was assumed that stories like the legend of the Lion of Nemea were no more than that – legends – but recent archaeology suggests that lions were still roaming the mountainsides of southern Greece at the peak of the Mycenaean civilization. The bones of lions have been found in Mycenaean contexts at Tiryns and Kastanas.[33]

The agricultural calendar at first sight looks undemanding. Growing wheat or barley involved hoeing and sowing in October–December, harvesting and threshing in May–July. But growing olives involved hoeing in October, harvesting and pruning in November and December, and

Plate 4.1 Two men fighting two lions, the scene vividly depicted on the Danicourt ring, a gold signet ring made in about 1450 BC.

Figure 4.3 Wooden box with ivory dogs (or perhaps lions) standing on ivory plinths. The 11cm high box, found in Shaft Grave V at Mycenae, was probably made (of sycamore wood) in 1530 or 1550 BC.

hoeing and planting in February–April. Vines needed hoeing and pruning in February and March; harvesting and wine-making took place in September and October. Figs needed hoeing in February, harvesting in August and September, hoeing and pruning in October and November. Cultivating vines and olives with cereals therefore leaves very few slack periods in the working year.[34] The addition of vines and olives significantly turned agriculture into a full-time occupation, which it had not been before, and this in turn may have triggered another social and economic development, the emergence of full-time specialist craft workers and the development of town life.

While most Mycenaeans spent most of their time working in the fields, vineyards and olive groves near their villages, the routine of their rural work was doubtless broken frequently by visits to other settlements. From time to time they needed to buy fresh stock, or visit specialist workers in the towns to buy farm tools. From time to time they visited the shrines and temples in the towns; there were occasions, such as landmark birthdays, when special ceremonies had to be attended to mark rites of passage within the family. At certain points in the year there were major ceremonies to mark big communal festivals.

And on these occasions, town and country met.

5

EVERYDAY LIFE IN
THE TOWNS

Although the texture of life in the towns was different from that of life in
the country, with many new specialist occupations emerging, the people
working in the towns had a huge stake in the rural economy. Many of the
merchants and craftsmen, as well as the powerful administrators and courtiers, owned agricultural land and therefore derived both wealth and status
from food production. The natural rhythms of the countryside permeated
the towns.[1]

No Mycenaean town has been fully or even extensively excavated, on the
scale of Minoan Gournia or Palaikastro, for example, but towns certainly
existed next to each of the major citadels. There were towns at Mycenae,
Tiryns, Pylos and Thebes. Tsoungiza, not far to the north of Mycenae, is a
rare example of a settlement that has been excavated, though it consisted
of just a few hectares of houses. Tiryns is thought by some to have been
one of the biggest settlements, at eight hectares, but if the Kadmeia at
Thebes was continuously built over it would have been thirty hectares. The
town adjacent to Gla may have been even larger.

There is only patchy evidence of refinements such as organized street
layouts and fittings such as drainage systems. In the citadel at Mycenae,
there are drains designed to serve particular buildings, but there is no integrated drainage system. The way blocks of buildings developed suggests
that they expanded from original nuclei without considering any overall
town plan.[2]

HOUSES

The architecture of the town houses is unimpressive and there is a big gap
between the design of the 'palaces' and the design of ordinary houses. Houses
often consisted of a few rectangular rooms, rarely in any particular order,
and less advanced in terms of design and fittings than the Minoan or Cycladic
houses of earlier times. Some of the more imposing houses are of the 'corridor
house' type, with a series of large rectangular rooms contained between

Plate 5.1 The street between the House of the Oil Merchant (left) and the House of Shields (right). These two high-status houses looked across the main street of Mycenae towards the citadel.

flanking corridors, often with stairs leading up from the corridors to an upper floor.[3]

The plan of the main rooms in a Mycenaean 'palace' developed out of a Middle Helladic (2000–1600 BC) house plan, a long rectangular room with a vestibule at one end. Probably there was a lean-to porch in front of the vestibule; usually there was a store room at the back with a separate entrance. In the 'palace', this simple design was inflated into an impressive columned porch leading by way of a doorway into a vestibule, which in turn opened into the large main room. The store room feature was also retained at the back of the megaron at Pylos. Evidently, then, the monumental megaron was intended to look like a house, whether it functioned as a house or not. A fixed hearth was usually to be found in the Middle Helladic living room; in the later 'palace', this was inflated into a large and ostentatious circular fixed hearth in the middle of the main room. The earliest palace-style building known is 'Mansion I' at the Menelaion. This is a megaron with a room at the back with a separate entrance; it also has rooms on each side, reached across flanking corridors.[4]

The ground-floor walls of houses were solidly built of stone, their thickness varying according to the load they had to bear, in other words according to the number of upper storeys. Elaborate timber frames were built into the structure, evidently to give the buildings more flexibility and earthquake resistance. These consisted of vertical timbers set into the walls at intervals on both sides, interlaced through the walls by short cross timbers; they were also linked laterally with horizontal beams. The frame was covered by mud plaster on the ground floor and by painted plaster on the floor above. The walls of the upper storeys, the living quarters, were made of mudbrick, sometimes using sun-dried bricks 60cm long, sometimes using mud that had been poured like concrete into a wooden mould, sometimes using two skins of mudbrick walling filled with a rubble core.

Town houses probably had flat roofs, like many modern Greek houses. This is shown in a fresco of a warrior falling from a flat-roofed building and an image on the Siege Rhyton of a crowd of waving onlookers who are standing on flat roofs with parapets. Fragments of burnt roofing have survived, and they show impressions of brushwood and beams in the baked clay. The same technique was used for roofing in Mycenaean times as in recent village houses. A brushwood or wattle layer was laid across the joists and then a coating of mud plaster was added. This could serve as the floor of an upper storey if required. Floors in the houses of ordinary people were made of stamped earth, whereas the floors of the rich were of white plaster.[5]

One tablet refers to 'twelve wall-builders' sent off to do building work at four different sites. Another tablet lists building materials for a small hall or megaron, using technical terms the Mycenaean builders would doubtless have understood at once. A series of three entries lists twelve beams, four roof-beams, six cross beams, all described as being 'of the chimney'. This is the timbering for the lantern in the roof above the open hearth to let the smoke out. Blegen found the shattered remains of two smoke-stacks 65cm in diameter and 50cm long, which were presumably set in mud plaster on top of the lanterns. Six timbers are described as 'door posts', and John Chadwick suggests that these include the lintels. Two roof beams and a column are listed, presumably to make a porch or small vestibule.[6] The materials listed amount to a ready-to-assemble, prefabricated megaron kit.

The earliest really elaborate buildings appear between 2900 and 2450 BC (Early Helladic II, sometimes known as Lerna III). These are the first 'corridor houses', such as the House of Tiles at Lerna, the Weisses Haus at Kolonna, Megaron A at Akovitika. These special structures had tiled roofs, as did the Round Building on the site of the later 'palace' at Tiryns. This was a massive keep-like round building 28m in diameter (about the same as the length of the House of Tiles), with its exterior studded with bastions; it too had a tiled roof.[7]

FURNITURE

Very little of the Mycenaeans' furniture has survived, except the plastered bench, which is an architectural feature of the 'palaces' and some of the rich houses. The locations seem right for reception or waiting rooms, and might therefore fit what is emerging as a strongly bureaucratic society.[8] On the other hand, built benches were used differently in the archive room at Pylos; they were used there for stacking and storing archive tablets. By contrast benches in the Minoan temples were used as altars, so we cannot be sure, when we see a bench at Mycenae or Pylos, whether we are looking at a seat, a storage shelf or an altar.

We can assume that the Mycenaeans had beds and chairs, because the Minoans had them; a cast of a bed was found at Akrotiri. The large gold ring from Tiryns shows a goddess in profile, sitting on a chair. The slender elegant legs form a cross shape, like a folding camp stool, and the design is very reminiscent of the stools shown in Minoan frescoes. The goddess's feet rest on a low block which looks as though it may be a footstool, and indeed the Linear B ideogram for a footstool looks exactly the same shape, a low rectangle, with what looks like a leather handle on each side.[9] One series of tablets at Pylos proves that the Mycenaeans had chairs, stools and tables. One inventory entry reads, 'Footstool inlaid with a man, a horse, an octopus and a palm tree in ivory'. Remains of footstools have been found at Dendra and Mycenae. Some were expensively embellished. The many ivory plaques found in the West House complex at Mycenae may well have come from disintegrated furniture in a furniture workshop or warehouse; the small decorative ivory inlays represent sea urchins, shells and dolphins.[10] Nor was it just at Mycenae that such rich furniture was made. Inlays for furniture have been found in a workshop at Thebes, and ivory chair legs were found in a store room there.[11]

Wooden biers were used for transporting bodies to tombs for burial; this was essential when corpses were not enclosed in coffins or sarcophagi. There are small painted clay models of what may be either beds or biers, and armchairs too.

Small plain offering tables were also sometimes made of wood, like the two found in Shaft Grave V. They consisted of shallow bowls of pale cypress wood with mortises to receive the three legs, which were simple flat plaques.[12]

Tables usually had three feet, because they were more stable on uneven floors than tables with four. It is therefore particularly puzzling to come across, 'One table of stone with supports of ebony and ivory, splay-legged, with nine feet, worked with spirals'.[13] One suggestion is that the Mycenaeans were already using the foot as a measure of length, but it is not clear why the tables, and there are several in the inventory, should be six feet or nine feet long.[14] My own suggestion is that the standard table design was the tripod table; as with modern tables, the top might be fixed on or simply rest on the substructure. A rectangular trestle table would need to rest on two tripods, and would therefore be a 'six-foot table', a longer rectangular table top would need to rest on three tripods, and would therefore be a 'nine-foot table'.

What the furniture was made of we are usually not told, but presumably mainly wood. Two kinds of wood are mentioned. One is *kutisos*, a kind of laburnum wood, the other is box, and both have been used for making furniture in modern times. Table tops might well be stone; the tablets actually mention stone, and Blegen found fragments of a marble table top. The decoration is more specifically identified as being made of ivory, stone, rock crystal and gold (leaf?).

It is unfortunate that none of this furniture has survived, apart from the elaborate inlays. There were probably many other furnishings, besides chairs, stools and tables, that go unmentioned in the inventory, and it should be assumed that cupboards and chests existed for storage.

The precious metal objects deposited in the tombs of the wealthy show the sort of vessels that must have been in general use. The wonderful gold cup from the tholos tomb at Dendra near Midea shows the sort of design that was probably usually executed in clay. The cup is 18cm in diameter, shallow, with a circular handle-loop. The Vapheio gold cups, deposited in a tholos tomb near Sparta, are more nearly beaker shaped, with a squarish handle on one side, much like a modern mug or tankard. The quality of decoration is astonishing – and probably not at all typical of everyday wares – but the overall shape of the vessel reflects the design of contemporary drinking vessels. The range of utensils used in cooking and for serving at table included cooking pots of various shapes and sizes, cauldrons, jugs and amphorae, made in clay for ordinary people, and bronze for the wealthy.

METALWORK AND ARMOUR

The main metal in use was bronze, which provided the cutting edges for weapons and tools, though it looks as if there was no adequate source of copper, the main constituent of bronze, on the Greek mainland. There was copper in Crete, maybe enough to supply a small-scale bronze age industry, but it is likely that most was imported from Cyprus. A late bronze age wreck off the south coast of Turkey demonstrates how cargoes of copper ingots were transported. It is not clear where the tin came from: maybe Slovakia, Spain – or even Britain. The Pylos tablets list the smiths, their addresses and the amounts of bronze issued to them. They were allocated relatively small amounts, usually three or four kilograms, which suggests that they were not full-time blacksmiths; they probably cultivated land and grew their own food. There were probably as many as four hundred bronze-workers in the kingdom of Pylos, not scattered about like village blacksmiths but concentrated in groups of up to twenty-six. This large number of workers probably produced a surplus of metal goods, and these were exported.

Bronze was used to make sword and dagger blades, spear points, chariot wheel fittings, suits of armour, cooking pots and cauldrons. Some spears had composite shafts, made in sections; this made it possible to have very long spears. Homer describes Ajax defending his beached ship with a spear that was an astonishing twenty-two cubits long; this was normally used for sea-fighting, though it is not clear how effective such an unwieldy weapon would have been. Even so, some massive spearheads have been found, 60cm long, so very big spears were certainly made. Spears, bows and arrows were the main weapons at this stage. Many arrowheads were still made of Egyptian flint or Melian obsidian, which could be sharpened to finer points than metal. A special kind of whetstone for smoothing the shafts of arrows, the 'arrow shaft polisher', was imported from northern Europe.

The technology for making reliable and effective swords was still in an experimental stage. The fine-looking swords and daggers found in the shaft graves show the skilful use of complicated moulds for the relief decoration of blades and midribs, and in the covering of hilts with *repoussé* goldwork. So elaborate and beautiful are they that it seems likely that many of these were for ceremonial use; they look too good to have been used in battle. The large number nevertheless confirms the shaft graves aristocrats' preoccupation with fighting; at least ninety swords were buried with the three princes in Shaft Grave V. The long rapier, which was the commonest type of sword in the shaft graves, was a borrowing from Minoan Crete. These unwieldy weapons, a metre long, were good for thrusting like spears and stabbing, but they were prone to break if given a sharp blow on the blade edge; then they were likely to snap, especially at the tang, the thin spike which fitted into the hilt, and most of the rapiers found are broken in this way. There was also a short sword that seems to have been a Mycenaean invention, with a broader blade and a tang enlarged into a proper, stronger hilt; this was an altogether more serviceable weapon.[15]

Homer makes it clear that his heroes went to a great deal of trouble to take their opponents' armour from them.[16] It was not just a matter of killing the enemy, but of taking his weapons as trophies. It is very understandable, in the context of relatively scarce raw materials and the high technology involved in making the artefacts, that Homeric heroes would take considerable risks to acquire a fine set of armour and weapons. They might later be dedicated as thank-offerings to the gods. Pausanias mentions seeing in the front chamber at the Argive Heraion the shield that Menelaus had taken from Euphorbos at Troy and dedicated at the temple.[17] We can also see from surviving examples like the Lion Dagger that the swords of the aristocrats were objects of great beauty, which must also have made them great prizes.

Mycenaean warriors protected themselves with big rectangular tower shields or figure-of-eight shields. Both were in use at the same time, as we can see in the picture on the Lion Dagger. Both types of shield were large, and must have been made out of hide rather than bronze. The dappled texture shown in fresco images of the figure-of-eight shields proves that they were covered with cowhide. The hair was left attached to the hide, partly to save unnecessary work in removing it, but also because the bristles

Figure 5.1 Mycenaean warrior carrying a spear or staff and figure-of-eight shield, and wearing boots, a codpiece and a boars' tusk helmet. An ivory plaque from the Artemision on Delos, probably made in about 1250 BC.

deflected and absorbed a certain amount of the energy when a weapon struck them. The figure-of-eight shields as shown in frescoes had visible lines of stitching round the edge – three lines at Knossos, two lines at Tiryns. The stitching represents the strips of rawhide that were used to stitch the hide to the wooden frame.

Homer describes tower shields, but perhaps misleadingly; Ajax carries a long-shadowed spear and 'a shield like a tower, made of bronze and seven layers of leather'.[18] This would clearly be much too heavy to carry, and Homer probably conflated the leather tower shields of the Mycenaean period with the much smaller round shields of the eighth century, which were indeed made of bronze covered with layers of leather. Agamemnon is described as being armed with two spears and a round shield, which is eighth century, iron age, gear. Ajax's shield is also described as having a boss, which his tower shield (as big as a wall) would not have had. Both the figure-of-eight and the tower shields must have been very unwieldy. Hector's shield, slung over his back, bumps against his neck and ankles as he runs. Periphetes, a warrior from Mycenae, trips on the rim of his shield, which must therefore have been large, but could have been of either figure-of-eight or tower design. Curiously, Periphetes is the only Mycenaean

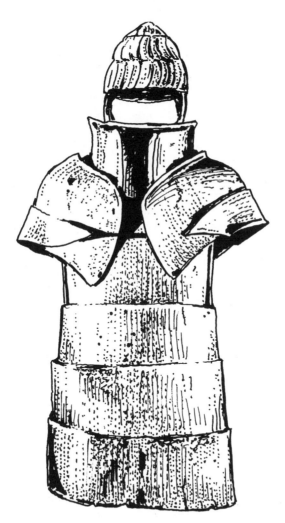

Figure 5.2 Suit of bronze armour from a tomb at Dendra (Midea).

121

(man from Mycenae) to be mentioned in Homer.[19] Elsewhere, Homer has warriors bearing round shields; Aeneas has one.[20] Round shields did in fact appear in the Mycenaean period, in the fourteenth century.[21] The tower shields shown on rings and other images are covered with dappled cowhide, just like the figure-of-eight shields, and they have semi-circular extensions at the top to protect the warriors' faces.[22]

Hector is 'covered with bronze all over'. At one time this was seen as an anachronistic description of hoplite armour from a later period, but the discovery of a bronze suit of armour at Dendra has changed all that.[23] Hector could indeed have been clad in a metal suit.

The most distinctive piece of Mycenaean armour was the boars' tusk helmet. This was made principally between 1570 and 1430 BC, but was still in use two hundred years later. Obviously, boars' tusks were not easily come by, and many were needed to make just one helmet; a boars' tusk helmet was a very expensive item, a family treasure. Homer confirms this; the boars' tusk helmet belonging to Meriones was stolen from Boeotia by Autolycus, given by Autolycus to Amphidamas of Kythera, and then by him to Molos, the father of Meriones. By the time Meriones gave it to Odysseus it was a priceless heirloom.[24] Tusk plates have been found in two shaft graves at Mycenae and in chamber tombs at Asine and Prosymna. Few warriors would have been able to afford these helmets. Probably most had leather helmets, perhaps with bronze discs or plates sewn onto them.

Leather leggings were in regular use by warriors from 1450 through to 1150 BC. The way the frescoes often show these in white and projecting up to protect the kneecap suggests, as mentioned already, that shining metal greaves had already been invented. Greaves were worn by warriors to protect their shins from disabling slashing by enemy swords, but also to stop them from being chafed and bruised by the lower edges of their huge shields. Greaves would also have been indispensable when hunting on foot in scrubland.

Large vessels such as cauldrons, kraters and large jugs, were made of several sheets of bronze held together with rows of rivets.

Gold is referred to in the Pylos tablets as *khrusos*, a loan-word from the Levant, in terms that suggest that an extraordinary levy was being raised, perhaps at a time of crisis leading up to the palace's destruction; it seems improbable that large amounts could have been levied, even on the rich, on an annual basis. It may even have been a Danegeld to buy off pirates.

Elaborately decorated gold cups were deposited in late high-status burials at each of the major centres. The wonderful gold cup found in a tholos tomb at Dendra near Midea and made in about 1400 BC is decorated with *repoussé* octopuses, dolphins and rocks; the style is accomplished, free and in the best Minoan style. The precious metal objects deposited in the tombs of the wealthy show the types of vessels that must have been in general use. The Dendra cup shows the sort of design that was probably usually executed

Figure 5.3 A warrior wearing a boars' tusk helmet. This ivory plaque made around 1250 BC (8.5cm high) was possibly an inlay for a casket or a piece of furniture, and was found in a chamber tomb at Mycenae.

in clay. The cup is 18cm in diameter, shallow, with a circular handle-loop. The two Vapheio gold cups, deposited in a tholos tomb near Sparta, are more nearly beaker shaped, with a square handle on one side. Some scholars think the cups are likely to be imported Minoan creations; others think the cups were made in Greece but by migrant Minoan craftsmen; others think that by this time Mycenaean craftsmen were able to produce this kind of artwork for themselves.[25] The quality of decoration is astonishing – and probably not at all typical of everyday wares – but the overall shape of the vessel reflects the design of contemporary drinking vessels.

Even the early high-status burials, the shaft graves, contained gold cups. Shaft Grave IV at Mycenae yielded a fine gold kantharos with two big

Figure 5.4 Gold cup from Shaft Grave II at Mycenae, beaten out of a single sheet of gold, with a handle riveted on. It is decorated with an architectural motif, an arcade of pointed arches, which may be a reference to a particular building.

handles and a single-handled gold goblet. They were both of high-quality, probably Minoan, workmanship – and they were entirely undecorated. A third cup, a one-handled electrum goblet inlaid with gold and *niello*, has a discreet and delicate picture of a fern-like dittany plant growing in a pot, which is repeated three times round the rim.

A gold-plated hexagonal wooden box was found in Shaft Grave V. Several of the rectangular faces are decorated with scenes of lions attacking their prey. Both the brutal subject and the stylized, rather crude execution are Mycenaean. The gold funeral masks covering the faces of the royal dead in the shaft graves, in both grave circles at Mycenae, are a uniquely Mycenaean creation. Nothing like this was ever done on Minoan Crete. The faces were evidently made by hammering a gold sheet over a carved steatite mould.

The range of utensils used in cooking and for serving at table included cooking pots of various shapes and sizes, cauldrons, jugs and amphorae, made in clay for ordinary people, and in bronze for the wealthy.

Silver has fared less well with time than gold, but a few objects have survived. Shaft Grave V at Mycenae yielded a silver jug. There was a silver funnel-shaped rhyton in Shaft Grave IV. It was decorated in *repoussé* with scenes of battle and a city under siege. Its conical shape meant that it could be used in a purely functional way as a funnel for pouring oil or wine.

The same grave yielded two more very fine rhytons, one in the form of a bull's head, the other in the form of a lioness's head; these could not have been used to guide the pouring of liquid into another vessel, and can only have been used for pouring libations. It is assumed that this whole family of expensive decorative rhytons was made exclusively for use in religious ceremonies. It is, moreover, another importation from Minoan religious practice.[26] A fine silver cup from Mycenae was decorated in gold and *niello* with a row of bearded male heads. Similar heads, separated from their background setting, were found at Pylos, which dates the Mycenae silver cup to the thirteenth century BC.[27] Although silver is found in the archaeological record, it is strangely absent from the tablets, which is another reminder that the tablets do not document the Mycenaean economy comprehensively.

Iron technology was in its infancy and only a few iron items were made, mostly simple hammered rings. A single iron point was found in the jewellery workshop at Thebes; it seems to be the earliest example of iron used in a practical context in the Mycenaean period.[28]

ARTS AND CRAFTS

The visual arts were not centred on stone carving, to judge from the meagre remains that survive. The Mycenaeans appear to have shared the Minoans' lack of interest in large-scale sculpture; it is a lack that binds Minoan and Mycenaean civilizations together, and distinguishes them from the neighbouring civilizations of Egypt and Anatolia, where life-sized and larger-than-life statues were popular. The earliest efforts seem to have been the grave markers, remarkably like modern gravestones, erected to mark the positions of the shaft graves. The carving on these limestone stelae was crude. There are running spirals copied from some Minoan original – it was a favourite Minoan fresco ornament, and this one is very similar to a plaster relief ceiling in the Knossos Labyrinth. Interestingly the sculptor at Mycenae was more comfortable carving his copy of a Minoan original than he was the adjacent figurative scene of a charioteer. But we have to remember that this was only the start; we are right at the beginning of a long tradition of Greek sculpture that would culminate in the work of Pheidias in the fifth century BC.

There is little evidence of stone carving again until the stone lionesses were hoisted onto the Lion Gate in 1250 BC. The sculpture shows two heraldically opposed lionesses, one on each side of a Minoan column supported on a pair of Minoan incurved altars placed side by side. Their front feet are resting on the altars. The heads, which must have faced outwards, have been lost; they were probably carved out of steatite and attached with dowels. They were presumably 'collected' in antiquity, though at some time after the visit of Pausanias in the second century AD; let us hope they will one day reappear. On top of the column is a row of four discs, representing the ends of rafters. These in turn supported some further ornament which has been destroyed. The design was not new – in fact it can be seen on fifteenth-century Minoan seals – what was new was its translation into a major monumental composition. There are several Mycenaean artworks related to the image on the Lion Gate. One, on a gem from Mycenae, shows a single incurved altar with two lions mounting it in the same way as on the Lion Gate; their faces, like their altars, fuse into one as they face us,

Figure 5.5 Headstone (stela) from Shaft Grave V. It is 1.35m high. Seventeen of these stelae were found in Grave Circle A.

which makes a strikingly surreal effect.[29] There are many other pieces of Mycenaean artwork which share the theme of opposed animals, such as two lambs facing a column and two sphinxes facing a sacred tree.[30] The Lion Gate sculpture marks a great leap forward to a monumental style that is noble and majestic in conception and holds a genuine promise of the classical tradition to come.[31] High up on the lintel, the sculpture remained visible through many of the succeeding centuries. It was certainly seen by Pausanias in the second century AD.[32]

A significant amount of sculpture must have been lost during that time. Low-relief carvings must have filled the relieving triangles above the doorways of all of the tholos tombs. Fragments of the carved façade of the Treasury of Atreus have survived, mostly more of the Minoan-inspired running spirals, though there are two pieces of a gypsum low-relief bull-leaping scene. More low-relief stone carving came in the form of triglyphs. The triglyph was a popular decorative feature of the Minoan temple-palaces, usually forming a kind of skirting along the base of a wall or forming the front face of a bench-altar; it occupied the same position in Mycenaean architecture, and was another straight borrowing from Crete. The triglyph consisted of three vertical fillets flanked by half-rosettes, and was carved in bold relief.[33]

The making of stone vessels was another feature of Minoan civilization taken over by the Mycenaeans. When the Minoan civilization went into decline, stone vessel production stopped on Crete and continued at only a few mainland Greek centres like Mycenae. Some quite elaborate stone jars and rhytons, made mainly of serpentine, have been found in the House of Shields at Mycenae, dating from around 1300 BC. It is thought that this kind of work was focused on just one or two workshops.[34] Flakes of gold leaf have been found adhering to some of the stone rhytons, and it would seem that this was a cheap way of producing gold ritual vessels.[35]

There is surprisingly little Mycenaean sculpture in the round. There are some large cult statues from Keos, a stuccoed and painted head of a goddess from Mycenae, and some small idols from Mycenae, Tiryns and Phylakopi. There is also the small ivory group, which is carved in the round. It seems likely that there were other sculptures in the round to create a tradition out of which the Lion Gate lionesses could eventually be produced, but they have simply not survived. Maybe more was created in clay or painted stucco, and it has simply disintegrated. There were the large antithetic sphinxes mounted over the porch at Pylos. The painted plaster head found in a house at Mycenae just south of Grave Circle A dates from around 1225 BC. It is just under life-size, and is a rather severe female face with staring eyes, an unsmiling mouth with down-turned corners and harsh colours. A curious rosette motif is painted on each cheek and the chin; possibly these were beauty spots. The face clearly belongs to a forbidding idol of some kind, perhaps a sphinx or a goddess.[36]

Figure 5.6 The richly carved doorway of the Treasury of Atreus (reconstructed). Note the relieving triangle over the door lintel and the attached half-columns (after Wace 1949).

Plate 5.2 The House of Sphinxes at Mycenae. View northwards, with the House of the Oil Merchant in the background.

There is clearer evidence of a well-developed tradition of carving in low relief, as in the many ivory reliefs. The ivory pyxis from Routsi carries a pattern of well-carved running spirals. The ivory pyxis lid from Ras Shamra may be a piece of Syrian craftsmanship, but it uses and develops a Mycenaean composition. A bare-breasted goddess stands between two rampant goats, which she is feeding. Syria was probably the source of the ivory the Mycenaean craftsmen used. Elephants lived in Syria until the ninth century BC.[37]

The art of fresco painting was imported from Minoan Crete, probably initially using Cretan artists, undergoing little change along the way. We tend to associate the frescoes with wealth and value them for the huge amount of information they can give us about the culture that produced them, but one of the major reasons for the development of the art was that painted plaster was a good way of covering up poor building materials. The best stone was kept back for corners and door jambs, and the rest of the wall was often no more than rubble, which had to be plastered.[38] At Mycenae it was not just the 'palace' that had wall paintings, but houses and other buildings both inside and outside the walls of the citadel.[39] The wall was first levelled up with coarse stucco, then finished with a fine lime plaster. Paint was not usually applied to the wet plaster, as in true fresco painting, but to the newly dried surface. In some Mycenaean frescoes the composition

Plate 5.3 The carved lions on the Lion Gate.

was sketched in monochrome outline on wet plaster, and these lines have bonded into the plaster even where the later coats of paint have flaked off. The palette consisted of black, white, red, yellow, blue and green, using carbonaceous shale, lime, haematite, ochre and copper silicate as raw materials.[40]

The first known wall paintings on the mainland were created between 1550 and 1450 BC – in the 'palace' at Mycenae. These, the fragments found under the floor of the East Lobby on the building's southern edge, were dated by associated pottery to 1550–1450 BC. Another group of early frescoes at Mycenae was found, again in a very fragmentary state, under the floor of the Ramp House. These too date to 1550–1450 BC as far as the pottery goes, and are likely to belong to the beginning of that period because of the many points of similarity with Knossian frescoes, especially the famous Bull-Leaping Fresco. Miniature frescoes at Tiryns may go back to this same early date, 1550–1500 BC.[41] The House of the Oil Merchant at Mycenae has yielded remains of frescoes of two distinct periods. The later frescoes were evidently on the walls when the house was destroyed, around 1280 BC. The earlier ones came from a deposit under the floor of a corridor together with pottery which dates their destruction to around 1350 BC. The styles of the two lots of frescoes correspond to earlier and later fresco styles discernible at both Pylos and Tiryns.

The earlier frescoes, which were evidently painted in the period 1500–1350 BC, are very similar to the Minoan frescoes with which they are contemporary. A good example is the bull leaper from Pylos. The later paintings, such as those that were on the walls at Tiryns and Pylos when those

Figure 5.7 The head of the goddess modelled in painted plaster from Mycenae. One of the few surviving examples of Mycenaean sculpture in the round. It dates from 1300–1200 BC and is 16.8cm high.

'palaces' were destroyed at the end of the thirteenth century, were made after the last of the Minoan frescoes and were extremely crude. From 1450 BC onwards, processions in the Egyptian manner were a popular theme, both in the Minoan and in the Mycenaean frescoes.[42]

At the Mycenaean centres, the frescoes were coarser than on Minoan Crete, where great refinement and delicacy were achieved. Black outlines, which became heavier with time, were added, and the colour green was added to the palette too, but in other respects there is little to differentiate the techniques.[43] The subject matter is slightly different. There is less in the way of religious exultation and exuberant celebration of natural landscape, more in the way of warfare, hunting and a rather stiff-necked stateliness, and it may be that these contrasts reflect real differences in the preoccupations and mindsets of the two civilizations. From the megaron in the citadel at Mycenae comes a fresco showing a citadel containing three-storeyed buildings under siege: possibly the citadel of one of Mycenae's rivals, possibly the citadel of Mycenae itself. There are some everyday scenes, as we see in fresco fragments from Knossos, such as ladies gossiping and horses being groomed, and even bull-leaping. Some scenes may show incidents in

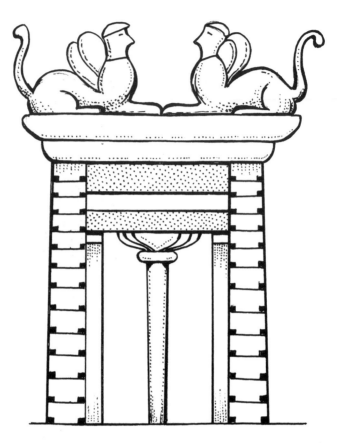

Figure 5.8 The Sphinx Gate at Pylos. A fragment of fresco from the north-east (right-
hand) wall of the Propylon, showing what the propylon itself looked like. It
was two storeys high with a tall central pillar topped with an elaborately
fluted cushion capital. The walls to each side were painted black and white.
The heavy corniced roof was topped by a pair of huge sphinxes, perhaps made
of clay coated with painted stucco. The heraldic composition is strongly
reminiscent of the Lion Gate at Mycenae.

mythology. A fresco at Tiryns may show Pandora's box; a fresco at Pylos
may show Orpheus playing his lyre. A rare explicitly religious fresco from
the Room with the Fresco at Mycenae shows two goddesses. Some frescoes
imitate the texture of marble and wood, just as they do on Crete and Thera.
The symbolic rendition of rocky landscapes, sky and cloud have been
borrowed intact from Crete; for skin colour, the symbolic use of Indian red
for men and white for women has been borrowed from Egypt by way of
Crete. As in the Minoan frescoes, there are marine motifs, especially at coastal
Tiryns.

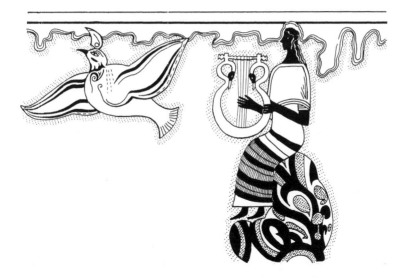

Figure 5.9 The bard and a crested bird in a rocky landscape: fresco from the Throne Room at Pylos. The lyre (or phorminx) is white, the bird and the bard's robe are cream, and the background is scarlet.

The style of the later Mycenaean frescoes is rather formal, static and hieratic compared with the Minoan, Theran and early Mycenaean frescoes, which seem more spontaneous, joyful and full of zest. The female adorant offering crocuses from a frieze in the Palace at Thebes is well-built, heavy and rather solid, typical of the evolving Mycenaean formal style; she formed part of a remarkable frieze of female worshippers, all carrying offerings, painted in around 1400 BC and destroyed shortly afterwards. The frieze was over forty metres long.[44] The fact that the joints on the women's fingers are indicated by two short brush strokes, both at Thebes and at Mycenae, though never in Minoan Crete, shows that the Mycenaean painters were developing their own divergent conventions.[45] The women in this procession carried offerings for a goddess, including flowers, serpentine jars and ivory boxes. The background consists of wavy bands of colour, which in a Minoan or Theran fresco would indicate a mountainous landscape, and may or may not mean that in a Mycenaean fresco. Similar processions were painted on the walls of the palace-temples at Tiryns and Pylos, and it is likely that they show the real-life cult processions that took place in the spaces in front of them.

Similar fresco techniques were applied to some of the floors of high-status buildings. The palace-temples at Mycenae, Tiryns and Pylos all had painted floors. The idea evidently started with imitations of stone pavements, and many of the square compartments drawn on the floors are filled with geometric designs developed from the veining of gypsum slabs. But they also contain images of marine creatures, in imitation of the marine floors of Minoan Crete. In the throne room at Pylos there is a solitary octopus in the rectangle right in front of the throne. Elsewhere in the palace-temple at Pylos there are several octopuses and dolphins.[46]

The last frescoes that we know of, from Mycenae, Tiryns and Pylos, show a sharp decline in skill and craftsmanship. The drawing is often crude and careless, with figures often heavily outlined in black. Even so, the images have a certain charm and they can still tell us much about the Mycenaeans and their way of life. There are hunting scenes from Tiryns, including a hunter walking along with two spears over his shoulder, at least six chariots, a stag, a bevy of watchful deer, and some improbable pink and blue hounds chasing wild boar.

Motifs from fresco art began to transfer from walls to pottery after the fall of Knossos. Men, birds and animals start to appear, as if in some way to commemorate the loss of the images from the walls of the Minoan temples. For whatever reason, chariot scenes and 'antithetic' animals are lifted off the walls and applied to the pottery.[47]

As the Mycenaean period opened on the Greek mainland, some of the very finest Minoan pottery was being produced on Crete. The Floral Style (1550–1500 BC) featured informal representations of flowers, reeds, grasses, applied to tea-cups, jugs with cutaway or horizontal spouts, rhytons and large pear-shaped storage jars. Two generations later, this ware was joined by another distinctive and vivid ware, the Marine Style (1500–1450 BC), in which nearly every conceivable form of marine life is depicted: argonauts, dolphins, fish, starfish and octopuses all swim among coral, rocks and sea-weed. On the mainland, similar pottery was produced, in a more provincial idiom, but on a fabric that is actually finer than the Cretan. There is also an extra pottery shape, the goblet. The Mycenaean pottery dating from 1550–1450 BC is so different from what went before that we have to assume that Cretan potters were actually brought in to centres like Mycenae, Pylos and Thebes to create the new styles for the Mycenaeans.[48] A clay potter's disc of Cretan type has been found on the island of Aegina, along with imported Minoan ware, which strongly suggests the arrival of Cretan potters. The earliest Mycenaean ware may have been made in the vicinity of Mycenae, but it appears almost at once in Messenia and seems to have spread quickly through the area that was about to become Mycenaean Greece.[49]

In 1450 BC another new decorative style emerged, this time distinctively Mycenaean, known as Palace Style. It re-uses motifs that are seen in Floral and Marine Style vases, but in a stiff, static and formal way. The Mycenaean motifs stand to attention, whereas in the Minoan style they are at ease. Exuberance is replaced by restraint and discipline. Liveliness is lost, but a certain majesty is gained. Palace Style decoration was applied mainly to large jars. Another popular shape was the Ephyraean goblet, named after Ephyra (Korakou has been speculatively identified as Ephyra), the site near

Corinth where it was first recovered; it was probably manufactured somewhere in Argolis. This was decorated in an entirely new way, with a single motif on each side and a small ornament under each of the two small handles. This style was imitated at Knossos, but not well.[50]

In the Late Mycenaean period (1400–1200 BC) Mycenaean pottery was similar across a wide area and it may be that this reflects a political and economic union of some kind, perhaps centring on Mycenae.[51] The same style spreads right across the eastern Mediterranean basin from Sicily to the Levant, in effect marking the extent of the Mycenaean trading empire. Significantly, only the pottery produced on Crete remains distinct, suggesting a certain level of autonomy there.

Stemmed cups evolved out of Ephyraean goblets; the stem became longer and the bowl shallower, like a champagne glass and standing about 20cm high, and this became the standard type of drinking cup from the fourteenth century onwards. The vessels were usually completely plain except for a single decorative motif, a stylized octopus, shell or flower, on the side facing away from the drinker. A fine collection of these stemmed cups, or kylikes, was found at Zygouries, not far north of Mycenae; the site, known as the Potter's Shop, may actually be part of a minor 'palace' centre.[52] One of the commonest vessels was the stirrup jar, invented in Crete back in the sixteenth century and widely used by the Mycenaeans from 1400 BC onwards for storing and transporting wine and oil. These were often globular or pear-shaped. At the top is a solid pillar of clay, which looks like the spout but is not: it is in effect the anchor for the two handles. The true spout sticks up vertically beside it. The Mycenaean name for the stirrup jar was *ka-ra-re-u*, something like *khlareus*, which is close to a modern Cretan word *khlaros*, meaning 'oil vessel'.[53] Another storage vessel was the alabastron, so called because some were carved out of alabaster; these are distinctively flattened, squat vessels with three small lugs. Large bowls used for storing dry goods were decorated in Pattern and Pictorial Styles. The Minoan motifs had by now been thoroughly absorbed and were becoming more and more stylized. A large white jar from Ialysus has a stylized, meticulously symmetrical brown octopus painted on it. By the thirteenth century, the stylization is so extreme that the origin of the motif is unrecognizable. A kylix found at Corinth has a red cuttlefish design painted on the buff fabric.

Large kraters decorated in Pictorial Style are found almost exclusively in Cyprus, and for a long time it was naturally assumed that they were manufactured there, but a few examples have been found on the Greek mainland, mostly near Mycenae, and it has now been established that they were all manufactured at workshops close to Mycenae, probably at Berbati just to the east of the city, where there are the right clay sources. The ware was probably specifically made for export to Cyprus, where they were used as centrepieces for drinking ceremonies.[54] The decoration appears to have been painted on at high speed and the effect is sometimes crude; Reynold Higgins

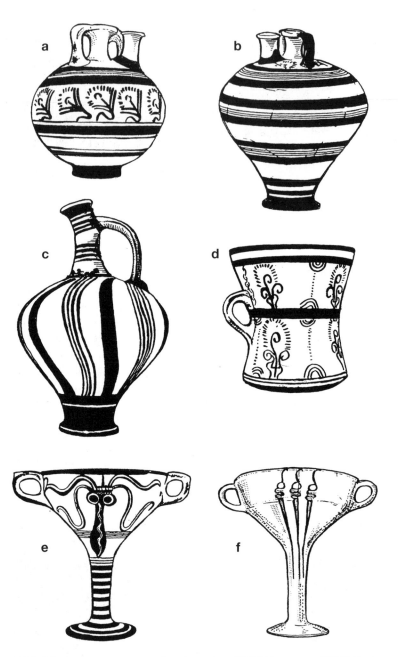

Figure 5.10 Mycenaean pottery. a & b: stirrup jars (LHIIIA), c: ewer (LHIIIA), d: mug (LHIIIB), e: kylix (LHIIIA), f: kylix (LHIIIB).

Figure 5.11 A mythic scene: two charioteers pursued by a whale! Painting on a Mycenaean vase exported to Cyprus in about 1250 BC.

calls it 'barbarous', which is a fair description, but the scenes showing warriors, horses and chariots can still tell us much about everyday life in Mycenaean Greece, and as much again about Mycenaean religious beliefs and mythology. One krater from Enkomi in Cyprus shows a charioteer with his groom riding along, perhaps into battle, while a long-robed god, Zeus perhaps, stands in his way holding the scales of destiny that will decide his fate.[55] It is an archetypal scene reminiscent of several in the *Iliad*, where the gods are shown intervening in battle and deciding the outcome.

Another Mycenaean vase from Cyprus shows a chariot being driven away from what appears to be a whale in hot pursuit. Yet another shows a rural scene in which two well-fed bulls, beautifully patterned with rosettes, are either grazing or more likely squaring up to each other ready to fight – one has his horns lowered threateningly towards the other – while birds hop round them.

Figure 5.12 Bulls with birds, painted on a Mycenaean vase exported to Cyprus in about 1250 BC.

The most famous example of Pictorial Ware is the Warrior Vase from the citadel at Mycenae, showing eleven fully armed warriors marching off to war. They carry their spears over their shoulders and tied to their spears are pouches containing, perhaps, their day's food ration. A woman waves goodbye.[56]

Another set of images shows animals and birds, often in pairs and facing each other, like the sphinxes on either side of a tree from Enkomi.[57] The figures are drawn in outline and filled with regular patterns of lines, dots, crosses or chevrons; probably these images were borrowed not from frescoes but from textiles.

The Mycenaean pottery painters liked zoning, dividing the vessel up into horizontal bands. This restricting and disciplined approach reached a climax in the Close Style, which evolved in Argolis in the thirteenth century. Pots were substantially covered by zones of geometrically patterned borders, sometimes including a pictorial zone of birds, which are also geometrically patterned.[58]

Small amounts of pottery were imported. Canaanite pottery, found in the South House annex at Mycenae, was imported as an élite good. One Canaanite amphora contained resinated wine. Some pottery was imported from Cyprus. Around fifty pieces of exotica altogether came to Mycenae from Egypt, the Levant, Mesopotamia and Anatolia, though none of them arrived in the thirteenth century; all are associated with that earlier, more impressionable, phase in the development of the civilization, when foreign influences were very strong.[59]

Though the Mycenaeans left no written music, we know they had musical instruments of considerable sophistication, and therefore music of some sophistication too. A few fragments have been found, and from these we can reconstruct a range of instruments. A parabola-shaped lyre was in use, probably imported from Minoan Crete. Its frame might have been made of wood, tortoiseshell or even alabaster and it had seven strings.[60] The phorminx was a distinctive Mycenaean development of the Minoan lyre. A large phorminx was also made in the fourteenth century, after the fall of Knossos, when it also appeared in Akhenaten's Egypt; the Egyptians of those times (the 1350s) mentioned that the large phorminx had been 'introduced by foreigners', who were presumably Mycenaeans.

The phorminx was an elaborately constructed lyre, roughly u-shaped overall, with a crescent-shaped soundbox at the bottom to amplify the sound. Played only by men, and probably only by seated men, this instrument rested on the lap and reached the chin. It was gripped against the left side of the chest with the left arm and plucked or strummed with the right hand, while the left hand damped the four or seven strings. It was made of polished oak-wood with ivory decorative attachments. The arms were made in two sections, the lower one in an s-shaped curve and decorated with a duckhead finial, the upper one straight and ending in a flower or animal-

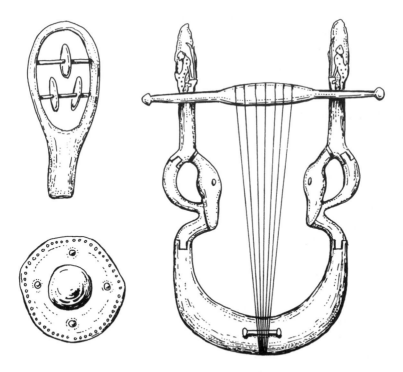

Figure 5.13 Musical instruments. Upper left, sistrum, found at the Phourni cemetery, Arkhanes; lower left, finger cymbal found on the Ulu Burun wreck; right, phorminx or lyre, based on parts found and the lyre-player fresco at Pylos (after Younger 1998).

head finial. The phorminx was probably used by bards to accompany songs and may have been used as a solo instrument or in consorts with other instruments.

The main wind instrument was the aulos. This consisted of two tubes made of cane, metal, wood, ivory or bone, each with a cane reed in the mouthpiece. There were two types of aulos, the clarinet type with a single reed and the oboe type with a double reed. In the classical period they came in different sizes, giving different registers. The tubes were fitted into bulbs at the mouth end; round these a leather strip was fitted and tied round the back of the head like a gag to hold the instrument in position. The outer ends of the tubes, which were up to 60cm long, were supported in the crook between fingers and thumbs. The fingers were used to stop the five finger-holes.

The sistrum, another Minoan import, was shaped like a table-tennis bat with horizontal rungs supporting small cymbals or bobbins. The sistrum was shaken and made a sound something like a tambourine.

Probably all of these instruments were used together in a band to make a blend of sounds. Music was used in religious ceremonies to heighten the sense of otherworldliness, just as it has been used across subsequent centuries. Some of the sounds will have had a specific purpose; the triton shell horn was used perhaps to call the faithful, the lyre to accompany women's voices, the phorminx to accompany the bard. Music was used as an accompaniment to work, to keep warriors marching in step, to keep rowers together, to generate atmosphere at ceremonies, to drown the sounds of sacrifice – and not least for communal entertainment.[61]

THE 'PALACES'

We cannot leave a discussion of life in the towns without mentioning the buildings almost invariably referred to as palaces. A significant portion of the Mycenaean economy revolved round these high-status building complexes. Each town had one of these complexes, which acted as a major social, religious, economic and political focus. The 'palace' had its own internal economy, which involved supplying the everyday needs of the élite group of people who evidently ruled from it, the palace staff and the dependent work groups. The 'palace' was also involved in a range of prestige activities: providing festival food, general hospitality, conspicuous consumption, exports, gifts to local élites and – not least – offerings to the gods.[62] At least 8,500 pottery vessels were in use at the Pylos 'palace' at the time of its destruction, neatly stacked on shelves according to type. They were used in a highly organized and efficient system of catering of a very specialized kind. In one pantry off the Main Court were around six hundred kylikes. In the store room next door there were wine jars. The implication is that short-term visitors to the megaron beyond the Main Court were supplied with a goblet of wine before entering.[63] Whether this was merely a hospitable welcome or part of a religious ceremony is an open question, but a very significant question, and one that leads on to the more fundamental question of whether the buildings we have been calling 'palaces' were really temples.

6

RELIGION

PROBLEMS IN INTERPRETATION

What did the Mycenaeans *believe*? Who were their gods – and how did they worship them? These are questions we are bound to ask, but the answers are hard to find. We can attempt a reconstruction of Mycenaean religion, but several major obstacles stand in our path.

One is that the sources are largely external. The remains of shrines, surviving figurines, idols and religious paraphernalia, images of ceremonies on seal-stones, signet rings and frescoes – all that these sources can supply is some of the outer surface of religious practice. Their interior meanings and the belief system behind them remain frustratingly difficult to reach.[1]

A second obstacle is the apparent similarity between Minoan and Mycenaean religions, which tempts us to assume they were the same. The religious scenes portrayed in frescoes and other artwork imply that both had tree and pillar cults, triple shrines and sacral horns, a goddess as a principal deity, with a subordinate god playing a secondary role as son and consort. Yet the picture that Homer gives, just five hundred years after the putative reign of Agamemnon, is of a very different religion. By then, Zeus is Father of all and supreme ruler; his wife Hera is chief among goddesses but subordinate to Zeus; the deities have no mystique or mystery about them; they are mere mortals writ large.

One way of explaining this has been to represent the Minoan religion as the shared patrimony of the Aegean region, in effect the inheritance acquired by the ancestors of the Mycenaeans when they migrated into the region. At the same time, the ancestors brought in with them a pantheon and a belief system of their own, a legacy of their Indo-European origin. The process was then a complex accommodation between the two religions.[2] This syncretistic model has been challenged repeatedly over the past sixty years, partly because of the lack of evidence to support it.[3] Many scholars have become uncomfortable about accepting Arthur Evans' views of the shared patrimony, based as they are on Frazer's *Golden Bough*. Did everyone in the eastern Mediterranean region and the Near East believe in a Mother Goddess and a Divine Son fated to die at the death of the old year and be reborn every spring? A major difficulty here is that the Evans–Frazer model does not accord well with what has been learnt subsequently of bronze age religion in the Near East.[4]

A third obstacle is that a great deal of evidence is available for religious beliefs and practices in Greece in the classical period, and this may mislead us. Some of the deities worshipped then and some of the religious practices too had an ancestry reaching back to the Mycenaean period. It is nevertheless not safe to assume that deities, even bearing the same names, had the same attributes or that religious practices had the same meaning or purpose.[5]

It is hazardous territory, and both the content and development of Mycenaean religion remain remarkably obscure. Tsountas, Picard, Evans, Nilsson and Mylonas have all pored, century-long, over the puzzling relationship between Minoan and Mycenaean religions and failed to reach a conclusion.[6] The distinctive flavour of Mycenaean religion at the close of the period suggests that the religion practised on the Greek mainland may have been fundamentally different from the Minoan throughout the late bronze age; perhaps the Minoan overlay was mainly iconographic, decorative – superficial, even – and a temporary craze only.[7]

What are the Mycenaeans *likely* to have believed? In common with other early farming communities, they are likely to have believed in supernatural powers that could control the weather, the fertility of their flocks and herds, the productivity of their soils. They will also have believed that the supernatural powers needed to be propitiated if natural processes were to continue working in their favour. This led to the orchestration of public ceremonies, with some level of communal participation, at which the gods were invoked with displays of respect; there were offerings of food, drink, living creatures, music, dance and drama. Alongside these public ceremonies, which would inevitably follow a seasonal calendar, there would have been household rituals, involving private acts of magic and superstition, but with the same general intention. Probably there were also secret ceremonies carried out by priests and priestesses, which only they knew about; it is common for priesthoods to try to make themselves indispensable in this way. In general terms, those are likely features of the Mycenaean religion. We can take several steps further, though, by observing that the Mycenaeans seem to have seized the Minoan belief system with enthusiasm in the Early Mycenaean period. It evidently filled a vacuum, as there is little evidence for religious practices before that time on the mainland. It is also clear that the Minoan 'package' was adopted first in Argolis, which is where the earliest Minoan-style ritual vessels are to be found.[8]

Minoan religion revolved round a Great Goddess with several transformations and several names. To what extent these transformations became separate goddesses in people's minds is impossible to tell; it is like disentangling the mystery of the Christian Trinity. The goddess Eileithyia may have been an aspect of the Great Goddess, or a separate goddess of childbirth. Maybe the one Minoan goddess with several manifestations was changed, progressively, into a multiplicity of Greek deities during the Mycenaean period. At the Cretan peak sanctuaries, she was worshipped as Mother of Mountains and Mistress of Animals. A seal from Knossos shows her standing regally on a mountain top with a lion on each side, perching like the lionesses on the Lion Gate.[9] The recurring question is whether this was a single goddess known by several names or many lesser goddesses with separate identities. Evans corresponded with Nilsson about this very question; he was uncertain.[10]

Some of the gods and goddesses of the classical period had already emerged by the time Pylos fell. The tablets speak of Zeus, Hera, Athene, Artemis, Paiawon (Apollo), Enualios (Ares), Poseidon and Hermes. Artemis appears as *A-ti-mi-te* at Pylos (PY Un 219), Hera as *E-ra* (just once, on PY Tn 316) and she is associated with Zeus.[11] It is not possible to tell whether these deities had the characteristics and responsibilities attributed to them later. It is nevertheless clear that three aspects of the Minoan Great Goddess stand out – Mistress of Animals, Goddess of Vegetation and Household Goddess – and that these correspond to three of the greatest goddesses of the classical period, Artemis, Demeter and Athena. A fourth aspect, represented by Hera the later spouse of Zeus, would have been less relevant in the Minoan religion, though she seems to have become more and more important on the mainland as the transplanted religion took root. But at least the Minoan and Mycenaean gods and goddesses had responsibilities for various aspects of the natural world, and those not only survived into the classical period but were vividly recalled in Homer, where we hear of Poseidon the Earth-shaker and Zeus the Cloud-compeller, Zeus of the Lightning Flash.[12]

There were also deities in the Mycenaean religion who seem to have no later equivalents: shadowy figures such as Marineus, Diwia, Komawenteia and a *Di-ri-mi-jo*, who is the son of Zeus.[13] The name Diwia is a female equivalent to Diwe, Zeus, so she may be assumed to be Zeus's consort, who would later be known as Hera, if indeed she is the same deity. Diwia may even be an additional name or title for Hera – 'Mrs Zeus'. Zeus was a member of the Mycenaean pantheon, but he was by no means the chief god. It is clear from the scale of offerings that Poseidon was regarded as the chief god. The fourth-century BC historian Ephorus observed, 'The Peloponnese in the olden days seems to have been the dwelling place of Poseidon and the land was considered sacred to him.' This is consistent with the idea of *Pa-ki-ja-ne*, the holy city of Pylos, and apparently not far from Pylos, being the seat of the goddess Potnia, where there was a large estate belonging to the 'wanax'.[14]

We have already seen that 'wanax' can refer to Poseidon, the Heavenly King. The Sumerians called him Lord of the Earth, the Hittites Earth-King.[15]

Plate 6.1 Two seated goddesses with a divine child. One goddess has her arm round the other and they share an elaborately textured and tasselled shawl, clearly visible in this back view of the ivory group, carved before 1300 BC. They are probably 'The Two Queens' to whom offerings were made at Pylos. This beautiful ivory statuette, only 8cm high, was found in the temple-palace at Mycenae.

If 'wanax' can mean either a king or a god, logically the female form 'wanassa' can mean either a queen or a goddess. One of the Pylos tablets includes a dedication *wa-na-ka-te wa-na-so-i*, 'To the King and the two Queens'. If the King is the chief god, Poseidon, the two Queens must be the chief goddesses.[16] They may perhaps be the same two goddesses depicted on the fresco at Mycenae, Hera and Athene.

SHRINES

We know that there were priests and priestesses, as they are mentioned in the Pylos tablets (e.g. Tn 316).[17] Identifying their shrines and temples helps to clarify the nature of the religion. An Early Mycenaean outdoor altar where fires were lit and double-axes of bronze and sheet-gold were deposited has been found near Epidauros. It stood at a shrine on the steep north slope of Kynorthion Hill close to the classical Sanctuary of Apollo Maleatas. Bulls and goats were sacrificed here, and the site produced clay figurines of oxen and bulls. It is similar to a Minoan peak sanctuary, and it looks as if the Mycenaeans were borrowing the trappings if not the beliefs of Minoan religion. This shows the sort of 'high place' the Mycenaeans worshipped at, and it is likely that others will eventually be discovered.[18]

The cult of the goddess Demeter was thought, even in the early nineteenth century, to be pre-Greek in origin, but such speculations were not based on excavation. Then, in 1932, when the telesterion built at Eleusis in the time of Peisistratus, tyrant of Athens 546–527 BC, was excavated, the remains of a Mycenaean megaron were found underneath it, its 50cm thick walls still standing to a height of 0.6m. It was a rectangular building 9.5m long, 5.7m wide and consisting of one large room and a portico.

Figure 6.1 The Mycenaean temple at Eleusis. The ground plan is derived from the archaeological remains at the site. The steeply pitched roof, the square window in the gable and the two triangular windows in the side wall are all based on the clay model of a temple found at the Argive Heraion (after Rutkowski 1987). The plaster is partly stripped from the side wall to show the construction.

In front of it was a projecting platform, like the apron of a stage, with a recessed flight of steps on each side. The temple, in use from around 1450 to 1100 BC, was set in a rectangular enclosure about 20m across, bounded by a stout wall. Nilsson interpreted the Mycenaean megaron as the dwelling of the local ruler.[19] This idea contains the seed of another idea, that the classical Greek temple could trace its design back to that of the palace of a Mycenaean ruler. It also contains the seed of two further ideas, that the megaron may have doubled as royal dwelling and shrine, and that religious ceremonies were presided over by a priest-king. This web of associations and assumptions – which I believe to be poorly founded – has been very hard to disentangle. Mylonas took the simpler, and I think correct, view, that the megaron at Eleusis was a temple. It is too small to have been a king's house and the house of a lesser person would not have justified an enclosure wall. The temple is also built on an inaccessible hill slope, when there are better sites for dwellings nearby. The location is easily explained by the text of the Hymn to Demeter, which says that the temple was sited on the Kallichoron well. An early well, possibly the Kallichoron well, was discovered during excavations.[20]

Town shrines have been identified at Mycenae, Asine and Berbati in Argolis, and Malthi and Pylos in Messenia, but the remains at most of these sites are paltry. The Asine shrine consists of a small stone bench-altar with five small female idols on it; at Berbati and Malthi the traces are similarly scanty. The so-called 'shrine' at the palace at Pylos, a room only 3m square, has been identified as a shrine solely because it opens onto a courtyard where a rubble and mudbrick altar was built.[21] This is hardly adequate, especially given that no objects have been found in or near the room to indicate that it was used as a shrine.[22] The shrine on Keos consists of a narrow rectangular building with more than fifteen near life-size terracotta statues of worshippers. A painted stucco head is thought to belong to a cult statue of the goddess. A similar stucco head has been found at Mycenae.

It is in the citadel at Mycenae, in an area close to Grave Circle A, that the most evidence about shrines has come to light. A rambling and apparently unplanned series of rooms seems to resolve into four separate shrines on three different levels. In the west, close to the citadel wall and at the lowest level, is the Room with the Fresco. This is a long room, reached through an anteroom, with a bath for ritual washing in the middle of one long wall, an oval hearth in the middle and a narrow bench-altar stretching along the other long wall; this is clearly not a seat as it is too narrow. In one corner there is a substantial painted altar with a fresco behind it. The altar was painted with three pairs of sacral horns resting on a row of red and black discs, representing the roof joists of a building, in this case a shrine or temple. In the surface of the altar is a socket, presumably for a double-axe.[23] The fresco shows a small female worshipper or priestess approaching with offerings of bunches of wheat. Behind her is a galloping

Figure 6.2 Goddesses Fresco. Wall decoration scheme associated with the altar in the Room with the Fresco in the Cult Centre at Mycenae (thirteenth century BC).

griffin, associated with the goddess; the griffin does not signify that the small figure in front is a goddess, only that the goddess is nearby. At a higher level, as if standing on top of the altar, are two much bigger females facing each other. These really *are* goddesses. They are big and dressed significantly differently from each other, one holding out her spear in salutation, the other carrying a sword with the point touching the ground.[24]

To the east, separate, about 2m higher and entered from a different direction altogether, is the Room with the Platforms. This has a low rectangular table or altar in the middle of the room, possibly for libations but, because of its similarity to the low altar at Anemospilia in Crete, it is more likely that it was used as a table for sacrifice. Beyond the sacrificial table, at the inner end of the room, is a series of bench-altars of different heights. Behind these, in one corner, is a window, not out to the sky but into the earth; it opens onto a steep outcrop of living rock, which presumably had something to do with the cult activity in the room. This is reminiscent of the outcrops of living rock deliberately incorporated within the open-air ceremonial enclosure at Kato Symi on Crete, and sticking up out of the floor of the Anemospilia temple right in front of the bench-altar in the central shrine.[25] The inclusion of a piece of living rock is another idea imported from Minoan Crete.

On the highest of the Mycenae bench-altars stood a large female idol (possibly a worshipper) with a table of offerings in front of it. The idol was hidden from the doorway by the three columns running down one side of the room. Behind the columns a narrow stairway leads up to a small square room which was a store for clay idols, offering tables, bowls and kylikes –

Figure 6.3 Painted clay idols from the Room of the Idols at Mycenae. Left: LHIIIA goddess holding her breasts (33cm high). Right: LHIIIB priestess with arms raised in adoration (29cm high).

in effect a sacristy. Some of the clay idols were older than the room, which was not built until about 1290 BC, so they must have been brought from other sacred sites.[26] There were many beads of glass paste, carnelian, amber, rock crystal and lapis lazuli; probably many of the idols represented worshippers, bearing offerings of necklaces for the goddess. The faces of the idols look like masks, and they may mimic the masks worn by priestesses during ceremonies.[27]

Immediately to the east of the Room with the Platforms and 3m higher up the slope was a large rectangular building. Little was found here, but in the centre of the large room at the inner end, 4m by 5.5m, was a large square hearth. Finds in the basement suggest that the walls were decorated with a procession fresco. Although the building was in a poor state when excavated, there is general agreement that it was a megaron. Curiously, archaeologists seem to be able to agree that this whole area, megaron included, was given over to religious cult activity, yet not make the logical next step, which is to consider that the megaron on the summit of the acropolis had the same function.

To the east again is a ramp or processional way leading to a courtyard in front of a fourth shrine, in the Tsountas House. This consists of a room over 6m long, where Tsountas is thought to have discovered the plaque showing the War Goddess. It contained an altar coated with many layers of plaster. It is not certain whether this shrine was roofed or not. The 2m-wide processional way zig-zags up the steep slope towards the palace. About 10m along its second leg it passed through a roofed, plastered and frescoed gateway, which some have suggested marked the formal entrance to the Cult Area.[28] It may be so, but it is also possible that porches of this kind roofed in the roads at several other points round the citadel, either to improve access from building to building at first floor level or to improve military control of the site during emergencies. The single fresco of a procession of chariots is more in keeping with this last idea. The whole complex of adjacent small shrines was destroyed in around 1200 BC, when houses outside the citadel were being destroyed too.[29]

The shrines at Mycenae represent a small area of the citadel and they in no sense dominate the town. It has been observed that religion seems not to have dominated Mycenaean society as it dominated Minoan society.[30] But that may be because some important evidence has been overlooked.

Just inside the Lion Gate, on the left, is an odd little niche 70cm wide and 1m high, too small to be a guardhouse. It is much more likely to have been a gate shrine dedicated to whatever deity presided over the citadel.[31] The Mycenaean west gate at Athens too had its gate shrine. The Athenian gate was protected in the same way as the Lion Gate, by a massive projecting bastion on the south side, and it had a shrine at its outer end; it was set in a recess in the bastion, its roof supported by two columns.[32] There was something similar at Troy too.

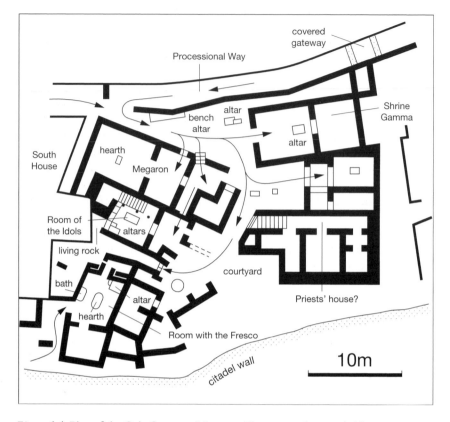

Figure 6.4 Plan of the Cult Centre at Mycenae. The arrows show probable access routes.

At Tiryns, there was a cult area that was similar in several ways to that at Mycenae. It was an unplanned huddle of irregular buildings comprising small, irregular-shaped chambers; it was in the lower citadel; it was close to the citadel wall; it was close to an open square. The Tiryns sacred area also housed clay idols of goddesses and adorants, including a beautiful figurine of a young smiling goddess with raised hands.[33]

The idols found in the shrines were based on wheel-turned clay cylinders, which formed the bodies and dresses, and these were based on a type of clay idol that was common in Minoan Crete. A different type of clay figurine, a distinctively and uniquely Mycenaean type, was the small clay female figurine. This has been found all over Mycenaean Greece, often with child burials. Some have seen these figures as Divine Nurses, to protect the children on their journey; some have seen them as no more than toys. They were first made in around 1430 BC and they gradually became more stylized. The upper body was simplified into a disc, the lower body into a column. In the last stages the uplifted arms made a crescent, making them look a little more like the larger idols.

In Minoan Crete the triple shrine was a common feature, seen in some of the peak sanctuaries and most conspicuously of all in the Bull Court at Knossos. Gold images of triple shrines made out of sheet gold were found in Shaft Graves III and IV. They show the three compartments of a triple shrine, side by side, each containing a straight-sided Mycenaean pillar behind a pair of sacral horns. The central compartment carries an elaborate altar on top with a triple cornice crowned by more horns of consecration. Two birds alight on the shrine, to indicate the presence of the deity. These objects seem to tell us that the Mycenaeans built triple shrines just like the Minoans, but the fact is that at this rather early stage (1600–1500 BC) it is more likely that the artwork was imported from Minoan Crete and therefore tells us nothing about architecture in Mycenaean Greece.[34] The one slight misgiving I have springs from the shape of the pillars; they are not thick, tapering downwards, but relatively thin and parallel-sided, more Mycenaean than Minoan.

CEREMONIES

On signet rings and frescoes, religious ceremonies are often shown taking place in the open air. This may not always reflect what actually happened; the scene shown may be an idealized landscape, the imagined dwelling place of the deity, while the ceremony took place indoors and somewhere else. This can be seen very clearly in the Throne Sanctuary at Knossos. The throne was a seat of honour for a priestess who, when properly prepared, was transformed into an epiphany of the goddess. The peculiar wavy shape of the throne's back is nothing other than a representation of a mountain peak; a rhyton from the temple at Zakro shows a very similar form to indicate the summit of a mountain rising behind an elaborately designed peak sanctuary, leaving no doubt that the throne represents the mountain-top domain of the goddess. The fresco behind the throne was a re-creation of the wild setting of the Cretan mountainsides. The room as a whole was designed as a symbolic habitat for the goddess as Mother of Mountains.[35] Sometimes the open-air setting is more literally right, as in the miniature frescoes from Knossos, where great crowds assemble to watch a great spectacle – probably bull-leaping – in the Central Court at Knossos itself. Other scenes show women dancing in front of crowds in what is clearly intended to be the West Court.

Where people are joined by mythical creatures, we are on surer ground. The presence of griffins is a reminder that the goddess is present; her heraldic griffins are never far from her side, which is why they were painted on the walls of the Throne Sanctuary at Knossos. The emblems and insignia of the

Plate 6.2 The landscape, especially of Argolis, was steeped in myth and legend. This is the spring at Lerna where Heracles killed the Hydra.

deities are not always so clear, though. The Goddess of War is symbolized by her huge figure-of-eight shield. In one fresco, she is almost totally obscured by the shield; in many Minoan and Mycenaean images the shield alone is shown, sometimes floating in the sky as a reminder of her invisible presence. A frieze of figure-of-eight shields was found on a wall in the South-West Building at Mycenae. This is the house where Mylonas believes the High Priest of the Cult Centre of Mycenae lived, so it would be appropriate that his house walls were decorated with the special symbol of the Goddess of War, a goddess particularly venerated by the Mycenaeans.[36]

The appearance of gods among mortals seems extraordinary to us, but the idea of epiphany was common in antiquity. Under special conditions, ordinary people might be possessed by gods or, put another way, gods might appear to people in the form of a person they knew. In Homer, Athena appears at the palace of Odysseus on Ithaca in the form of the chieftain Mentes, which means that her presence was completely undetectable.[37]

The great Minoan religious symbol was the double-axe, the emblem or sceptre of the Great Goddess Potnia, The Lady. Like the figure-of-eight shield, it could appear with the goddess, or in her place. Tiny double-axes made of gold foil were found in the shaft graves at Mycenae. They were degenerate forms and probably local artists were using a fashionable motif with little or no understanding of its meaning on Crete. Some scholars have observed that the double-axe is completely absent from Mycenaean contexts after 1450 BC, and that the symbol never really took root on the mainland at all. If that is true, its presence on some artwork found on the mainland must be the handiwork of Minoan craftsmen who simply added symbols that meant a great deal to them, though not to their clients. A stepped pyramidal stone base was nevertheless found at Mycenae, and it was of Late Mycenaean date; stone bases of this kind, with square sockets in the top, were usually used as stands for ceremonial double-axes by the Minoans.[38] It seems likely therefore that the Mycenaeans did use the double-axe as a religious symbol, if less frequently than the Minoans.

The same is probably true of sacral horns. The Minoans, with their focus on the bull-leaping ceremony, naturally adopted symbolic bull's horns as a decorative and architectural feature. The Minoans built horns of various sizes, usually of stucco, sometimes carved in stone, and mounted them in places of honour, often on the tops of altars or even in rows along the cornices of shrines and temples. It is curious that none have so far been found at Mycenae, Tiryns or Thebes, though fragments have been found at Gla and Pylos. They nevertheless are shown on various artworks and it is clear from the small amount of evidence surviving that the Mycenaeans did adopt the sacral horns.[39]

The gods and goddesses shown in procession frescoes were probably priests and priestesses disguised as deities; dramatic enactments like this were certainly performed in late antiquity.

The body language of religious gesture can also be read from the frescoes. Gods and goddesses made a particularly imperious commanding gesture. They stood up very straight, threw their head back, held a spear or staff vertically at arm's length in front of them, with the arm a little above horizontal; the left arm was crooked, drawn back as if about to throw a punch.[40] One of the gold rings from Mycenae shows three women approaching a sanctuary to worship. The one in front bends her right arm sharply back at the elbow, with her forearm extending forwards and her hand down. The woman in the middle raises her left arm and plants her fist on her forehead, a characteristic Minoan gesture of adoration. The third woman has her arms hanging at her sides; who knows what that means?[41] A procession of grieving and lamenting women painted on the side of a clay larnax shows them with their hands reaching up to the crowns of their heads, though interestingly they have their breasts covered.[42]

There are veiled references to ceremonies in the tablets, and the language used is revealing. The Olive Oil tablets refer to the Spreading of the Couch. This is a spring ceremony that was widespread in the Near East, and the couch is specifically for the Sacred Marriage of the Goddess and her risen consort, so that the fertility of the earth can be renewed. There is also a reference to 'dipsioi', The Thirsty Ones, a euphemism for The Dead.

Figure 6.5 Procession of women lamenting at a funeral, painted on a clay sarcophagus in a chamber tomb at Tanagra.

Di-pi-si-je-wi-jo is therefore the Festival for the Dead, not dissimilar to the Athenian All Souls Day, which was the third part of the three-day Festival of Anthesteria. The Spreading of the Couch was the second part. The first part, The Opening of the Jars, finds its equivalent in the tablet entry, 'new wine'. Palmer argues neatly and convincingly that the three adjacent entries on the tablets refer to the three consecutive parts of the religious festival that would later be known as the Anthesteria. So, rather surprisingly, there is some evidence that at least one major classical festival was fully formed by 1200 BC.[43] There were other festivals too. One of the Olive Oil tablets refers to a ceremony called 'the pulling of the throne', which may have involved carrying a dignitary on a palanquin.[44]

It is possible that the Mycenaeans imported the bull-leaping ceremony – not a sport but a religious ritual – from Crete. A bull-leaping fresco was found in the citadel at Mycenae. It probably dates from 1450–1400 BC, when the Minoan frescoes were still visible in Crete and therefore available for copying. It does not prove that bull-leaping happened at Mycenae and may simply be another religious image borrowed from the much admired older culture.[45] Another fresco showing a bull-dancer balancing on the back of a galloping bull was found at Tiryns.[46] The pose is extraordinary. The man is poised on his right knee and toe, hanging onto the bull's horn with his right hand and with his left leg thrown high in the air behind him – a real circus act. The horizontal stripes round the acrobat's legs are probably leather thongs or laces used to secure the shoes round the ankles and again just below the knee.

An integral part of religious observance in the bronze age world was sacrifice, and in this the Mycenaean civilization was no exception. A gold ring from Mycenae shows a male worshipper approaching a walled sacred tree with a handsome goat, evidently for sacrifice. A gold ring from near Thebes shows a bull lying down next to an altar, and tethered to it, awaiting sacrifice. A gem from a chambered tomb at Mycenae shows a standing bull with its head severed, two heads of boars over its back and the severed leg of another animal underneath it. The so-called Montigny gem, found at Mycenae, shows a goat lying on a sacrificial table with a dagger sticking into its neck and its tongue protruding.[47] Several images of sacrifice are associated with the figure-of-eight shield, implying that the sacrifice was to the Goddess of War.[48] Finds of animal bones and ash at the peak sanctuary near Epidaurus provide archaeological confirmation that the Mycenaeans sacrificed animals. The *Iliad* tells us that Agamemnon sacrificed lambs and bulls,[49] and the *Odyssey* describes Telemachus reaching Pylos to find the inhabitants on the beach sacrificing black bulls to Poseidon.[50]

Human sacrifice also took place and the Mycenaeans may have had the same ambivalence about it that the classical Greeks were later to have. 'Better minds' thought it was a horrible practice, but it was nevertheless seen as a cruel necessity on certain occasions.[51] Human sacrifice is described in Homer

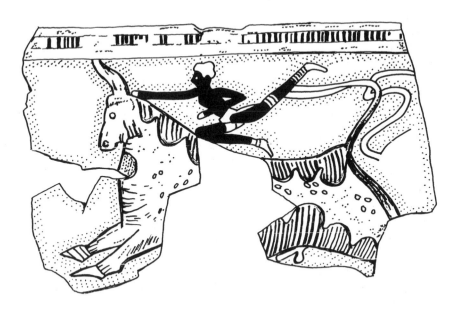

Figure 6.6 Bull-leaping fresco from the temple-palace at Tiryns (after Schuchhardt 1891).

as if it was an integral part of the world of the bronze age heroes. Agamemnon was prepared to sacrifice his daughter Iphigenia to appease Artemis, who had quelled the wind and prevented the fleet from sailing to Troy. Iphigenia was fetched from home and sacrificed at Aulis, where the Mycenaean fleet was assembled.[52] In Homer, the young son of Andromache, Astyanax, was thrown to his death from the walls of Troy. Since sixth-century BC images of the incident show the boy being killed on an altar, it was evidently construed at that time as a human sacrifice rather than a murder. Priam too was shown meeting his death on an altar, in an act of sacrifice rather than revenge.[53]

Some of the Linear B tablets imply human sacrifice. There are Minoan tablets from Knossos listing offerings to named gods and goddesses, and the offerings include people. One Pylos tablet (Tn 316) belonging to the final days of Pylos is scrappy, incomplete, but begins with a date and a place, and the name PYLOS is written on it six times, huge to the point of paranoia, on the left hand side. The text refers to the bringing of offerings and includes an unknown word, *po-re-na*, that seems to mean 'sacrificial victims'.[54] After a repeating opening formula there is a list of deities, some familiar (Zeus and Hermes), others unfamiliar. Each god receives a gold vessel, and in nine of the thirteen entries the gold cup is followed by the name of a person, most often a woman, in two places a man. The women are offered to goddesses, the men to gods. The tablet could be interpreted as an offering of slaves as temple servants, but equally it could describe the arrangements for human sacrifice. In the circumstances, it probably represents a last-minute attempt to enlist divine aid. Perhaps the final attack came before the sacrifices could be carried out.

> In the month of Plowistoios,
> At Pylos, he consecrates (or sacrifices) at Sphagianes and he brings gifts and leads the sacrificial victims: to Potnia one gold cup, one woman;
> To Mnasa one gold dish, one woman; to Posidaia one gold dish, one woman;
> To Thrice-Hero one gold cup; to Dopotas one gold cup.
> At Pylos.

On the back of the tablet, the list continues:

> At Pylos, he consecrates (or sacrifices) at the shrine of Poseidon, and the town takes part.
> And he brings gifts and leads sacrificial victims: one gold cup, two women to Boia and Komawenteia.
> At Pylos. He consecrates at the shrines of Perse, Iphimedeia and Dia.

And he brings gifts and leads sacrificial victims: to Perse one gold
    dish, one woman;
To Iphimedeia one gold dish; to Dia one gold dish, one woman;
To Hermes Areias one gold cup, one man.
At Pylos. He consecrates (or sacrifices) at the shrine of Zeus, and he
    brings gifts and leads sacrificial victims;
To Zeus one gold dish, one man; to Hera one gold dish, one woman;
To Drimios son of Zeus one gold dish.
At Pylos.[55]

Several sacrificial victims are mentioned, with an official to attend them.
The *porenes* were a recognized group at Pylos – and Thebes too – so it seems
that human sacrifice was institutionalized and part of a set administrative
procedure for dealing with crises. Very likely a squad of sacrificial victims
was kept fed, clothed and available at all times at each of the centres. Who
these people were we can only guess. They may have been bought slaves,
prisoners of war, civilians taken captive in raids, or given as some kind of
tax obligation by their families. It may be that the word for sacrificial victim
did not survive the end of the Mycenaean civilization, as if both the idea
and the word had become taboo.

Animal sacrifice was a commonplace ritual of propitiation. Achilles sacrificed four horses and two dogs on Patroklos' pyre, followed by twelve Trojan
prisoners. Later Priam's daughter Polyxene was sacrificed on Achilles' tomb;
by this act of appeasement the Greeks hoped to gain a fair wind for the
voyage home. Menelaus resorted to a similar rite in similar circumstances,
sacrificing two children when he was detained in Egypt for a long time by
storms.[56]

Smaller-scale offerings that did not involve death might be left on offering
tables, three-legged altars of clay often coated with plaster and painted. One
from Mycenae was painted with a flame pattern round its edge, which makes
it look like the huge circular hearth at Pylos, but with legs.[57] Is it possible
that the hearths were only occasionally used for burning and that they were
regularly used as giant offering tables? Mylonas mentions that the hearth
in the Mycenae megaron had 'signs of smoke and fire on its sides and the
top, indicating its use', which persuades momentarily, until we remember
that the paintwork on the adjacent walls was also severely damaged by fire;
it was the fire that destroyed the building.[58]

The sacred enclosures are by their very nature difficult to identify, and
the images on signet rings suggest that they might be found in almost any
type of open country. Just a few have been identified, like the one at Agios
Vasilios, beside the Mycenaean road from Mycenae to Corinth.[59] There were
also sacred enclosures at Delphi around 1300–1200 BC (on the site of what
would later become the sanctuary of Athena Pronaia) and about 1km outside
the modern village of Amyklai.

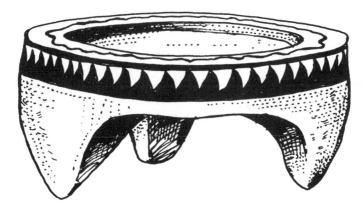

Figure 6.7 Table of offerings from Mycenae. Painted clay. The painted flame pattern is the same as was applied to the large hearths; are the large hearths really large offering tables?

In the enclosures were altars with cornices supported by pillars and often containing a central 'Minoan' pillar with a distinctive cushion capital. The altars were topped by sacral horns. Corniced walls were also built round sacred trees to protect them.[60] Models made by the Minoans imply a belief that souls and even deities might visit the everyday world in the form of birds, so a bird alighting in a tree might, under certain prescribed conditions, be interpreted as a visitation by a god. That might in turn sanctify the tree and form a focus for subsequent rituals. Pausanias describes an ancient sacred site in Arcadia: 'On Mount Lykaion there is an altar of Lykaion Zeus in the shape of a mound of earth. In front of the altar stand two pillars, on which there used formerly to be gilded eagles.'[61] This ancient shrine was located and explored in 1903. A circular feature, probably originally a mound, was discovered, and a little below the altar were the bases of two columns. Pausanias' description was accurate.[62] An ancient peak sanctuary, possibly conserving vestiges of a Mycenaean cult, stood on Mount Lykaion – and the real eagles alighting there were seen in ancient times as visitations by Zeus himself. In a similar way, I have seen eagles circling above the Diktaian Cave in Crete, the birthplace of Zeus, and been half-persuaded of a divine presence.

A gold ring found on the Mycenae acropolis translates a visit by worshippers to a sacred tree into a visionary experience. The Goddess of Vegetation herself is seated informally beneath the sacred tree, which is in full leaf, the overloaded boughs looking like gigantic blackberries. She is holding three poppy-heads, almost like wands of office, but perhaps hinting that this vision has been assisted along by opium. Two women worshippers and two children approach the goddess with offerings of flowers. A magnificent double-axe, which in Minoan Crete symbolized the Great Goddess, floats in the air in the centre of the rapturous scene. Above an undulating horizon are the sun and moon. Over on the right, on the edge of the field of vision, six animal heads show the sacrificial animals whose heads were perhaps mounted on the enclosure wall.[63] The centrality of the double-axe and the incredibly high quality of the craftsmanship – the ring is a masterpiece – have led Mylonas and others to propose that a Minoan master-craftsman made it. In 1500 BC, Minoan craftsmen were probably routinely travelling to Mycenae and other mainland centres to undertake commissions for wealthy rulers. At that time, the Mycenaeans were hungry for all things Minoan, and probably ready to pay handsomely for them.

Bogdan Rutkowski uses the image on the Dendra ring as evidence that substantial shrines were built in the rural enclosures, but that is unjustified, given the lack of vegetation.[64] The image probably shows a temple in one of the towns. There is a three-tiered altar-like structure standing inside a building with tall columns; the building has a flat roof with horns of consecration. The Dendra ring shows us one of the impressive urban temples that have so far gone unidentified.

The scenes on the rings and frescoes show that people processed to and assembled at shrines, enclosures and temples. They performed ceremonies of adoration, invoked the gods by dancing, propitiated the gods by offerings and sacrifices. Religious hysteria, possibly helped along by alcohol or opium, led to numinous experiences.

Certainly in the shrines and temples there were figurines and idols, some of them probably life-size and adorned with rich clothing, necklaces and other jewellery. There were doubtless ceremonies surrounding the donation of such adornments. In the *Iliad*, Hecuba chooses the longest and most richly decorated dress as a gift for Athena and goes to the Temple of Athena to present it.[65] Homer may well have been describing a Mycenaean practice: it was certainly a Minoan practice. The temple treasure at Knossos included faience dresses, offerings of token dresses to the goddess. There is also a seal impression showing a priestess or worshipper carrying a flounced dress, perhaps as a gift for the goddess, perhaps actually to dress the wooden idol of the goddess.[66] Practices like this were part of the classical system, and incredibly elaborate ceremonies surrounded the periodic presentation of new vestments to the goddess. Homer tells us that they were part of the system in the eighth century BC, or remembered through oral tradition from earlier. We know they were part of the Minoan system; so it is very likely that they were part of the Mycenaean system in between.

Homer mentions 'drink-offerings to the everlasting gods of Heaven'.[67] The many kylikes at Pylos suggest just this kind of socio-religious ceremony. Homer also refers to the rite of libation, a simple ceremony of pouring out a drink for the gods into a sacred vessel, or into a specially designed pit, or sometimes just onto the ground. Book 7 of the *Iliad* tells us, 'Not

Figure 6.8 Part of a solemn procession of women attending a ceremony. Fragment of a fresco in the temple-palace at Tiryns. The symbolic value of the exposed breasts in religious ceremonies is obvious from the way the painter has exaggerated their size. Note also the elaborate hairstyle, and the use of rings.

a man dared drink before he had made a libation [to Zeus]'. The necks of amphorae were set into the floor of the cult centre at Mycenae to receive libations. A mythic representation of the libation rite is shown on a gold ring from Tiryns. In this, a procession of demons approaches a goddess formally seated on a folding chair. The demons carry libation jugs to fill the huge goblet she holds up. In the background are mountains, vegetation, sun and moon, the natural landscape that is the goddess's domain.[68]

The Pylos cult centre at Sphagianes was a focus for religious ceremonies. One mentioned earlier (in tablet Un 2) may describe the coronation of a new king or a seasonal ceremony in the cult of Poseidon.[69] The quantities of food consumed at these festivals were considerable.

The overwhelming impression is of the importance of women in religious ceremonies, just as in Minoan Crete. The most complete fresco, from Mycenae, shows a meeting between two goddesses and what seems to be a priestess, a much smaller female figure, moving towards them at a lower level. Then there is the Procession of Women at Thebes. Not only were goddesses very important in the Mycenaean pantheon; their priestesses were evidently major figures in Mycenaean society.[70]

REDISCOVERING THE TEMPLES

One peculiarity of the Minoan and Mycenaean civilizations that has often occasioned comment is their lack of temples. In 1974, Monique Gérard-Rousseau commented that the Pylian tablet Tn 316 shows that the goddess *Di-wi-ja* had her own sanctuary, the *Di-u-ja-jo*, and that Zeus, Hera and *Di-ri-mi-o*, Zeus's son, also had a sanctuary, the *Di-u-jo*, both at Pylos. In addition there were at least three more, listed on the same tablet, the *Pe-re-82-jo*, *I-pe-me-de-ja-jo* and *Po-si-da-i-jo* (Posidaion) – all at Pylos. The frescoes at Pylos show processions of men and women with offerings, evidently going to the Pylian sanctuaries, and yet archaeologists have failed to identify any true Mycenaean temple, at Pylos or anywhere else. This is extraordinary, as we might expect the sanctuaries to be well-defined and substantially built structures.[71]

One explanation that has been offered is that the Mycenaeans were fundamentally a rural people and that, although they had sanctuaries in the towns, it was the rural sanctuaries that were the hub of their religious life.[72] Certainly there were rural sanctuaries in both Minoan and Mycenaean cultures: the sacred enclosures and peak sanctuaries. A simpler though more radical explanation is that the Mycenaeans *did* build monumental temples, just as the Minoans did before them, but we have been calling them palaces. I argued the case for reinterpreting Knossos as a temple at length in *The Knossos Labyrinth*, and have not been persuaded by subsequent counter-arguments from various quarters to change my mind.[73]

When we look at the archaeological evidence from the great building at Knossos, sometimes in antiquity called the Daidalaion, sometimes the Labyrinth, it points squarely to a primary use for religious cult. It is surprising that the building was initially identified as a palace, though the history of its excavation throws light on this. The first person to excavate at Knossos was an amateur archaeologist, Minos Kalokairinos, who believed he was uncovering parts of a palace, the royal palace of King Minos as he confidently named it on his sketch plan. Schliemann visited the site and adopted this explanation, expecting (in 1886) that Knossos would turn out to be 'a vast edifice similar to the prehistoric palace of Tiryns'. Arthur Evans visited both Schliemann and Kalokairinos before his first visit to Knossos, and therefore arrived at the site predisposed, even before his workmen started digging in 1900, to discover a great bronze age palace there.

In fact Evans was disappointed. As he extended Kalokairinos' excavations in the West Wing he uncovered yet more passages and store rooms. The Throne Room was welcome as apparent evidence of kingship but the adyton, the strange sunken lustral area, was a problem; the room was also small – only 6m by 4m, windowless and dark. Evans was relieved to have found a throne, but more pleased to find that the open space to the east was actually a huge Central Court with suites of rooms on its far side.

There, at last, he thought he had found the king's apartments, but they too were gloomy, windowless and claustrophobic, a semi-subterranean suite built into a cutting chopped out of the tell and buried deep under several storeys.[74] Evans seized on the four remaining steps next to the Throne Room, inflated them to twelve leading up to a first floor, then another eighteen to an imaginary second floor; Evans put his spacious, airy, well-lit royal apartments up there – a Sanctuary Hall, a Tricolumnar Hall, a Loggia, a Great Hall – in what is no more than thin air.[75]

The Palace of Minos, Arthur Evans's definitive account of his excavations and his interpretation of them, shows him preoccupied with King Minos and the building's royal connections, while page after page supplies evidence of the religious function of which he was fully aware. For Evans the Throne Room 'teems with religious suggestion'.[76]

Some observers saw the flaws in Evans's palace interpretation immediately. Revisionist voices challenged it from time to time during the twentieth century.[77] The architecture, the artefacts and the frescoes all lead to the irresistible conclusion that the building is a temple.[78] It consists of a series of more or less self-contained shrines, often with accompanying sacristies, vestries and stores of religious paraphernalia, many opening onto the Central Court, where certain large-scale semi-public ceremonies took place, including bull-leaping. There was also a West Court, for a different range of public ceremonies. In the north-east sector of the complex were workshops making high-status artefacts, perhaps for use as offerings, and kitchen stores. In the north, above a pillared undercroft, was a refectory, probably for drinking ceremonies – the rites of communion shown in several Knossian frescoes. Scattered round the Labyrinth were four adyta, which were used for individual initiation rites, such as the rites of passage from one age-group to another.[79] These rites have been made more explicit by the frescoes on adyton walls on Thera. The discoveries on Thera have, in effect, done much to corroborate the revisionist interpretation of the large building at Knossos as a temple.

The plan of the temple at Knossos was repeated with minor variations at other Minoan centres on Crete. Usually there was a major shrine and other religious cult installations along the west side of the Central Court, backed by corridor-like store rooms and a West Court behind these. Sometimes there were refectories on the north side (Knossos, Mallia and Zakro) and *polythyron* rooms (rooms with many doors) on the east side of the Central Court (Knossos and Zakro). There were individual differences. Knossos and Phaistos had ceremonial stepped entrances on the north-west: Zakro and Mallia did not. But there were enough recurring features to show that all the Minoan temples functioned in the same way. They were a focus for the reception, recording and storing of produce; they were a focus for the production of craft goods in gold, ivory and semi-precious stones, some of which may have been votives for worshippers to leave in the shrines; they were a focus for textile production, though it is not clear in which rooms this happened, probably the upper floors above the Great Goddess Sanctuary at Knossos, and these may have produced the dresses for priestesses to wear and for wealthy worshippers to donate to the cult images in the shrines. They were a focus for individual initiation ceremonies, and presumably families and sponsors came to the temples with children of various ages to see them through these rites of passage, as depicted in frescoes on the walls of Thera.[80] They were a focus for the veneration and propitiation of the gods and goddesses by various means including gifts and sacrifices. They were a focus for major public religious festivals that took place in the West and Central Courts. At most of these ceremonies, the fresco evidence tells us, it was the priestesses who dominated the proceedings; they were evidently held in very high esteem.

The fact that many people worked in the temple-complex does not mean that they lived there, any more than modern people live in factories or office blocks where they earn their living. Although a kitchen area has been identified at Knossos, it consists mostly of stores of utensils. There are no fixed hearths anywhere, which implies that no large-scale cooking went on there. There could have been no banqueting, in the modern sense of the word, in the banqueting halls; only special meals, like the symbolic wafer and wine of the Christian communion, would have been possible. Fitton's objection that changing the name 'palace' to 'temple' creates a new and symmetrical problem – where, then, are the palaces? – misses the main point, which is that we need to see the principal functions of the large, high-status buildings at the Minoan centres for what they were.[81] The kings may well have attended ceremonies at the temples and used them to enhance their status and impress their subjects, much as the British royal family uses Westminster Abbey and St Paul's Cathedral for state occasions that intermittently but effectively reinforce the socio-political pecking order. The underlying religious function is nevertheless the main function of these buildings.

This digression on the Minoan temple-palaces has obvious implications for any assessment of the Mycenaean culture, which borrowed heavily from the Minoans. The Knossos Labyrinth was developing, with several rebuilds, from 1900 BC until it was abandoned in 1380 BC; it was therefore available as a model to the Mycenaeans for the first two centuries of the civilization's development. To bring the matter down to a very specific level, if the Throne Room at Knossos, together with its antechamber, sacristies and vestries, is really a shrine, then architecturally similar suites of rooms at Pylos, Mycenae and Tiryns must also be interpreted as shrines. The Throne Sanctuary has several points of similarity with the Mycenaean megaron. There is an inner square room with a throne, entered from an ante-room which in turn is entered from a formal open space or court. At the back of the inner chamber are vestries and sacristies which may be reached by a separate entrance. This, with a porch added between the ante-room and the court, is not unlike the arrangement of the megaron at Pylos. The Cupbearer Sanctuary at Knossos, the site of which was vandalized by Evans to build a staircase, was divided into three rooms: an inner chamber, an ante-room and a porch, this time opening out of a corridor. It also had four columns, but two in the inner room and two in the outer.[82] The Great Goddess Sanctuary can be reconstructed as having an impressive flight of steps up from the court, a porch and a single big rectangular room with a central light well surrounded by eight columns. A statue of the goddess 3m high formed a focus for this sanctuary, instead of a living priestess as an epiphany of the goddess seated on a throne. The Knossos Labyrinth thus had some shrines that were similar in form to the mainland megaron. There were other shrines that were small, such as the Triton Shell and Late Dove Goddess Sanctuaries;[83] although these seem little more than broom cupboards, there is no doubt from the way they were equipped that they too functioned as shrines, and may have supplied a model for the sort of shrine we see in the Mycenae Cult Centre.

How does this apply to the 'palaces' at the Mycenaean centres? The Palace of Nestor at Pylos offers the most complete ground plan, and thus makes an obvious starting point. At first sight the Mycenaean 'palace' is very different from its Minoan counterpart.[84] There are no *polythyron* rooms (with partitions made of rows of doors) at Pylos. There are no pillar crypts (cellars with single central pillars and libation pits); nor are there any adyta (sunken lustral areas). The most conspicuous difference is the absence of a large central court. This implies that some major public ceremony or ceremonies that took place at the Minoan centres did not take place at the Mycenaean centres. Given that it has been proposed that the bull-leaping ritual took place in the central courts, it may be that the absence of bull-leaping on the Greek mainland gives us a straightforward explanation. With no bull-leaping ceremony to accommodate, there would be no need for a roomy central court. There is, nevertheless, a central court at Pylos, just 13m across and 7.5m deep, and the contrast between Minoan and Mycenaean courts should not be exaggerated. The big Minoan palaces had big central courts; Knossos, Phaistos and Mallia had very similar courts, about 50m long and 24m wide. There were more modest Minoan palaces, Gournia, Zakro and Galatas (at Kastelli, south of Mallia), with courts that were around 35m long and 15m wide. But there were also some small Minoan palaces with proportionately small central courts; Petras (near Sitia) and Makry-Giallos had courts that were 16m long and only 6m wide.[85] The Pylos courtyard is actually the same in area as the smallest Minoan central courts.

The courtyard was reached by way of an imposing gateway with two porches, each with a single column supporting a roof. The comparable entrance at Knossos is the West Porch, which has a single-columned porch opening from the West Court, and leads into a long Procession Corridor designed to delay, by exactly 100m, the worshippers' arrival at the Central

Court and its sanctuaries. At Pylos, there was less drama. People walked in a straight line into the court and from there into the megaron, with its two-columned porch, ante-room and large inner chamber. This is comparable, as described earlier, with the structure of the Throne or Great Goddess Sanctuaries at Knossos. As with the Throne Sanctuary, it is possible at Pylos to go round the side, along a corridor, and reach the sacristies and store rooms at the back of the megaron. The large fixed round hearth in the megaron is something new; the throne placed against the wall on the right is something familiar.[86] Room 46 at Pylos may have had a similar function to the Throne Room: it too has a round hearth. Interestingly, room 46 forms part of a suite that originally had its own independent access from outside, but was later walled in so that the access was from a courtyard (47) out into a walled enclosure. Something very similar to this happened at Knossos, where the 'King's and Queen's Apartments' were originally open to the east but were later shut in by a high enclosure wall. Possibly both temples were built at times of peace and optimism, and both were adapted later, in a time of greater uncertainty, to make them more secure when there was a threat of attack.

The large round hearth at the centre of the throne room has been generally assumed to prove a domestic, residential function for the megaron as a whole. Commentators have imagined a huge fire blazing in the hearth, warming the king and his courtiers on winter evenings. But there are problems with this. One is the excessive size of the hearth. With a diameter of 3.5m, or more at Mycenae, it is really too big to have served this purpose. If fires blazed in the hearth, the elaborate paint work round its edge would

Plate 6.3 The hearth in the Throne Room at Pylos.

have been quickly spoilt. It is true that the decoration was redone several times, but a large fire would quickly have undone the work. The portable bronze tripod cauldrons would have made more effective braziers, giving heat exactly where it was needed, and it is far more likely that they were in general use for heating. The closeness of the four structural wooden pillars to the hearth also argues against large fires. It seems more likely that the round hearths were large versions of the stuccoed clay offering tables, some of which were painted with the self-same design. If the 'hearth' was really a large offering table, its function was closer to that of an altar.

This is not to say that small fires were not occasionally kindled on it, for 'burnt offerings', and the stylized flame design painted on the hearth rim suggests this. There has been a long association of fire with sacrifice. There were earlier Minoan fires of sacrifice at the peak sanctuary on Mount Juktas in Crete. There were later offering fires in the Dreros temple, built in about 800 BC; this temple, with its hearth and presumed smoke-hole above, supported on two columns, has been described as one of the earliest known temples in Greek lands.[87] It can instead be seen as a degenerate successor of the larger and grander Mycenaean temples of five hundred years earlier. The ashes found in the Sub-Mycenaean temple at Thermon in Aetolia were thought by the early twentieth-century excavator of the site to indicate a house, not a temple. Now we cannot be so sure. Temples with hearths have been found at Drera and Perachora. Hearths in the megara at Pylos, Tiryns and Mycenae are not necessarily inconsistent with their use as temples.

An underlying problem is that designs for temples evolved from designs for houses. It was natural to build a 'house for the god' that was a special version of the houses of ordinary people. The megaron evidently began as a house for mortals and was gradually taken over and developed into a house for immortals; the megaron design was such that it could easily be developed into either a house or a temple.[88] The Sub-Mycenaean temple at Thermon had a colonnade round it, just like the later Hellenistic temple built on the same site, but the Sub-Mycenaean colonnade had elliptical ends; this was a deliberate reference back to the apsidal ends of the early houses.[89]

Pylos, like Knossos, had its cache of archive tablets. It also had stores of cups for drinking ceremonies. There is no big Central Court where these ceremonies could have taken place and no formal West Court either, so it seems likely that the relatively informal spaces, courts 63 and 88, might have been used in this way.

The main block of the 'Palace of Nestor' was evidently designed as a unit, but it was added onto the north-east side of an earlier unit, sometimes referred to as the 'Palace of Neleus' or South-West Building. This had a form of megaron with a large four- or six-columned chamber as its focus and a large porch arranged at right angles to it; this in turn seems to have opened from court 63, and may have had a formal entrance complex in rooms 59–61. As with the later building erected alongside it, the principal suite was backed by a warren of small ancillary rooms. At Pylos a third building, the North-East Building, was erected on the far side of the 'Palace of Nestor', and was the last element to be built. This was a workshop complex; the chamber at its entrance, room 93, may have been no more than a porter's lodge or reception desk, similar to the archive rooms at the main entrance; like the Minoans, the Mycenaeans were sticklers for detailed administration. The workshop area is in a roughly comparable position on the north-east side of the main complex as at Knossos. The Wine Store was also built in a position comparable to the so-called 'kitchen' stores at Knossos.

There are conspicuous differences between the building complex at Pylos and the Knossos Labyrinth, not least in scale, but it is clear that there are also many points in common, including architectural detail – the use of façades of shaped blocks of stone, rubble walls plastered on the inside, mud brick upper storeys, timber framing and columns. There were even painted griffins facing the throne in both, and it is as if the griffins – known associates of the goddess – are telling us that an epiphany of the goddess sat on the throne; the composition was not complete until the central figure was present. Overall, it seems more likely than not that the 'Palace of Nestor' was a temple complex similar in type to the Minoan temples. The scheme of the wall paintings would have told us much about the purpose of the

Plate 6.4 An apsidal house at Lerna.

Plate 6.5 Corner of the Throne Room at Pylos, showing slots in the walls for timber framing.

complex if it had survived. It is clear from analyses of the wall paintings at Knossos and Thera that they sign the ancient use of the spaces beside them, either literally or metaphorically. Unfortunately there are only a few fragments from Pylos, but enough to indicate a cult use.

A problem arises because the Mycenaean temple-art has been to a significant extent copied from the Minoan temple-art of a couple of centuries earlier. The earliest Mycenaean frescoes so far discovered come from a fragmentary dump deposit at Mycenae and they seem to date from the decades around 1500 BC, when frescoes were still being painted in the Minoan temples. The Pylos frescoes, whether found in dumps round the palace or still on the walls, all date to 1250–1200 BC. They show much the same imagery as was used in Crete 1750–1380 BC, and therefore show a remarkable tenacity of tradition that can be compared with the bardic poetry tradition that was generated at about the same time. The repetition of images in the Mycenaean frescoes suggests the existence of pattern books of some kind. Alongside the maintenance of tradition over long periods would have come misunderstanding. The iconography might be repeated, but eventually without conveying the original meaning, rather as in Homer Odysseus is described as 'hiding' his gift of tripod cauldrons in a cave, when in fact his proto-historic equivalent was probably dedicating it to the gods in a cave sanctuary. The Minoan ritual of bull-leaping was probably not practised by the Mycenaeans, so the fresco images could never have meant anything real to them. This in turn could easily explain the unusual compositional aspects of the painted scenes. It is a short step to argue, as Mabel Lang did, that the Pylos frescoes were probably decorative, that they did not indicate the characteristic activities that would have taken place in adjacent spaces.[90] On the other hand, large images of lions and wingless griffins are only to be found in cult rooms with large circular hearths. Griffins are directly and explicitly associated with the epiphany of a goddess in the Theran frescoes, and this missing link explains the prominent position given to the griffin in frescoes at Pylos, Knossos and Mycenae. Griffins flanked the throne at Pylos, so a female must have sat there.[91]

Processions of large-scale human figures cover the walls of the porch and ante-room immediately preceding the throne rooms. Marine motifs are normally depicted on the floors, as in Minoan Crete. The images in the frescoes at Pylos and other Mycenaean centres were placed with deliberation and care. I do not believe that Lang's view that the Pylian frescoes are little more than wallpaper is justified.

In two areas at Pylos, the inner propylon and Room 20 (fallen in from the first floor), a broad frieze seems to vindicate Lang's wallpaper idea. The frieze of solid colour is scattered with small, apparently unconnected scenes – shrine façades, grazing animals, pairs of women in conversation – rather like graffiti. But this may be to misread the images. The chatting women may in fact be priestesses, like the group shown in the Grandstand Fresco at Knossos, in which case the shrine image would represent the temple where they officiated, and so on. It would be unwise to deny the frescoes their meaning.

The ante-room of the Pylos megaron was decorated with a scene showing a procession of men and women worshippers accompanying a huge bull on its way to sacrifice; the worshippers carry boxes, vases and bowls as offerings and the two leading figures are on the point of passing through a corniced doorway – presumably the adjacent doorway of the megaron.[92] The main wall of the megaron had the throne at its centre, and huge representations of a lion and a griffin were painted on at least one side, probably both. In the panel outside this heraldic image of the deity's mythic attendant beasts, a huge bull awaits sacrifice. There are also smaller images that are hard to relate to the overall picture, a repeating vignette of pairs of men seated at tables and the lyre player with a bird. Possibly the seated men represent the ritual feast that followed a bull sacrifice and the lyre player is reciting poetry to his own music. Possibly the seated men represent something more serious and religious in tone, the rite of communion that is shown in a similar way in frescoes at Knossos.

The porch to the main megaron had a procession fresco showing worshippers arriving with offerings. The larger porch to the banquet hall in the so-called 'Palace of Neleus' (Room 46) also had a procession fresco, although

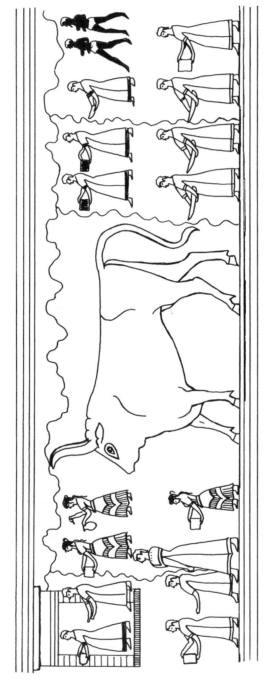

Figure 6.9 Procession fresco in the ante-room of the megaron at Pylos. Worshippers carry offerings into the temple. The context implies that the bull is a sacrificial offering. The doorway top left is probably a depiction of the adjacent doorway into the throne room (after Piet de Jong's drawing in Lang 1969).

it may be that these fragments fell from the destroyed chamber above. This fresco shows rows of worshippers arriving. One is an attendant leading a pair of gigantic hounds who are evidently harnessed to something we can unfortunately no longer see, perhaps a chariot carrying an important adorant, a priestess, or even a deity. The row below consists of a procession of male attendants carrying tripod cauldrons. As we know from the Polis Bay cave sanctuary on Ithaca, tripod cauldrons were regarded as eminently suitable offerings to gods. Interestingly these male attendants are all wearing greaves, suggesting that they are warriors or perhaps have travelled across open country. There can be no doubt that these images signal the use of the adjacent chambers, courts and corridors at Pylos for religious ceremonies.

The workshop area, the North-Eastern Building, can be regarded as a temple workshop of the same type as found at Knossos. The tablets mention artisans who 'belong' to a god or goddess; presumably these were the people who worked in temple workshops.[93]

The tholos tomb at Pylos was in use right through the Mycenaean period, and it was built in a very significant location, with its dromos on a direct alignment through a monumental gate in the fortification wall to an older entrance, fifty metres further west, in the temple-palace itself. Although we cannot see anything of the original structure that preceded the Pylos temple-palace it is clear from this alignment that a structure of profound ritual importance existed on the hill, on the site of the later temple – presumably an earlier temple something like the Menelaion.[94] The way the tholos tomb faces and respects the early building suggests that it may have been a temple.

A large tablet (Jn 829) in the archive at Pylos records contributions of bronze from thirty-two different officials. It is described as 'temple bronze', which suggests that in the emergency that brought about the fall of Pylos temple treasure was being surrendered for the war effort – and it was justified as specifically 'for points for javelins and spears'. A point that has been glossed over is that the tablets refer to temples, which must therefore have existed. The Mycenaean word na-wi-jo seems to have meant temple.[95] Phrases incorporating the word for 'house' also refer to temples: 'the house of Marineus' and 'the house of Potnia' at Thebes.[96]

The way the 'palaces' have been reconstructed on paper is tendentious. Piet de Jong's beautiful and justly famous paintings of Knossos and Pylos have established an image of the buildings as palaces, but they can be depicted differently. To take the Mycenaean megaron on its own for a moment, we can make it look quite different according to the type of roof we give it in our reconstruction drawings. Many Minoan and Mycenaean buildings had flat roofs, as shown in the frescoes. When the megaron is drawn with clean lines, two plain flat oversailing cornices and a flat roof, the Tiryns megaron can be made to look rather Egyptian in style.[97] The same building can be made to look more Minoan if the cornices are topped by rows of sacral horns. Significantly, it can be made to look like a classical Greek temple if it is given a shallow pitched roof, especially if some decorative features are added in the triangular gable over the porch.

The 'palace' at Mycenae is less easily examined than the one at Pylos because so much has been eroded off the summit of the acropolis and part of the megaron itself, including two-thirds of the circular hearth, has slid down into the ravine. It is also clear that the design of the complex has had to fit into a confined and difficult hilltop site. Even so, it is possible to see points of similarity with the Pylian concept of a temple. The double-porched 7m-square propylon was built on the course of a much earlier pathway snaking up onto the summit. A few steps had to be provided to reach its floor level. From the formal entrance gateway a procession corridor, probably open to the sky, passed round the western side of the hill inside a retaining wall, which also functioned as the west boundary of the 'palace'. The West Passage sloped up to the great West Portal, where it widened to make a kind of West Court, with a commanding view across the citadel and town, and the Plain of Argos beyond. Little of the Portal survives, but it is known to have had doors. Inside, there was access to at least three corridors, one of them leading into a corner of the Main Court (11.5m by 15m). This is reminiscent of the way the Procession Corridor at Knossos arrives in the south-west corner of the Central Court. The court is small when measured against the great Minoan temples of Knossos, Mallia and Phaistos, but comparable with other Mycenaean courts; Tiryns is 16m by 20m, Pylos 13m by 7.5m. The Minoan courts were paved; this one was painted stucco, the same chessboard pattern as the megaron floor at Pylos. Beyond is the megaron, which was 23m by 11.5m, similar in layout to the one at Pylos, a rectangular roofed unit with porch, ante-room and large square inner room with round hearth, four columns and a chimney. Curiously, the doorway into the inner room was not fitted with doors – there are no pivot holes in the threshold – so it may have been closed by curtains.[98] This is suggestive of ritual use rather than living accommodation, and conjures images of the Biblical 'veil of the temple'.

The Pylian megaron has a corridor running along each side, giving access to smaller rooms beyond. Something of this survives at Mycenae, but only on the north side and it seems unlikely that there was ever a corridor on the south side. The north corridor originally led uninterrupted from the Portal along the side of the Main Court, past the porch and into a suite of rooms to the north of the megaron. Later on, perhaps with the same mounting need for security that we saw at Knossos and Pylos, this was blocked off and access was only by way of the porch. Tsountas thought this corridor led to the domestic quarters, but only fragmentary remains survive, not enough to reconstruct a plan. Mylonas speculates that there may have been a second megaron, at right angles to the first, opening from the South Corridor. Wace thought a shrine might have existed there, on the summit of the acropolis.[99] Whether there was a shrine in this location, the layout of something like half of the area of the 'palace' of Mycenae – the northern half – remains in doubt.

The House of Columns, sixty metres away, should probably be treated as part of the 'palace' at Mycenae and, as we have already seen, its layout has points in common with that of the main temple-palace, though half the size and rotated through ninety degrees. A north-east to south-west corridor runs along one edge of a court, which in turn has a megaron at one end and a block of rooms at the other. If the main part of the 'palace' at Mycenae functioned as a temple, the House of Columns is likely to have functioned as a temple too.

The megaron had its origins in an early house design, a room with a porch, and it was a design that leant itself to development into a great hall or a sanctuary.[100] It has been assumed that the domestic origin of the megaron means that the 'palatial' megara must also have been residential, but the same design was to become the model for the classical temple. Uncertainty surrounded the Trojan megara from the time of their discovery by Schliemann; initially they were interpreted as temples, and later reinterpreted as residences. The ground plan alone is insufficient evidence of function. At Thermon in Aetolia the long, narrow Sub-Mycenaean megaron called Megaron B, built in the eleventh century BC, was almost certainly a temple; it had a colonnade round it just like the classical temples, and a colonnaded Hellenistic temple was built exactly on top of its remains.[101]

Plate 6.6 The citadel wall at Tiryns.

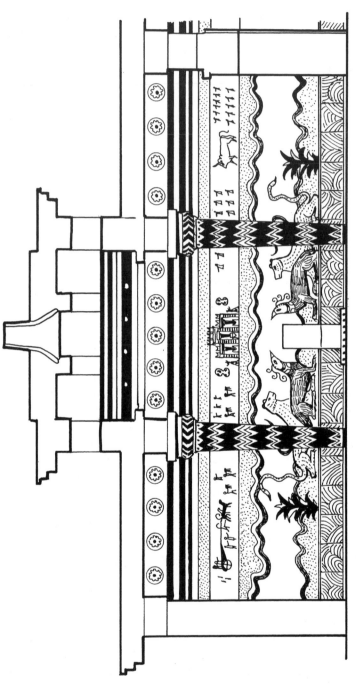

Figure 6.10 The throne room in the megaron at Mycenae: a reconstructed section. The overall decorative scheme of the south wall is speculative. Paired lions seem to have been a heraldic device special to Mycenae. Paired griffins were the companions of the goddess. The decoration is likely to have been in three zones, a main one with a frieze above and a dado of imitation marble below. The zig-zags painted on the columns are inferred from the carved zig-zags on the half-columns at the Treasury of Atreus. The overall effect must have been overwhelmingly rich.

Clearly the Mycenae 'palace' was different from the palaces at Pylos, Tiryns, Athens, Thebes and Gla, which all stood on level ground, and the architectural differences can be explained by topography and erosion. The House of Columns should be seen as the second megaron which at Tiryns, in 1400–1200 BC, stood immediately beside the main megaron but set back a little to the north-east. For all the destruction we now see at Mycenae, it was probably a much richer building than Pylos; for instance, we know that its columns had small stone capitals decorated with elaborately carved leaves, and that the threshold and dado slabs were of high quality. Tiryns too was probably more elaborate and opulent than Pylos, with its great court colonnaded on three sides.

Some things the Mycenaeans of the fourteenth and thirteenth centuries were doing were significantly different from the Minoans. The proportions their architects used were divergent. The average beam span in Minoan buildings is 2.0–2.5m, while the average span in Mycenaean buildings is 3.5–4.0m – significantly longer. There were differences in the proportions of their columns too. The typical Minoan column was five times taller than its diameter, whereas the Mycenaean columns shown on the Treasury of Atreus and Tomb of Clytemnestra were twelve or fifteen times taller than their diameter – much taller and thinner. This becomes significant when we have only column bases from which to reconstruct a building's elevation. It has also been observed that the height of a column is between 1.25 and 1.66 times the length of the span it supports. The spans separating the four columns of the domos at Mycenae are known, and it has been calculated that the columns must have been 4.5m high. Given that there is no other evidence for a second storey or gallery to the megaron at Mycenae, it should be assumed that it was a tall, single-storey structure.[102]

The Pylos tablets identify large numbers of people as priests, priestesses and male temple attendants (*hieroworhgoi*).[103] The shrines identified at Mycenae, Tiryns and Pylos were very small and could not have accommodated a large priesthood; large numbers of priests could only have been employed in a temple.

Homer mentions temples, yet even if there is some genuine Mycenaean material in Homer a certain amount of material from later centuries is also present and little can be argued from the poems unless it is corroborated. Lord William Taylour thinks the references to temples 'seem more at home in the period after the tenth century BC'; but if the buildings we have been calling palaces up to now were really temples, a little more of Homer is rooted in the sixteenth century.

Isabelle Ozanne comments that there were no temples, that the essential ritual acts were performed in the main room in the palace. In support of this idea, she mentions the ritual appurtenances of the megaron at Pylos: the libation channels cut into the floor beside the throne, the offering table in the foyer, the griffin mural. But it is clear that, as we saw at Knossos, this evidence can be used equally to support the idea of the palace as a temple.

Sacred sites often display continuity across cultural and political divides and sometimes even major changes in religious beliefs. Maybe we can infer something of the reputation of the site of the palace-temples by looking at the way in which they were developed in later centuries.

As we have just seen, a Sub-Mycenaean megaron (= temple) at Thermon was replaced by a much more recognizable temple in the Hellenistic period, on almost exactly the same ground plan. Four to five hundred years after the fall of Mycenae, an Archaic temple was built right in the middle of the remains of the Mycenaean temple-palace. Raised in about 625–600 BC, it had a sculpted frieze on its south façade, which included warriors and a goddess dressed as a bride. It is thought she was Hera.[104] The emphasis on Hera might suggest that Mycenae had control over the Argive Heraion at that time, part of the fatal rivalry with Argos.[105] The emphasis on Hera might equally be a relic from the earlier period when the Mycenaean temple was also dedicated to the goddess. In the classical period, Hera was revered across most of Greece, yet even then the Argive Heraion never lost its primacy; it remained the principal temple of the goddess. She was

Plate 6.7 The Heraion. The foundation platform for the Old Temple of Hera. The masonry may be Mycenaean in date.

Figure 6.11 Hera as a bride at Mycenae. This sculpted head 32cm high is from the Archaic temple built on the acropolis at Mycenae. Was Hera perhaps honoured here in the Mycenaean age too?

worshipped all round the head of the Gulf of Corinth, at Sicyon and Corinth itself, lands that were all once part of the kingdom of Mycenae.[106] Mycenae's Archaic temple stood until 468 BC, when the Argives slighted the citadel, breaking down the walls in two or three places and probably destroying the temple. The Argives had a change of heart in the third century BC, repaired the walls of Mycenae, and rebuilt the temple on the same site again.[107] We do not know to whom this Hellenistic temple was dedicated, though it seems likely that it was Hera.

There was a small, possibly medieval, church on top of the ruins of the temple-palace at Tiryns. It was unceremoniously removed by Schliemann during his excavations of 1876 and 1884; unfortunately Schliemann's Tiryns diary and the excavation diaries for this period have disappeared.[108] Whether there was a temple on the Tiryns acropolis in the Archaic or Hellenistic period is uncertain, but Pausanias comments that in his day, the second century AD, the Argives *still* had the wooden idols of Hera and Apollo they had taken from Tiryns, presumably in 468 BC, and presumably from a shrine or temple there.[109]

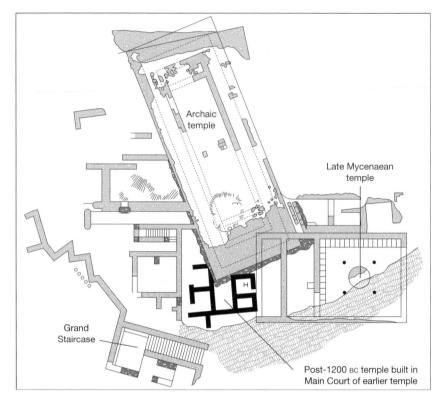

Figure 6.12 The summit of the acropolis at Mycenae. The Archaic temple was built
directly on top of the ruins of the Mycenaean temple-palace. In the courtyard can be seen the remains of a post-1200 BC temple building.

Pylos had a different history, sinking into complete obscurity after its
destruction in 1200 BC. There was a re-occupation of the site by squatters
in the Sub-Mycenaean period. Between 1100 and 900 BC, people moved in
and reused some of the walls of the old temple-palace to make their houses.
Substantial lengths of wall must still have been standing, and the sheltered
space between the South-Western Building and the 'Palace of Nestor' was
occupied. So too was the space between the 'Palace of Nestor' and the North-
Eastern Building. The main court and the megaron porch were turned into
a house, and so was the main chamber of the megaron.[110] At first this
suggests that the site did not retain any aura of sanctity, but a temple was
raised *next* to it – a Sanctuary of Hera.[111] Pausanias says of Pylos, 'there
is a Sanctuary of Athene there with the title Koryphasian Athene, and
what they called Nestor's House, which has a picture of Nestor in it'. Prom-
ising though the sanctuary and its association with Nestor's House sounds,

Pausanias was probably describing Coryphasion near the coast rather than the site on the Englianos ridge. Even so, it may speak of an ongoing tradition of a major cult of a goddess in the area; the Koryphasian Athene appears on the coins of Pylos.[112]

A later Greek temple dedicated to Rhea was built across the south-west corner of the 'palace' at Knossos, covering the remains of the Cupbearer and Destroyed Sanctuaries, in much the same way that the Archaic and Hellenistic temples were built over the temple-palace ruins at Mycenae. Evans used the damage done by the insertion of this Greek temple as an excuse to dismantle the area, using the stone from the Greek temple to build his monumental staircase.[113] Resonances of the Great Goddess of the Minoans can be felt in later goddesses such as Athena, Hera and Rhea. Rhea incorporated the Minoan Goddess of Caves, known in the fourteenth century at Knossos as Eleuthia;[114] Rhea was the goddess of childbirth, the Divine Mother, the Mother of Gods. A temple to Rhea raised on the site of the Labyrinth strongly suggests a tradition reaching back to the Lady of the Labyrinth, and a memory of the site as a holy place dedicated to a great goddess.

The Athenian Parthenon was built beside the remains of an Archaic predecessor which in turn is believed to have been built on the site of the Mycenaean temple-palace, but twice its width. The Archaic and Mycenaean temples stood on the Acropolis in what is now the space between the Parthenon and the Erechtheum. The reconstruction of the Athenian megaron is based on fragmentary remains such as two column bases, which are assumed to be two out of the four surrounding the circular hearth. In front of the Mycenaean megaron there was a large courtyard 25m long, in which a square altar stood, directly in front of the megaron's porch.

Orchomenos had a later Sanctuary to Dionysos, but in Pausanias' time the oldest sanctuary that could be recalled was the one dedicated to the Graces.[115] Whether either of these stood on the site of the temple-palace at Orchomenos is not known.

Thebes was to have many shrines and sanctuaries. The old Mycenaean citadel, known as Kadmeia after its legendary founder, Kadmos, was full of sacred associations. As Pausanias commented, 'Kadmos made a splendid marriage if he really married a daughter of Aphrodite and Ares as the legend says'.[116] Close to the High Gates of the acropolis was the Sanctuary of Zeus All-highest; near the Elektra Gates was a shrine to Apollo; near the Proitian Gates was the shrine dedicated by Heracles to Glorious Artemis. In the Theban acropolis, Pausanias had pointed out to him the place which in ancient times had been the House of Kadmos, in other words the Mycenaean temple-palace.[117] The site of the second 'palace' was occupied by a Sanctuary of Law-giving Demeter, Demeter Thesmophoros.[118] Close beside it were 'the ruins of Harmonia's bride-room'. Harmonia was the bride of Kadmos, the daughter of a god and a goddess, no less; her bridal chamber was a

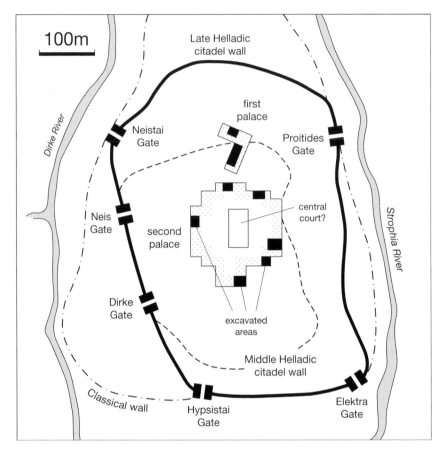

Figure 6.13 The citadel at Thebes, with its two bronze age 'palaces' (after Symeonoglou 1985; Marazzi 1994).

shrine. It was said that the Muses themselves sang at her wedding.[119] This may have been part of the second palace. There was also the site of the bride-room of Kadmos's sister, Semele, no longer a ruin but a space 'which to this day they keep untrodden by human steps'. This was the site of the first 'palace'. It is easy to understand how a cult of Dionysos would have continued on the site of the building where the god had been born. There was an open-air sanctuary dedicated to Dionysos on the site in the fifth century BC, as depicted in the *Bacchai*, and in the second century BC when Pausanias visited Thebes. A third-century BC inscription from the Treasury of Thebes at Delphi also identifies the Sanctuary of Dionysos Kadmeios as an open-air sanctuary. The site is known to have remained open until the Byzantine period.

The sites of the ancient temple-palaces in the citadel of Thebes were evidently remembered as very special and holy places. The area was ideal for religious observance because it was already saturated with memories of religious ritual and powerful mythic associations. It is easy to understand how a religious cult centre would continue on the site of a Dionysos cult, among the ruins of the building where he was born. The birthplace of Heracles was also pointed out in Kadmeia on the site of the 'House of Amphitryon', possibly another Mycenaean ruin, and there were sanctuaries to Zeus Homolois and Zeus Hypsistos, but it was the two great open-air sanctuaries to Dionysos Kadmeios and Demeter Thesmophoros that dominated.[120] The goddess Demeter was venerated there especially, and almost two kilometres to the south of Thebes there was a grove sacred to Demeter and the Maid; in Pausanias' day the place was still called Potniai, 'The Goddesses'.

In the medieval period there was a small church on top of the temple-palace at Tiryns. It was unceremoniously removed by Schliemann during his excavations of 1876 and 1884; unfortunately, as mentioned earlier, Schliemann's Tiryns diary and the excavation diaries for this period have disappeared. Whether there was a temple on the site in the Archaic or Hellenistic period is uncertain, but Pausanias comments that in his day the Argives still kept the wooden idols of Hera and Apollo they had taken from Tiryns in 468 BC, presumably from a shrine or temple somewhere on the acropolis.

Plate 6.8 The Menelaion at Therapne, near Sparta, a later monument to Menelaus.

The early temple on the Menelaion was not reoccupied later, which is how its remains survived, but the classical monument to Menelaus was built next to it, and shows that the site was treated with great reverence in later centuries, perhaps continuing a sacred site tradition.

The evidence is patchy but, at those sites that went on being urban centres in late antiquity, and even at those that were abandoned, it does seem that a memory was kept alive that the huge and costly building complexes we have been calling palaces were temples. And a goddess in particular was remembered: Athena at Athens, Demeter at Thebes and at other sites large-eyed and queenly Hera.

7

A MYCENAEAN
SEA-EMPIRE?

LONG-DISTANCE TRADE ROUTES

Before the dawn of the Mycenaean civilization, in the early bronze age, long-distance trading was already under way across northern Europe, from the Atlantic seaboard to central Germany. In the middle bronze age, developing north-to-south trade links brought Greece into closer contact with that northern world. Amber from Denmark was traded south to the upper Danube valley. The Carpathian bronze-working communities also became more active, establishing trade links down the lower Danube to the Black Sea, and from there it was possible for central European groups to make contact with Mycenae, by this time a dynamically evolving culture feeding off contacts with other cultures. A gold dagger found in Romania shows the influence of Mycenae in its hilt design. Then amber necklaces complete with spacer beads appear in early Mycenaean royal graves; Mycenae was ready to tap the European hinterland.

In about 1700 BC, amber appeared simultaneously in graves at Mycenae (Shaft Grave O in Grave Circle B) and Pylos (one of the early tholos tombs). It arrived in possibly only three consignments, one each for Mycenae, Pylos and Kakavatos in Messenia. The next consignment need not have arrived until around 1200 BC, this time possibly through middlemen in Aetolia and Epirus. The early consignments may have come to the Peloponnese by sea, possibly from Britain, given the remarkable similarity between Mycenaean and British spacer plates. The later and much smaller consignment may have travelled overland to the head of the Adriatic, then along the east coast of the Adriatic. Significantly, in the fifteenth century BC the 820 pieces of amber found in Greece are all confined to Argolis and the Pylos area in Messenia, apart from a few pieces at Thebes. The total haul of amber from bronze age Greece forms a distinct belt running from Pylos across Laconia to Mycenae and on to Boeotia and Attica. The first appearance of amber at Knossos in 1420–1380 BC has been taken as evidence that mainland Mycenaeans were occupying Crete, and taking amber with them.

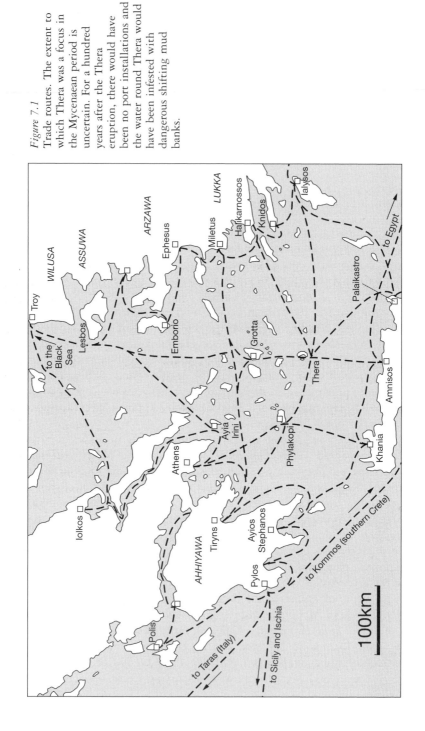

Figure 7.1
Trade routes. The extent to which Thera was a focus in the Mycenaean period is uncertain. For a hundred years after the Thera eruption, there would have been no port installations and the water round Thera would have been infested with dangerous shifting mud banks.

By the late bronze age and the flowering of the Minoan and Mycenaean civilizations, trade seems to have radiated mainly from foci in the Aegean. By the fourteenth century, folding stools, a symbol of power in the Mediterranean world, were traded as far north as Denmark. But these appearances in the archaeological record are only odd items. It does not look as if there was enough contact between the northern and southern worlds for there to be any transformation of the one culture by the other. There was no social or economic or political interdependence of the sort that was to emerge in the first millennium between urban southern Europe and the 'barbarian' north.[1] At the same time, an amber bead with gold casing found in a sixteenth-century BC context in Zurich must have been made in Wessex and exchanged or traded halfway across Europe, and probably others like it travelled further still. There are clues here to networks of trade and exchange among élite groups from one side of Europe to the other.[2] Although the daggers carved on Stonehenge are *not* Mycenaean and the sarsen trilithons are *not* modelled on the Lion Gate, the possibility remains that the kings of Wessex and the kings of Mycenae were doing business with each other.

Several objects, such as the crescentic earring from Wilsford Barrow G8, faience beads, the Bush Barrow bone mounts and amber necklace spacer plates, find tellingly close parallels in Mycenaean Greece. Perhaps the Greek amber was traded via Britain, and the first appearance of amber in Greece in around 1550 BC is certainly compatible in date with the Wessex Culture in England. Close inspection reveals dissimilarities, though. There are indeed bone mounts in Shaft Grave Iota at Mycenae, but 5cm in diameter compared with the 2.6cm diameter of the Bush Barrow mounts; local comparanda suggest that the mounts were generated locally – and independently.[3] There is not much to connect Britain with Mycenae, but just enough. Amber was sought by the élite groups in both Wessex and southern Greece in the second millennium BC, and the gold-wrapped amber bead found halfway between Wessex and Greece confirms that Scandinavian amber was acquired by Wessex craftsmen and traded on across Europe.

Mycenaean trading was largely by sea. In the island-studded Aegean, land was seldom out of sight, so it was easy to create safe and reliable trade routes east of Greece. Towards the end of the fourteenth century, political links with Egypt and the Levant were developed, and by the thirteenth century the Mycenaeans had gained control of the eastern trade routes; there was a marked increase in the number of oriental objects and raw materials arriving in Greece. The main route from the east was from Ugarit to Cyprus, then bay-hopping along the southern Anatolian coast, carried along by the east–west current. From Triandha on Rhodes ships sailed westwards across the Aegean to Thera (at least until the caldera eruption, after which the island was avoided) or Melos and from there to Nauplion and Tiryns.[4] The journey out might have been via one of the ports of Crete (Amnisos on the north coast or Kommos on the south) and from there

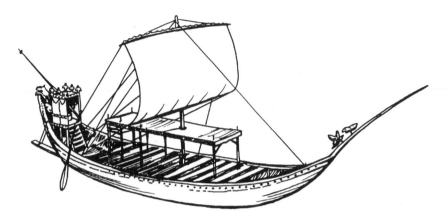

Figure 7.2 A sixteenth-century ship, reconstructed from a Theran fresco.

south-eastwards to Egypt. This route exploited the north-west winds that commonly blow in September. From Egypt, sea currents carried the vessel north to Ugarit.[5]

Travelling west was more dangerous. In classical times the conventional route was to follow the coast of western Greece through the Ionian Islands as far as Corfu, then strike west for Italy across the narrowest part of the Adriatic. The voyage from the island of Othonoi to Otranto in Italy is about 80km. The Mycenaeans probably used this route too.

SHIPS AND PORTS

Mycenaean ships were similar to Minoan ships. The earliest representation of a Mycenaean ship is on a vase fragment from Iolkos in Thessaly, where, aptly, Jason's *Argo* was built. The Iolkos ship had its keel extended to make either a ram or a landing gangway. It also had many pairs of oars and, just like other ships of this period, a big oar-rudder at the upcurved stern. The rowers were 'numbed in leg and arm by the toil of smiting the sea-water with their blades of polished pine'.[6] A prominent zig-zag pattern is shown as if painted on the side of the ship, though this may be an attempt to show waves. Images on seal-stones show additional features, a captain's cabin in the stern and a single square sail mounted on a single central mast. The ships were shallow-draught vessels and could be beached in sandy bays. Homer describes the Greek ships as being dragged up onto the beach and held upright with props.[7] He also repeatedly describes the ships as 'black'; possibly they were commonly painted black or had their hulls waterproofed with pitch. Other hues were possible: Odysseus refers to crimson-painted ships.[8] The Thera frescoes, dating to around 1550 BC, show that there were several different types of ship in existence in the Aegean at this time.[9]

The late thirteenth-century wreck at Cape Gelidonia adds little to our knowledge of bronze age ships. Virtually nothing of the hull was left because of the rocky bottom and the strong currents which dispersed the silt that might have preserved the timber. It is thought to have been quite a small vessel, 9–10m long. The main cargo was copper and bronze ingots, mostly of the four-handled so-called oxhide type, each weighing about 20kg and measuring 60cm long. They had apparently been stacked with layers of matting between them; sticks underneath them were probably placed there to stop the shifting cargo from abrading the hull. There were also bronze tools, originally stored in wicker baskets, a few scarabs, a cylinder seal from Syria and domestic pottery.[10] The distribution of the finds suggests that the ship was 10m long. A cylinder seal, weights and traces of food (fish bones and olive pits) were found at one end, suggesting that a cabin was located there, probably the stern. The Cape Gelidonia wreck was a small merchant vessel, involved in a widespread and crucial trade, the transport of metal. Oxhide ingots of the same type have been found in Syria, Cyprus, the seabed off Anatalya and Kas, Crete (Palaikastro, Zakro, Mochlos, Knossos, Kommos and Ayia Triadha), Sicily, Sardinia and mainland Greece (Mycenae and the seabed off Euboea). Most came from Cyprus. Oxhide ingots are shown in Egyptian wall-paintings from around 1450 to 1200 BC.

The Ulu Burun wreck near Kas has been dated to 1310 BC. This ship was wrecked along the same stretch of the Anatolian coast as the Cape Gelidonia ship, on its way from Cyprus to the Aegean. Its cargo included 354 copper ingots amounting to over 10 tonnes in weight, a few ingots of tin, for use in making bronze, and some ingots of blue glass. There were many Syro-Palestinian amphorae, standard storage vessels, in this case used for transporting terebinth resin that was intended for use in dyeing cloth. The ship carried Mycenaean and Cypriot pottery and some Egyptian scarabs; it has been suggested that the crew was multinational.[11]

A painting on the side of a clay box from a twelfth-century tholos tomb at Tragana shows a ship in the period immediately after the collapse of the Mycenaean civilization. It shows what a large Mycenaean vessel would have looked like. The rigging is carefully painted in, including the stays for the single central mast. The stern has a high stern-post terminating in a fish-tail or possibly an animal head. Also at the stern are a large steering oar and a square cabin. At the prow there is another cabin and an elaborate forecastle with some kind of banner mounted on top. A raised gangway runs the length of the ship, presumably to allow deck-hands to move up and down the ship without interfering with the oarsmen. A single sail billows in the wind, and the ship's wake zig-zags away from the stern.[12]

Pylos tablets list thirty men as oarsmen, who come from five different places; they are 'rowers to Pleuron'. It has been suggested that thirty rowers

constituted the crew of one ship and that the number of rowers listed altogether in the tablets implies a force of up to twenty ships.[13] There were
ships of different sizes, and therefore different numbers of oarsmen.[14] The
coast of Pylos was divided into ten sectors, each with an official in charge
and an allocation of men. This was the coastguard, the force of eight hundred
men charged with defending the coastline from attack (An 657, 654, 519,
656, 661).

Mycenaean ports were mainly based on natural harbours. Nauplion, in a
sheltered corner at the northern end of the Bay of Argos, made a perfect
haven for ships and there was a Mycenaean citadel for its defence on the
hill above. But not all the harbours were natural. Given the Mycenaean will-
ingness to change the landscape at Ayios Adrianos by damming and
diverting a river, it is not surprising to find ambitious coastal engineering
works at Romanou, the port of Pylos. The Selas River was diverted from
its natural outlet into the north end of Osmanaga Lagoon so that it flowed
westwards through an artificial rectangular dock basin 320m by 230m. To
prevent the basin filling with sediment, an artificial lake was created as a
sediment trap. This was done in 1400 BC. For around two hundred years
after that the flows of water were carefully managed so that only clean water
went into the artificial harbour; sediment-laden flood water was diverted
down the natural river channel into the lagoon. This expert management
stopped in around 1200 BC, after which all the river water went into the
harbour and both harbour and lake became silted up.[15]

REACHING OUT

As one might have expected, the Mycenaean kingdoms traded with each
other. A Linear B text found at Mycenae documents a shipment of cloth
from Mycenae to Thebes. Transactions like these appear rarely in the archives
because the shipments were sent off seasonally and the archive tablets refer
only to the recent past.[16]

One of the main reasons why the Mycenaeans reached out to other lands
was the poverty of their own. Neighbouring civilizations (Babylonian, Egyptian and Hittite) built great wealth out of their own natural resources. Greece
was always poor in resources; its potential for wealth lay in the ingenuity,
ability and single-mindedness of its people. Mycenaean Greece can be
compared with the Venetian republic or with modern Singapore, states
whose wealth depends on commercial enterprise, on human resources.[17]
Their particular interest was in acquiring metals. The gold they wanted is
believed to have come from Nubia. It has been suggested that Egyptian
gold was earned by mercenaries ready to fight for Ahmose against the Hyksos
invaders in the sixteenth century. It is quite possible that Greek warriors
did fight as mercenaries, but the payments involved could not account for

the enormous wealth that was pouring into Mycenaean treasuries. Exactly how the Mycenaean rulers became so rich is something of a mystery. The Minoans became rich on the back of large-scale wool production, and the environmental conditions in mainland Greece were similarly favourable to wool production. There was a ready-made market for wool and woollen cloth in the cold winter regions of central Europe lying just to the north of Greece, so it may be that Mycenaean wealth was built, like Crete's, on wool. It may also have been built in part on the slave trade. We know from the Pylos tablets that large numbers of slaves were systematically captured from the Anatolian coast; some were taken home, others may have been sold in Crete, for example, or the Cyclades.

Before 1600 BC, the Greeks concentrated mainly on subsistence agriculture; foreign trade was not at that stage a priority. But from 1600 onwards, as a hierarchical society evolved, with more power and status in the hands of the few, there was a progressive interest in international trade. In many societies this has, at least initially, to do with the acquisition of conspicuously rare and unusual materials and artefacts, the possession of which confers enhanced status. As we have already seen, one of the first conspicuous exotic arrivals at Mycenae was amber. The wearer of an amber necklace was immediately identifiable as a high-status individual, because the source of the amber was on the other side of Europe; it had been brought unimaginably far. But how was the necklace paid for?

Spices are known to have been produced and they were used to make unguents. Unguents were manufactured at or near Mycenae, and probably exported to Egypt and the Levant in stirrup jars.

Something of the shape and complexity of the trading system can be seen in the patterns of traded goods. Mycenaean pottery, such as Pseudo-Minyan ware, is to be found at Mycenaean sites on mainland Greece (Mycenae, Aegina, Athens and Iolkos); it was also traded west to southern Italy and the Lipari Islands, and east to Khania, Kommos and Knossos on Crete, Kos and Rhodes. Imports flowed into Mycenaean Greece by a variety of routes. Canaanite jars, a high-status import, were traded from Canaan to Cyprus, along the south coast of Turkey to Kommos, now emerging as a key *entrepôt* in the Mycenean trading network, and from there to the wealthy classes at the mainland centres (Athens, Eleusis, Mycenae, Tiryns, Argos and Pylos).[18] Scholars have traced a variety of imports and exports, revealing a complex and far-reaching trade network. Exports reached Saqqara in Egypt and Amman in Jordan. It has been argued that eighteenth-century texts at Mari show weapons, textiles and pottery coming from Crete that might have originated at Mycenaean centres, but there seems no reason to think this; the texts actually refer to Crete, where all of these things could well have been produced, and the date is really too early for the Mycenaeans to have been involved.[19]

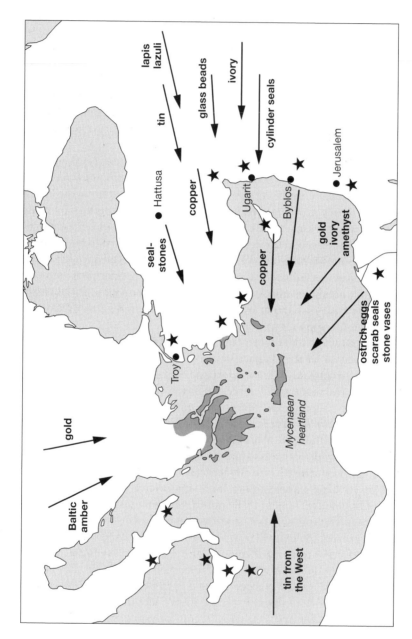

Figure 7.3 The Mycenaean trading empire. Arrows show imports to the Aegean. Stars indicate finds of fine pottery exported from Greece.

THE COLLAPSE OF THE MINOAN SEA-EMPIRE

The Mycenaeans took over a well-developed Minoan trading operation at a time when the Minoan civilization underwent a weakening crisis, the precise nature of which is still not understood. It was not unlike a modern business take-over. The result was the creation of a vigorous and well-organized trading empire similar in geographical reach to the Minoan empire it replaced. The Mycenaeans started to develop trading operations in the Aegean region in around 1500, the expansion phase lasting from 1450 BC until the final fall of Knossos in 1380 BC. During the fifteenth century, the Minoans seem to have retained commercial control of not only Crete but the eastern Aegean, including the colonies on Rhodes and at Miletus.[20]

What precipitated the collapse of the Minoan civilization? One problem in our path is the uncertainty that still surrounds the date of the Thera eruption. Those following tree-ring and ice core evidence argue for a date in the 1620s; those looking for compatibility with the chronology derived from Egyptian king lists argue for a date a hundred years later. At present, the arguments for 1520 create fewer problems. The effects on Crete, at either date, would have been profound. A west or west-north-west wind was blowing at the time of the eruption, taking much of the ash to the east and south-east of Thera. Ash fell over a large area, most of it sea, but the eastern half of Crete was covered to a depth of 1–10cm. This is enough to put farmland out of production for a year or two and would have created a major economic setback for eastern Crete. Many will have starved. The ash veil will have reduced temperatures, perhaps locally as much as 5 degrees Celsius, also having an effect on food production. The Thera eruption will have caused tsunamis too, giant waves 10–20m high that must have swept across the coastal settlements of northern Crete twenty-four minutes after leaving Thera. Towns and harbour installations were damaged, the ships the Minoan sea-empire depended upon destroyed. Though it certainly did not destroy the civilization, this series of disasters must have weakened the Minoan economy considerably.[21] Other blows raining down on it during the next hundred years were to exploit that weakness. Among the first to take advantage of Crete's decline were some Anatolian colonists who arrived in the early fifteenth century and founded settlements in southern Crete.

There is vivid evidence of the switch from Minoan to Mycenaean influence at Phylakopi on Melos. In the Late Cycladic city of Phylakopi I, Minoan pottery was in use and a wall was decorated in Minoan style with the famous Flying Fish Fresco. In Phylakopi II, a megaron with hearth was built in mainland Greek style, and all the pottery was from the mainland, not Crete.

In the fifty years after 1380 BC there was a dramatic increase in the number of Mycenaean sites round the Aegean. By 1330 BC, when the empire reached its fullest extent, there were twenty-four sites on the island of Rhodes alone.[22] The Mycenaean heartlands consisted of the Mycenaean territories or homelands, the kingdoms of the Peloponnese and the southern part of central Greece. Beyond this core was a region that was so strongly acculturated with Mycenaean elements that some scholars have proposed conquest, others large-scale colonization; this consisted of all the islands of the south and central Aegean, including Crete, and the south-west coastline of Anatolia. Further

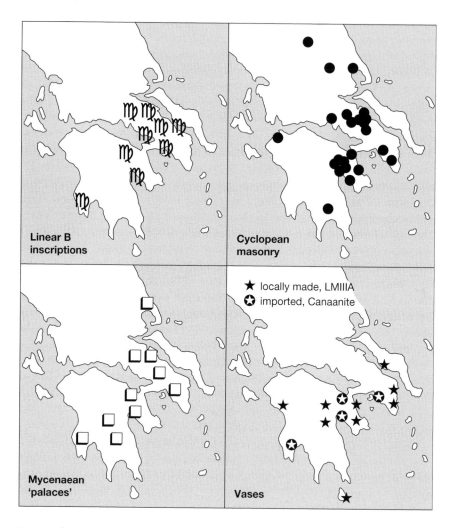

Figure 7.4 Defining the Mycenaean heartland: four indicators. The 'palaces' (temple-palaces) include the newly discovered site at Pellana and the high-status site at the Menelaion.

out still, there were areas where there was trading but only limited diffusion of Mycenaean culture; north-west Greece, south-east Italy, eastern Sicily, Tuscany, Sardinia, Cyprus, the Levant and the Nile Delta. It is by no means clear what Mycenaean traders were doing in Sardinia, as they were not taking any metal ores from that island; the ingots found in Sardinia are of Cypriot copper.[23] In northern Greece and the Balkans there were even more limited contacts, but a certain amount of exchange. The north-eastern Aegean was dominated by Troy. Scattered through the trading empire were trading posts, some of them home to sufficient numbers of ex-patriot Mycenaeans for them to be regarded as colony-communities.[24]

The exact nature of the relationship between Crete and the Mycenaean mainland in the fourteenth century remains elusive. Many Mycenaean cultural elements came in, an obvious one being the style of the new frescoes in the Labyrinth at Knossos. There was also a significant level of destruction at many Minoan centres. These facts have led some to argue that the Mycenaeans invaded and conquered Crete. This seems unlikely. The level of destruction is actually much greater than would be needed to take over political control of Crete; earthquake, insurrection, civil war, socio-economic collapse, or indeed several colliding factors would seem more likely causes.[25] The damage at Ayia Irini looks like earthquake damage; the damage at Pyrgos, where the 'villa' was burnt but not the ordinary houses, looks selective and deliberate. The extent of the conversion to Mycenaean culture on Crete is also not as great as in other parts of the Aegean region, which became more culturally homogeneous than at any time so far. This implies that Crete was to a considerable extent left alone to work out its own troubled destiny under its own Minoan élite.[26] No doubt there were powerful traders and magnates, and perhaps administrators, who came across from the mainland – the fact that mainland burial practices, including chamber tombs, were adopted suggests that some mainlanders arrived to exploit the Minoans' problems. But the temples went on much as before.

The Knossos Labyrinth was modified, but only in minor ways, with new, more formal and magisterial frescoes. It has been said that the Throne Sanctuary was decorated with a fresco of heraldically opposed griffins, a popular Mycenaean motif, but not seen before in Crete.[27] There was, in fact, one griffin facing the throne and that was painted on the west wall of the sanctuary. The fragments surrounding the throne on the north wall show a riverside landscape with luxuriant vegetation; the 'griffin's paws' on one side of the throne were merely broadly brushed-in foliage. The heraldically opposed griffins in the Throne Room were never at any stage part of the prehistoric design; they were imported not by the Mycenaeans but by Sir Arthur Evans and Emile Gilliéron, his artist, in 1913.[28]

Much has been made of the Minoan sea-empire, partly perhaps because Thucydides wrote about it, putting it on the map long before archaeologists discovered the Minoan civilization. The Mycenaean acculturation of the Aegean was more thorough and pervasive, yet has attracted less attention.[29] This is odd, because Homer alludes to the existence of a Mycenaean sea-empire in his reference to Agamemnon's 'empire over many islands and all the Argive lands'.[30]

There is no reason to suppose that there was any political unification of the empire. There is no hint in the Pylos tablets that Pylos was subordinate to any other mainland centres; equally, there is no reason to suppose that Crete or any of the islands in the Aegean were under political control from the mainland. Pylos was autonomous; so was Knossos.

The exact nature of the trading empire is also elusive, and it almost certainly changed year by year according to the exigencies of local political developments. There were also different kinds of trade going on. Trade at places like Ugarit in the Levant was probably organized by freelance traders operating according to the local pattern of exchange. In Egypt, Mycenaean goods arrived in a completely different way, as part of a formal exchange of 'royal gifts', described by the Egyptians as 'tribute', which implies that the Mycenaean centres were subject to Egypt, which they certainly were not. The temple-palaces, as in Minoan Crete, were centres for the organization and recording of trade; trading done under their auspices held some sort of formal accreditation. Shipwrecks like the one at Cape Gelidonia show that another form of trade, by 'tramp' merchants, was also going on.[31] But for the chance survival of a handful of wrecks, this type of trading would not have been suspected; we are probably seeing only part of an extremely complex regional economy.[32]

There is little evidence of social or cultural impact on more distant places. In the far west, substantial amounts of Mycenaean pottery have been found in southern Italy and Sicily, but with no other trace of Mycenaean culture. By the end of the thirteenth century, there were the beginnings of some Italian influences on the Mycenaeans, who adopted swords, fibulae and axes in styles from the Po valley; Adriatic trade was on the increase during the closing years of the Mycenaean civilization. Further to the west and north-west there is no sign of any influence at all, in either direction; the complex economic and social patterns developed in the Aegean had little to offer that was relevant to the pre-urban communities of north-west Europe.

The Mycenaean colonies in Anatolia were emphatically confined to a narrow coastal strip in the west.[33] There were community-colonies at Ephesus, Iasos and Miletus, but they had little effect on the interior; no doubt the Hittite rulers resented Mycenaean interference on the coast and took action to prevent any further encroachment.[34] The Hittites must have regarded the Mycenaean colonies as a thorn in their side, resenting Miletus in much the same way that the Spanish resent Gibraltar. More is being discovered about the Anatolian colonies all the time. Kilns have been found near the

Archaic temple of Athena at Miletus, where Milesians were making their own 'Mycenaean-style' pottery, some of it of high quality. Some of the poorer coarse pottery that was at one time assumed to be the local ware was actually imported from mainland Greece – the containers used to transport wine, olive oil and other commodities to Miletus.[35]

One thing is clear from the archaeology, and that is that the Mycenaean civilization became the dominant culture throughout the whole Aegean region by the fourteenth century BC. Whether it should be seen as a trading empire or more neutrally as a 'koine', an area of shared culture, is still a matter for discussion. Certainly the Mycenaean civilization was seen as dominant in the Aegean by contemporary Egyptians. The wall paintings in tombs of officials in the reign of Tuthmose III show codpiece-wearing Cretans among the processions of tribute bearers. The tomb of Useramon, dating from 1451 BC, is one of these. Just a generation later, the tomb of Rekhmire shows tribute bearers initially with codpieces, but then over-painted with kilts. By changing their costume, the artist changed the visiting Minoans into visiting Mycenaeans. The Minoans had been supplanted in the trading system by the more important Mycenaeans. Pharaoh Amenophis III encouraged long-distance contact. Several scarabs bearing his names reached Crete and Greece in the fourteenth century. He was named on the faience plaque found in the Room with the Fresco at Mycenae. Here is a hint – appropriately, at Mycenae – of the formal, royal gift-exchange type of trade between the great Mycenaean centres and the Egypt of the pharaohs.[36]

The Mycenaean kings and their merchants were able to exploit the fall of Knossos, which they may even have engineered, and then reach out and take over the Minoan trading operation. By the end of the fourteenth century, political links with Egypt and the Levant had been developed, and by the thirteenth century the Mycenaeans had gained control of the eastern trade routes. This was marked by a significant increase in the number of oriental objects and raw materials arriving in Greece. But there were other changes in progress too. While the Mycenaeans were opening up routes to the east, the Cretans switched their attention to the west; there was a dramatic increase in Italian imports to the Aegean, and mainly to Crete. It may be that the by now less ambitious Minoan traders felt more comfortable working the western trade routes, leaving the more unstable and increasingly dangerous trade routes in the east to the more aggressive Mycenaeans.

It was only certain Minoan and Mycenaean centres that had large quantities of orientalia and occidentalia. The trading must have been carefully organized along specific directional lines, with specific points of entry. Most of the exotic material has been found at six centres, Ialysos on Rhodes, Zakro, Kommos and Knossos on Crete, and Tiryns and Mycenae in Greece. Each centre specialized in certain goods. Cypriot goods are common at Tiryns but not at Mycenae, Egyptian goods are relatively common at Mycenae but not at Tiryns, the patterns suggesting that centres developed specific trading relationships with distant producers: Mycenae with Egypt, Tiryns with Cyprus, Thebes with Assyria, Kommos with Italy. The merchants must have grown very rich on these ambitious enterprises. The kings increased their international status by joining in the trading at the highest level, engaging in the most elevated form of commerce, exchanges of royal gifts.[37]

THE TROJAN WAR

HOMER'S VIEW OF THE WAR

Homer's version of the Trojan War is familiar enough. Paris, the son of Priam king of Troy, has abducted Helen, wife of Menelaus king of Laconia. The Achaeans (Greeks from all the kingdoms of central and southern Greece) plan to sack Troy and bring Helen back. The confederation is led by King Agamemnon, brother of Menelaus, as commander-in-chief. There is an initial quarrel among the Greek leaders over two more abductions. King Agamemnon has taken Chryseis the daughter of the priest Chryses; he then takes Briseis away from Achilles when he is forced to give Chryseis up. Achilles appeals to the gods to inflict loss on the Achaeans, and Zeus is won over to his cause. The voyage to Troy is not described at all; the action moves immediately to the Troad. The Greek warriors disembark on the beach in front of Troy and there is an exchange of taunts between Greek and Trojan heroes, after which Menelaus engages Paris in single combat. Paris loses, but his life is saved by the goddess Aphrodite, who spirits him from the field of battle back inside the walls of Troy.

The Trojan leader Hector, Priam's son, drives the Achaeans back to their beached ships, and they are forced to build a defensive wall and ditch. Urged by his chieftains, Agamemnon sends envoys to Achilles, offering him rich rewards and his daughter's hand in marriage if he will return to the front line. Achilles refuses, but decides to stay his hand until the Trojans reach his own ships. Battle recommences and the Trojans breach the wall and threaten the ships. Agamemnon and Menelaus are wounded in the onslaught and Achilles' closest friend Patroklos, who has seen the mayhem, pleads with Achilles to relent. Achilles agrees only to let Patroklos fight, in Achilles' armour. The appearance of Achilles is enough; the Trojans turn back, but Patroklos is killed by Hector, who takes Achilles' armour and wears it himself.

Achilles' rage is now turned on Hector, who has killed his friend, and he is reconciled with Agamemnon. His mother brings him a new suit of armour made by the god Hephaestus, and he goes into battle, killing Hector.

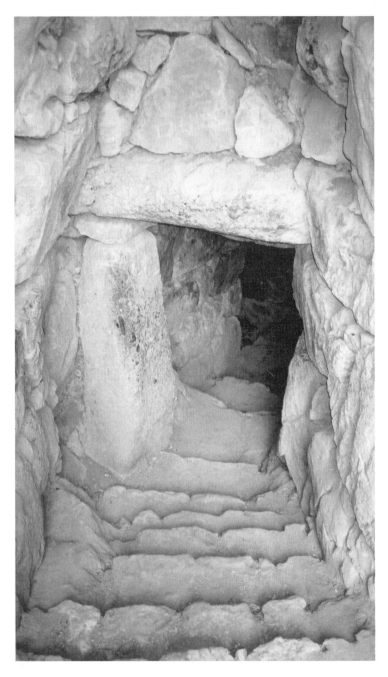

Plate 8.1 Halfway down the staircase to the secret water cistern at Mycenae. Mycenae too was equipped to withstand a siege. Note the inner doorway with its heavy lintel and relieving triangle, reminiscent of the much bigger Lion Gate.

After dragging Hector's corpse behind his chariot, Achilles holds a lavish funeral for Patroklos, complete with human sacrifice. Achilles is persuaded to return Hector's body to the Trojans, but does not expect Priam himself to come to his tent in the night to plead for his son's body. Achilles sends Priam safely back with Hector's body. With Troy's main defender dead, the city must fall to the Achaeans. It has already been predicted by Thetis that 'hard on the heels of Hector's death, your death must come at once'.[1]

This outline is but a skeleton of the poem, which extends to over 15,600 lines. It was first written down in the eighth century BC and has been known as the *Iliad*, 'The Poem concerning Ilium', since at least as early as the fifth century BC, though it could as well be entitled 'The Wrath of Achilles' and some commentators have argued that it started off as a shorter poem with that title. The poem seems straightforward enough, yet it raises many questions.

Is it a work of fiction based on poetic invention much later than the events described, or a genuine historical inheritance from the bronze age, or a mixture of the two? Was Homer an historian or a pseudo-historian? It is self-evident that it would be unwise to cite Homer as a source without corroboration. There is some evidence from the Linear B tablets to suggest that elements of the story were authentic survivals from the bronze age. The phrase 'Athana potnia' which is found on bronze age Linear B tablets of the thirteenth and fourteenth centuries BC is very close to Homer's phrase 'Potni Athenaie', and means the same thing, 'the Lady Athena'. If the story of the Trojan War as told in the *Iliad* is fact, when is it likely to have occurred, how and why? Were Atreus and Agamemnon historical figures, real rulers of Mycenae?

Homer may have been reflecting the concerns and interests of the eighth century. The dialect and geographical knowledge suggest that the 'final' form of the epic poems was arrived at on the west coast of Greek-colonized Ionia. That the *Iliad* and *Odyssey* were tailored to an audience of ex-patriot Greeks in Anatolia would fit very well; the *Iliad* tells a story of successful Greek conquest in Anatolia and the *Odyssey* a story of an ultimately safe passage home to Greece, so the bard was tailoring his material to suit the interests of his audience.[2]

Sources other than Homer fed the tradition. When the Greeks were returning from Troy, they were deliberately shipwrecked by old Nauplios, to avenge his son Palemedes. He showed lights, which lured the fleet onto rocks at Kaphereus on the southern tip of Euboea. The survivors who reached land were cold and hungry, and fed on some goats sheltering from the storm in a cave sanctuary of Dionysos. The Greeks took the wooden idol with them back to Argos and installed it in a temple there.[3] None of this is in Homer. Pausanias may have picked up a local legend here – Euripides used it too – or it may have been an episode in the *Nostoi*, one of the lost poems of the Epic Cycle. Homer represents part of a larger oral and written tradition, and we should expect that other parts of the tradition survived independently, even if they have not survived right down to the present day.

The later Greeks had an illuminating view of Homer. Herodotus gives an alternative version of the abduction of Helen by an unnamed man and the arrival of Helen and her lover at Memphis in Egypt, where they were judged by Proteus. Herodotus comments, 'I think Homer was familiar with the story, for, though he rejected it as less suitable for epic poetry than the one he actually used, he left indications that it was not unknown to him'.[4] Herodotus goes on to quote passages in the *Deeds of Diomed* and the *Odyssey* where Helen's excursion to Egypt is mentioned. Herodotus asked the Egyptian priests if the Greek version of what happened at Troy had any truth in it and they gave him information they claimed to have had direct

Figure 8.1 The silver Siege Rhyton found in a shaft grave at Mycenae. In the background is a walled city or citadel, with corniced flat roofs at several different levels. In the foreground, ordinary people defend it; they are not dressed as warriors, but naked.

from Menelaus; Menelaus told them that after his wife was abducted the Greeks sent a strong force to the Troad in support of his cause. Immediately the Greeks landed, ambassadors, including Menelaus himself, went within the walls of Troy to demand the restoration of Helen and the treasure that Paris had stolen. The Trojans gave an answer that they always stuck to afterwards: that Helen and the treasure were not there – both were in Egypt, where they were held by King Proteus. The Greeks assumed this was a lie and laid siege to the city. The lengthy discussion in Herodotus shows not only that varying traditions of the Trojan War existed in antiquity, but that the ancient Greeks were aware of them and knew that the epic poems contained a not always consistent amalgam of these traditions. Herodotus also shows us, conversely, that a substantial part of the story as told in the *Iliad* was thought, by historians with a very different perspective from the Greeks and access to different sources, to be substantially true.

GREEKS AND TROJANS ACCORDING TO THE HITTITE TEXTS

In 1906–8 ten thousand clay tablets inscribed in eight bronze age languages were discovered at the Hittite capital of Hattusa. This huge resource opened up the possibility that something of the political history of bronze age Anatolia would be learnt. Early on, Winckler found a letter from the Egyptian pharaoh Ramesses to the Hittite king Hattusilis about their joint treaty. The Hittite royal archive collection is not only much larger than the one at Pylos, it contains details about diplomatic crises, rivalries, negotiations with foreign powers, snubs, apologies; in some there is even a personal content and an emotional charge. The widow of Tutankhamun and teenage daughter of Akhenaten and Nefertiti, Ankhesenamun, wrote to the Hittite king, Suppiluliumas I, to ask if one of his sons would marry her and become king of Egypt. 'My husband is dead. I have no son. You, so they say, have many sons. Were you to send me one of your sons, he would become my husband.' This obviously opened the door to Egypt becoming a satellite of the Hittite king. It was an extraordinary prospect, and Suppiluliumas hid neither the pleasure nor the great honour he felt at this request, he, already High King of a great empire. 'I have never encountered such a thing in all my life.' It was unheard of for a non-Egyptian to become pharaoh, and this helps to explain Suppiluliumas's surprise. In fact it ended badly with the chosen son, Prince Zannanza, being murdered on the journey to Egypt by a rival court faction.[5] The tablets were so detailed and so many that there seemed a strong possibility that the Greek expedition and the fall of Troy would be there, somewhere in this huge royal archive.

Emil Forrer's 1924 paper equating the Ahhiyawans of the Hittite texts with Homer's Achaeans caused a sensation. Forrer collected and published all the available historical texts of the Hittites and reconstructed a complete regnal list of the kings of Hatti, then he announced that he had found in the Hittite texts references to the Achaeans, the Homeric Greeks, and even specific personalities such as Eteocles of Orchomenos and Atreus of Mycenae. Forrer's claims were hotly disputed by Friedrich in 1927 – Forrer's paper was 'mistaken in its main conclusion' – and the debate has continued unresolved ever since.

The controversy revolves round one word in particular in the Hittite texts, the name of a country of unspecified location, 'Ahhiyawa' or 'Ahhiya'. This, especially the short form, is phonetically close to 'Achaea', though the short form occurs in only two texts, the Indictment of Madduwattas, dating to the reign of Arnuwandas I in the fifteenth century BC, and an oracle text probably of the same period.[6] 'Ahhiya' may be seen as the older form of the name. The Indictment of Madduwattas has a king called Attarissiyas the 'man of Ahhiya' driving Madduwattas from his kingdom so that he had to seek asylum at the Hittite court. The writer's father, probably Tudhaliyas I, gave Madduwattas land in the mountainous 'land of Zippasla', but here too he was attacked by King Attarissiyas. The Hittite king's response was to send an army. In the battle that followed, Attarissiyas deployed a hundred chariots and an unspecified number of foot-soldiers. Afterwards, Madduwattas joined forces with Attarissiyas in an attack against Alasiya, Cyprus, an attack which must of necessity have been seaborne and involved a fleet of ships.[7]

The question of Ahhiya and the Ahhiyawa remains unresolved, but one reference to the Ahhiyawa has been noticed on Linear B tablet C 914 at Knossos. A hecatomb of cattle is sent to Akhaiwian (A-ka-wi-ja-de), which seems to be a unique Cretan reference to the mainland Greeks. The mainland Greeks referred to the Cretans as 'Kretes'.[8]

In the mid-fifteenth century, the Hittite kings began to lose control of the western Anatolian coastlands. Assuwa, a coalition of twenty-two states in north-west Anatolia, right next to Troy, became a thorn in the Hittite king's side. Tudhaliyas II was an active and highly successful Hittite High King who controlled a huge empire stretching from the Aegean coast all the way to Aleppo. In about 1450 BC Tudhaliyas in person led his army against Assuwa and inflicted a resounding defeat. The Hittite annals claim that ten thousand Assuwan soldiers were taken back to Hattusas as prisoners, including the Assuwan king Piyama-Kal, his son Kukkuli and other aristocrats. Tudhaliyas appointed Kukkuli king of Assuwa, which became a vassal state. Kukkuli rebelled and was executed. It was political instability of this kind, not just in Assuwa but all along the Aegean coast, that the Mycenaeans were able to exploit. One fragmentary letter mentions Assuwa and Ahhiyawa together, implying that the rebellion of Assuwa may have been supported by the Mycenaeans. Another (ambiguous) letter says 'the king of Ahhiyawa withdrew or retreated' or someone 'relied on the king of

Ahhiyawa', so the Mycenaean king was either leading his army in Anatolia or supporting rebellion from afar.[9]

One document (KUB XXIII 13) tells of events in the time of King Tudhaliyas IV, around the time of the Trojan War. Possibly it describes events that found their way into the Homeric epic.

> Thus speaks tabarna Tudhaliyas, the Great King. The Land of the Seha River transgressed again for a second time. They said: 'In the past, the great-grandfather of His Majesty [King Muwatallis?] did not conquer us by force of arms; and when the grandfather of His Majesty [King Mursilis III?] conquered the countries of Arzawa, he did not conquer us by force of arms. He would have conquered us, but we erased him for his transgression.' Thereafter Tarhunaradu [king of the Land of the Seha River] waged war and relied on the king of Ahhiyawa. And he took refuge on Eagle Peak. But I, the Great King, set out and . . . raided Eagle Peak. And five hundred teams of horses and . . . troops I brought here to Hatti, and Tarhunaradu together with his wives, children and goods I transported to . . . and led him to Arinna, the City of the Sun-goddess. Ever since the days of Labarna no Great King went to the country. I made a descendant of Muwawalwi . . . in the Land of the Seha River king and enjoined him to deliver . . . teams of horses . . . .[10]

Tarhunaradu was king of the Land of the Seha River in 1240, around the time when Troy VI is thought to have been severely damaged by an earthquake. Ore Hansen suggests that 'Eagle Peak' was Troy itself, which means that the Hittite account can then be made to describe an attack on Troy, but the connection is hard to see. No one could ever have described the low flat-topped hill of Hisarlik as a peak.

Some scholars have seen evidence in Homer of events that date from earlier than the Trojan War of 1250 BC. There was, for instance, an earlier and unsuccessful expedition to rescue Helen which resulted in Achilles and other Achaean warriors fighting in Teuthrania.[11] This may have happened months or years before the events described in the *Iliad*, and was described in the *Kypria*. Some elements in Homer, like Ajax's tower shield and the use of silver-studded swords, date from several centuries before the Trojan War. It is possible that some episodes embedded in the Epic Cycle originated in earlier epics describing the era before the Trojan War; certainly the expedition to Troy was not the only Mycenaean adventure in Anatolia.

In year three of the Annals of Mursilis II (c.1330 BC), comes the first indication of a connection between Ahhiyawa and the country (or later) city of Millawanda. Unfortunately both this reference and another in the following year are on broken, incomplete tablets, and the whereabouts of Ahhiyawa are left unspecified; one reference nevertheless does mention a ship, which would support Forrer's idea that Ahhiya was overseas. Mursilis fell ill and the divination priests opened an inquiry into the cause of the divine anger. A large tablet records the questions put to the oracle, and the answers. It mentions the god of Ahhiyawa and the god of Lazpas, whose statues were taken to Hattusa to succour the sick king, and questions are asked about the rituals appropriate to these honoured foreign gods.[12] The divination tablet confirms friendly relations between the kingdoms of Hatti and Ahhiyawa. Since Lazpas is almost certainly Lesbos, there is an implication that both gods came overseas from lands to the west of Anatolia.[13] At this stage, some seventy years before the Trojan War, Hittites and Ahhiyawans were on friendly terms. Some Greeks even gave their children the name of the stammering Hittite king, Mursilis (Myrsilios).[14]

Another document that is very important in this debate is the Tawagalawas Letter, addressed to the King of Ahhiyawa by an unnamed though elderly king of Hatti, and dating to around 1250. The letter covered at least three tablets, of which only the third survives intact; there are fragments of the first two. The letter is hard to understand, but it seems that a Hittite prince called Piyamaradus had turned to banditry and was causing disaffection in the Lukka country.[15] The exact location and extent of this territory are not known, but only part of it lay within the Hittite empire.[16] Piyamaradus's base was the adjacent city of Millawanda, which was outside Hittite control but under the indirect control of the King of Ahhiyawa. The Hittite king had written the letter to press the King of Ahhiyawa to hand over Piyamaradus and so restore peace in the Lukka Land; it was an extradition request. The people of the Lukka Land had already on their own account written appealing to Tawagalawas, the brother of the King of Ahhiyawa, probably because he was currently living in Anatolia and therefore likely to be able to help them. On another occasion, when the Lukka city of Attarimma was attacked, they called on the Hittite High King to help them. Everything points to the Lukka Land being a buffer zone between Ahhiyawa and Hatti, probably with poorly defined frontiers.

Piyamaradus was well enough established in the Lukka Land to apply to the Hittite king for recognition as a vassal. The Hittite king was apparently willing to agree to this, and sent his son and heir to fetch Piyamaradus, but Piyamaradus, sensing either weakness or treachery, refused to accompany the heir to his father's court and insisted on recognition on the spot. After the Hittite king had suppressed the revolt in the Lukka Land, he received a message from the King of Ahhiyawa telling him that he had instructed his agent (regent?) in Millawanda, a man named Atpas, to hand Piyamaradus over. The Hittite king arrived in Millawanda to discover that Atpas had allowed Piyamaradus to escape by sea, naturally the subject of a further complaint. The letter has by this stage confirmed not only that the King of Ahhiyawa was in control in Millawanda but that Millawanda was on the coast. The rest of the letter consists of reasons why the King of Ahhiyawa should accede to the Hittite king's request to hand over Piyamaradus. Among the suggestions is that the messenger bearing the letter should be kept as a hostage for Piyamaradus' safety. 'The messenger is a man of some importance; he is the groom who has ridden with me in my chariot from my youth up, and not only with me, but with your brother Tawagalawas.' This speaks of a close relationship between the dynasts, implying that in times past, the King of Ahhiyawa's brother had driven in the Hittite king's chariot, perhaps even at the Hittite king's side; it is not possible to infer whether this was during their youth and Tawagalawas was as a favour given driving lessons by the best groom in Hatti, or in later years and the two had driven side by side for diplomatic reasons on some ceremonial occasion.

The Tawagalawas Letter contains two hints that Hittites and Ahhiyawans had already come to blows over Wilusa.

The tone of the letter is respectful and friendly. The Hittite king, probably Hattusilis III, even goes as far as apologizing to the King of Ahhiyawa for his 'soldierly' turn of phrase in case it is interpreted as aggressive.[17] He tactfully implies that his brother-king cannot be fully aware of the situation and will surely act appropriately as soon as he understands it. At the same time there is the clear implication that the King of Ahhiyawa is a *long way* from the scene of the events described. He is a remote figure, has probably been fed distorted and inaccurate information by his underlings and is not in direct personal control of what is happening at Millawanda.[18] The date of the letter, around 1250, is in legendary chronology close to the reign of Atreus or Agamemnon.

The reference to the King of Ahhiyawa as the Hittite king's 'brother' has been widely discussed, as it states that the Hittite king regards the Ahhiyawan king as his equal. The letter was not the only communication between the two kings on the Piyamaradus affair, and it is evident that a letter from the Ahhiyawan king must have contained some reproof for the content and tone of a still earlier letter. Hattusilis is conciliatory and defensive:

> If any of my lords had spoken to me, or even one of my brothers,
> I would have listened. But now my brother the Great King, my
> equal, has written to me, shall I not listen to the word of my equal?

Interpreting this is not easy, and it is possible to hear heavy sarcasm in it. Hattusilis was undoubtedly exasperated with Ahhiyawan interference in western Anatolia, and may well have felt that the King of Ahhiyawa was seriously overreaching himself – a jumped-up Great King, not a real one. This may have been in Hattusilis's mind as he himself was a usurper; he had deposed his nephew who, significantly, appealed to Ahhiyawa for help.

Hattusilis was extremely sensitive about his own status, and this may have driven him to be sarcastic about the pretensions of the Ahhiyawan king. Hattusilis received a letter from Ramesses II which he considered to be over-bearing and superior in tone, wrote back indignantly, and received a further letter from Ramesses:

> I have just heard all the words you have written to me, my brother, saying 'Why did you, my brother, write to me as if I were a mere subject?' I resent what you wrote to me . . . you have accomplished great things in all lands. You are indeed a Great King in the Hatti lands . . . Why should I write to you as though to a subject? You must remember that I am your brother. You should speak a glad-dening word: 'May you feel good every day' yet instead you utter these incomprehensible words not fit to be a message.

Hattusilis was over-sensitive about his own status as Great King and may well have been sarcastic about the status of other kings. He dismissed a request from the King of Assyria to be treated as an equal – 'Stop writing to me about brotherhood and Great Kingship: I have no wish for it.' Nevertheless, even after allowing for sarcasm and the occasional need for diplomatic flattery, it is clear that the King of Ahhiyawa was a king of high status, on a level perhaps with the King of Assyria.[19]

On a minor point, written communication between Hatti and Ahhiyawa would involve scribes at Hattusa being able to read and write Greek, or scribes at Mycenae and other Mycenaean cities being able to read and write Hittite. The occurrence of a couple of Hittite personal names in the archives at Knossos and Pylos lends support to the idea of diplomatic correspondence being conducted in Hittite.[20] It is very unfortunate that the Atreid royal archive at Mycenae has not survived.

Thus far, there are strong grounds for identifying Ahhiya with Achaea, and identifying Millawanda (in some places 'Milawata', suggesting an early Greek form 'Milwatos') with the major Mycenaean colony of Miletus on the south-west coast of Anatolia.[21] One objection that has been raised to Miletus as Millawanda is that Arzawa, a hostile country, would have separated Millawanda from the Hittites and prevented them from maintaining regular communication,[22] though this presupposes that we know exactly where Arzawa's frontiers were and that political alliances and frictions were clear-cut. Indeed, having an unco-operative buffer state between himself and the Hittite king may have helped Piyamaradus to develop his freebooting operation with as little hindrance as possible. From reconstructions of the likely location of Arzawa it in any case looks as if it would have been possible to reach Millawanda from Hattusa by passing to the south, through the land of Mira in the upper Meander basin.[23] Some positive support for Miletus as Millawanda comes from the tablets, where Millawanda is mentioned in association with the names of several places that can be located in the hinter-land of Miletus.[24]

Some scholars like to interpret Ahhiyawa as an Anatolian kingdom. But if that were the case, why would the King of Ahhiyawa be so out of touch with what was happening in part of his territory? The best explanation is that the king was separated from an Anatolian colony by a stretch of sea. The Ahhiyawan High King, or 'man of Ahhiya', is likely to have been the foremost among the Mycenaean kings, who is likely to have been the King of Argolis. Although some of the early tablets imply that 'Ahhiyawa' was in western Anatolia, that may mean no more than 'an American presence in Baghdad'; the ultimate power base was far away, and the Mycenaeans would have been able to make a very significant impact on the Hittite empire by operating through Rhodes, Miletus and Ephesus.[25]

The King of Ahhiyawa supported the powerful King of Arzawa in a war against Hatti in around 1320 BC. He also supported the King of the neigh-bouring Land of the Seha River in a similar war against 'the Great King of Hatti'. This repeated Greek interference in western Anatolia was on a larger scale than the slave raids suggested by the Pylos tablets, and is exactly the sort of background we would expect to an expedition against Wilusiya in the north-west in the thirteenth century.

Forrer invited opposition when he identified Tawagalawas as an 'Aeolian' prince. His only reason for proposing this seems to have been the slight resemblance between the name 'Tawagalawas' and an early version of 'Eteocles', the name 'Etewoclewes'. Forrer pressed this identification so that Tawagalawas might be the Eteocles who was the son of Andreus, King of Orchomenos in Homer, but in this some scholars felt he was trying to press too much Homeric allusion from the sources, causing them to reject his more important fundamental thesis out of hand. In Forrer's support, the Pylos tablets contain the name 'Etewokleweios', which seems to supply an evolutionary link to the name 'Eteocles'.

A fragmentary document records a letter from the Hittite king to an unnamed sub-king, possibly the ruler of Milawata, addressing him as 'my son'. Ahhiyawa is not mentioned, but there are references to the Piyamaradus incident as if it was a recognized precedent. The events relating to Piya-maradus would be well known in Milawata-Miletus, though less known outside the Lukka Land. There is also an implication in the friendly but proprietorial address that the outcome of the Tawagalawas Letter had been satisfactory from the Hittite king's point of view and that he had effectively gained, or regained, control over Milawata. Milawata's relationship with Hatti changed through time, and in around 1315 BC a Hittite army under Mursilis' generals arrived to sack Milawata.

By the thirteenth century, it is clear that Ahhiyawan interference in western Anatolia had become a continual problem to the Great Kings of Hatti. Ahhiyawa became a significant component in Hittite diplomacy.

In the 1260s, a deposed Hittite king actually requested help from the King of Ahhiyawa before going into exile in Syria. Shortly after this, Hattusilis was preoccupied with the sacking of his city of Carchemish by Assyrians in the east, but he was still aware, as the tablets record, of the Ahhiyawan threat in the west. Ahhiyawa was seducing and destabilizing one western kingdom after another. War with Ahhiyawa was to be avoided; where possible, the Hittite kings preferred diplomacy.

It was the thirteenth-century kings of Ahhiyawa who were accorded the status of 'Great Kings', by the Hittite Foreign Office in the reigns of Hattusilis III (1278–1250) and Tudhaliyas IV (1250–1220). These Ahhiyawan kings correspond with the kings of the Atreid dynasty at Mycenae. It looks as if it was the legendary Atreus and Agamemnon who worried the Hittites.

Another key Hittite document relating to the identification of Ahhiyawa is a treaty between Tudhaliyas IV (1239–1209) and a King of Amurru (Syria). In it, the Hittite king helpfully lists 'the kings who are of equal rank to me: the King of Egypt, the King of Babylon, the King of Assyria, and the King of Ahhiyawa'. Curiously, the words 'and the King of Ahhiyawa' have been deleted, implying that the Hittite court for some political reason at that time did not want to acknowledge the full international status of Ahhiyawa.[26] Nevertheless, although overruled, the scribe had placed Ahhiyawa in what was presumably a customary list of contemporary great powers, and the 'man of Ahhiyawa' was a High King or Great King of the same international standing in the eastern Mediterranean region as the Great Kings of Hatti, Egypt, Babylon and Assyria. Mycenaean Greece seems the most natural candidate for this missing power.

An objection to identifying the Ahhiyawans in the treaty with Amurru as Mycenaeans is that the treaty forbids the King of Syria to let Ahhiyawan ships trade through Syrian ports with Assyria. For this trade embargo to be deemed necessary, there would need to be substantial trade in Mycenaean goods east of the Euphrates, and there is little evidence of it.[27] On the other hand, absence of evidence is not evidence of absence, and cannot be used to refute the hypothesis. Such evidence as there is of Mycenaean trade in the Levant – and there is *some* – in any case suggests that it was indeed reduced around 1250–1230 BC, and the treaty drawn up at just that time may have been the reason for that reduction.

A fundamental linguistic objection has been raised: 'Ahhiyawa' is not the same as 'Achaea'. The earlier form of classical 'Achaia' would have been 'Achaiwia'. Sommer's argument against this is that the earliest authority we have, Homer, uses 'Achaiis', not 'Achaiia', and we have no reason to assume the use of the form 'Achaiia' before the seventh century BC. It can neverthe-less be counter-argued that Homer may have used 'Achaiis' for metrical expediency, and 'Achaiia' may have existed in prose usage;[28] on the whole, it seems safe to assume that 'Achaiwia' meant 'Land of the Achaeans' in Mycenaean Greek. This is the form in use at Knossos. It can be argued that 'Achaiwia' is not identical to 'Ahhiyawa'. If the Hittites were so familiar with the Achaiwia, the doubters cry, why did they persistently spell and therefore presumably pronounce their name wrongly, and over so long a period? Why did they substitute *hh* for *ch*, *iya* for *ai* (a familiar diphthong to both Mycenaean and Hittite), and *a* for the final *ia*? It is argued by Sommer and his supporters that the resemblance between 'Ahhiyawa' and 'Achaea' is superficial and coincidental: they are not the same place. Ahhiyawa was a territory situated entirely in the west of Anatolia.

In Forrer's favour, a great deal of archaeological evidence has subsequently emerged that supports the idea of Mycenaean contact and trade with the coastal towns of western Anatolia. Miletus carries the hallmarks of a Mycenaean colony or trading post. Conversely, Hittite control penetrated a long way west, into the Lukka Land, Seha River Land and Land of Zippasla; there was only a very small area left that could have been Ahhiyawa. If Ahhiyawa was only in Anatolia, how could it have become so important? How could it have been accorded the status and circumspection it evidently was? The tablet references to Ahhiyawan activity at sea, the major Cyprus expedition in particular but also the long-distance trading with Syria, suggest a significant command of the seas and some major power base. The Greek traditions of successive sea-empires or thalassocracies emphasize that there was only room for one such sea-empire in the Aegean at one time, and we know that the Mycenaeans dominated the Aegean Sea from around 1400 BC onwards. The Hittite tablets in any case frequently refer to Ahhiyawa as 'overseas', which points strongly to Greece.[29] There is a common sense argument too; given the assertiveness of the Mycenaean culture, the Hittites cannot have failed to make contact with the Mycenaeans in the eastern Aegean, western Anatolia and along the trade route to the Levant – exactly where the Hittite texts suggest contact was indeed made.[30]

The Hittite archives are telling us something very significant. If the Ahhiyawans were Mycenaeans or Achaeans, the texts provide positive evidence for repeated contact between the Hittites and Mycenaeans throughout the late bronze age. But if the Ahhiyawans were not Mycenaeans, the Mycenaeans go entirely unmentioned in the Hittite archives.[31] Given the scale of the archaeological evidence for Mycenaean activity in the Aegean region, this alternative looks untenable.

In the end, if it is only the linguistic objection that stands in the way, it is not a sufficient objection.[32] If there were different Hittite and Greek forms to the bronze age name of the Achaeans, then so be it: there are plenty of later parallels. The nineteenth-century British preferred to use anglicized forms such as Bechuanaland, Basutoland and Leipsic rather than Botswana, Lesotho and Leipzig. It was an expression of nationalism. The French call the British capital 'Londres' for the same reason that the British call the French capital 'Pa-riss', and it seems likely that things were not so different in the bronze age.

If we accept that Ahhiyawa was Mycenaean Greece as a working hypothesis, there are many implications. Perhaps the most striking is the Hittite picture of the unification of the Greek mainland kingdoms under a High King. This is the picture Homer gives us too, but the circumstances described in the *Iliad* appear exceptional, a relatively short-term coalition created to deal with a particular political and military emergency; it would not be surprising to find that in peace-time the twenty Mycenaean kingdoms went their several separate ways. Yet the Hittite archives imply that there was one man at the helm, a High King, an Agamemnon, throughout the centuries represented in the archive tablets. It is possible that the High King was the King of Thebes or Orchomenos, but it is more likely from the archaeology that, as Homer says, it was the King of Mycenae who held this office. The other significant implication from the Hittite archives is that the King of Ahhiyawa and his agents were busy along the western Anatolian coast, and that this disrupted the fraying western fringes of the Hittite empire. We hear of the King of Ahhiyawa himself campaigning on the Anatolian mainland. This brings us very close to the Trojan War.

Forrer was sure he had identified Troy (Greek 'Troia') itself in the Hittite archives, in the name 'Taruisa'. This might be pronounced Taruwisa, Tarwisa, Truisa or Troisa. Unfortunately it only occurs once, in the damaged annals of Tudhaliyas I (1420–1400), the first Hittite king to visit this region, in a list of towns of the Land of Assuwa, which itself is hardly mentioned again. It seems likely that 'Assuwa' was an early form of the name 'Asia' and that like Roman Asia, Assuwa was on the west coast of Anatolia. The towns are apparently listed in geographical order, starting from the border with the Lukka Land, and this puts Troisa, the last in the list, in a northerly location – in the Troad, in fact.

The problem with this identification is once again linguistic. According to the rules of Greek phonology it is not possible for Troisa to develop into Troia. There is nevertheless a way out, and that is to suppose that Taruisa was derived from a primary form Tariya, even though that has not been identified in any text. Just before Taruisa is the name *U-i-lu-si-ia*, pronounced Wilusiya, and this has been seized on as the Ilios of Homer. The name of the sub-king of Wilusa in around 1280 BC, in the reign of the High King Muwatallis II, was Alaksandus. This is of course the same name as Alexandros, also called Paris, and Alexandros was the prince of Ilios or Troy.

Wilusa features in the Hittite archives as a western Anatolian Arzawan kingdom, and it may be that Troy was a city of Wilusa. Homer uses another name, Dardanians, to describe some of the people of the Troad, and Egyptologists have pointed out that the contingent of 'Drdny' who fought as King Muwatallis's allies at the great Battle of Kadesh in 1275 BC might have been Dardanians. In other words, as part of the Hittite empire, Trojans fought for the Hittite king against Egypt. It is what one might have expected. It is an interesting thought that the fathers of Trojans who fought against Agamemnon in the Trojan War fought against Ramesses in the Battle of Kadesh twenty-five years earlier.

Muwatallis did not live long after the Battle of Kadesh. He was succeeded by Urhi-Teshub, Muwatallis's son by a concubine; he took the royal name Mursilis III. Meanwhile, Muwatallis's brother Hattusilis, still ruling his own kingdom in the north, felt he had been unfairly overlooked. Hattusilis encroached on his nephew's authority little by little, eventually, after seven years, imprisoning, deposing and exiling Urhi-Teshub to Syria. He became High King as Hattusilis III, concluding a peace treaty with Egypt in 1269.[33] The early decades of Hattusilis's reign represent a high point in Hittite power. In the south, he gave his eldest daughter Naptera as a bride for Ramesses II, the king of Egypt, where it was recorded:

> It was a great and singular occurrence, a great and unprecedented marvel . . . The daughter of the Great Prince of Hatti was fair before the heart of his Majesty. He loved her more than all else that had been bestowed on him.[34]

In the east, Hattusilis was safeguarding Syria against the growing might of Assyria by openly goading the Babylonians into attacking the Assyrians: 'Go now and plunder the land of the enemy . . . My brother, sit there no longer. March against the land of your enemy and vanquish him.'[35]

But this zenith was short-lived; a period of ferment and disintegration began, and the Mycenaeans seem to have played a part in it. The Tawagalawas Letter contains two hints that by 1250 the Hittites and Ahhiyawans had already fought over Troy, or at least over a town in the Troad. The Hittite king says: 'Tell him [Piyamaradus] that in the matter of Wilusa over which we were at enmity, he has changed my mind and we have made friends . . . A war is wrong for us.'[36] Later he refers again to 'the matter concerning the town of Wilusa over which we made war'. Another letter, from around the same period (about 1250), was from the King of the Land of the Seha River to a Hittite king mentioning that Piyamaradus had attacked Lesbos. Yet another document from the same period as the attack on Wilusa implies that the King of Ahhiyawa was himself present in western Anatolia. The document is damaged and incomplete:

> The Land of the Seha River again transgressed . . . 'His Majesty's grandfather did not conquer with the sword . . . He conquered the Arzawa lands . . . with the sword. We have . . . to him.' . . . made war. And the King of Ahhiyawa withdrew . . . withdrew, I, the Great King, advanced . . . then 500 horses I brought.

Many problems remain, since there is no certainty about the location or extent of any of the kingdoms of western Anatolia, and several entirely different reconstructions of Hittite geography are possible.[37] Scholarly opinion is still sharply divided over the whole Ahhiyawa question, with Oliver Dickinson representing the sceptics – 'it seems best to consider this an unproved theory' – and Lord William Taylour representing the growing body of scholars who believe that Ahhiyawa really was Mycenaean Greece:

> it is clear that [the Hittite documents] refer to a sea power . . . there can be no question that the real centre of power was Mycenae. The Hittites, being a land not a sea power, could have little knowledge of the territory that constituted the Achaean dominion or where its centre of gravity lay.[38]

MYCENAEANS AND EGYPTIANS

There is another strand in the evidence, this time from Egypt. As we have seen, the Hittite, Assyrian, Babylonian and Egyptian kings wrote to each other as brotherly equals, and there is a single tantalizing reference to the King of Ahhiyawa being an associate member of this exclusive jet-set of High Kings. Support for the identification of an Aegean location for this potentate comes from Egypt, which kept its own records.

A statue base from the mortuary temple of Amenhotep III at Kom-el-Heitan near Egyptian Thebes carries a list of names that have come from the Aegean. The list, which must date from the time of the pharaoh's death in about 1340 BC, opens with 'Keftiu' and 'Tanaja'. The first is known to mean 'Crete' or 'Cretans', and the second must mean 'Greece' or 'Greeks' as the word is very close to 'Danaans', Homer's name for the inhabitants of the Greek mainland. After thus distinguishing between Minoans and Mycenaeans, the inscription goes on to list the places from which those envoys had come; the Cretans had come from Amnisos, Phaistos and Kydonia (Khania), while the Danaans had come from Mycenae (Mukana), 'Deghajas' (unidentified), Messene and Nauplia in the Peloponnese. Then follow the island of Kythera, Wilia (surely not Troy?), then another group of Cretan town names, Knossos, Lyktos and Sitia. The ancient Egyptian name for Knossos was astonishingly close to the Minoan/Mycenaean name – Kunuscha. Amnisos too was very recognizable as Amnischa. Michael Wood suggests that the list is an itinerary of a bronze age voyage; it may be so, but the 'Cretans and Greeks' opening is more suggestive of a group of envoys arriving in Egypt.[39] Certainly the inscription implies that although the Minoans and Mycenaeans were recognizably distinct from one another, and it was important to distinguish between them, it was nevertheless possible to deal with them together, at least in the reign of Amenophis III.[40]

212

An inscription from seventy years earlier, year 42 of Thutmose III, around 1450 BC, refers to tribute sent by Danaja (Mycenaean Greece). This included a silver vase specifically of Cretan workmanship, which presumably either the Egyptians recognized from its style and quality or the Danaans were keen to point out. A similar list of tribute offerings from the reign of Amenophis III at Karnak mentions Danaja in a list with Ugarit and Cyprus, reinforcing the idea of the Mycenaeans operating in the wider eastern Mediterranean sphere.

A small amount of evidence from Crete and Greece confirms that a diplomatic relationship of some kind existed between Minoans and Mycenaeans and Egypt. Egyptian references to the Keftiu petered out after the Eighteenth Dynasty but imports of Mycenaean pottery continued.[41] An alabaster vase of Thutmose III and scarab of Amenophis III were found at Knossos, and a faience plaque bearing the name of Khanate was found at Mycenae. In the Linear B tablets from Knossos, a reference to 'the Egyptian' (*Ai-ku-pi-ti-jo*) suggests that there may have been small numbers of Egyptians, perhaps merchants, diplomats or agents, living as expatriates in Minoan and Mycenaean cities.[42]

Overall, the Egyptian evidence implies that the Mycenaean realm was regarded as significant in Egypt: significant enough to record. This in turn adds weight to the idea that the rulers of Hatti would also have been interested in the Mycenaeans.

THE TROJAN WAR: A TWENTY-FIRST-CENTURY RECONSTRUCTION

What follows is necessarily speculative. Although the Hittite archives span a couple of centuries of events, there are still many gaps. An outline reconstruction is nevertheless just possible.

From the Hittite royal archives, it is clear that in the thirteenth century the Hittite kings – Hattusilis III and Tudhaliyas IV in particular – had to push the resources of their empire to the limit to maintain their power. They were threatened continually by the Kaska peoples in the north; they were locked in continuing rivalry with Egypt in Syria to the south-east; they were worried by the increasing power of Assyria to the east; there was unrest in western Anatolia, where a powerful group of states was led in disaffection by the Arzawans. The Hittite kings adopted an elaborately refined diplomacy to deal with some of these problems, probably because they simply could not afford to react militarily on three or four fronts at once.

To this dangerously unstable situation we must add the increasing interest of the Mycenaeans in western Anatolia. For a long time, they had indulged in small-scale raids, taking slaves and probably other booty as well. As we shall see, they were raiding Anatolia in the fifteenth century, supporting the Assuwan coalition against the king of Hatti. But by the thirteenth century they had become more ambitious. The city of Miletus (Millawanda or Milwata) was well established as a Greek colony. The Hittite kings were understandably ambivalent about Miletus, but they were ready to concede that it and a certain amount of land round it were 'Achaean'. This concession may have hardened their attitude to the possibility of secession in the rest of western Anatolia, and they made it clear that they regarded Mira, Arzawa, the Seha River Land and Wilusa as vassal states of the Hittite empire. Any attempt at destabilization in those kingdoms would be met by force.

By around 1250 it is evident, again from the Hittite archives, that the Mycenaeans' activities in western Anatolia amounted to deliberate destabilization. It is as if the Mycenaeans sensed that the Hittites were more interested in the east than the west and were losing their grip on the Aegean coastlands; there was a power vacuum that might be exploited. The Mycenaean High King's brother was aiding Hattusilis's most dangerous enemy in the region. There had been a war between the Mycenaeans and the Hittites over a city in the kingdom of Wilusa, whose king was Alaksandus; it would not be long before the Wilusan royal family was moving into exile. The Mycenaeans' motives are unclear. They may have been keen to destabilize Assuwa as a step towards destabilizing Wilusa, the Troad immediately to the north, and the motive for that may well have been a desire to gain control of the Dardanelles. There is another possibility. There are mythic traditions of the Greeks that trace the bronze age dynasties at Argos, Tiryns and Mycenae back to Assuwa.[43] If there were blood ties between the royal families of Argolis and those of Assuwa, the Mycenaeans may have wanted to help their cousins to defend themselves against an invasion by King Tudhaliyas IV – an invasion of their own ancestral homeland. If so, they failed.

The forces gathered by Agamemnon in Homer are colossal. Some have suggested that the Catalogue of Ships was a poetic device, a means of drawing in as many famous heroes as possible, and not a factual piece of historical reporting.[44] The number of warriors seems grossly exaggerated. A hundred thousand warriors would not have been needed to take a relatively small citadel on a low, easily accessible coastal hill. The Pylos tablets mention forces guarding the Greek coast counted in hundreds, not thousands. On the other hand, the territories listed do coincide remarkably closely with the Mycenaean koine, so it is possible that the kingdoms listed really were part of the Achaean confederacy. The numbers of warriors and ships each contributed were probably much lower than Homer mentions, and some did not contribute any at all; Homer admits that land-locked Arcadia contributed no ships, and there may have been other kingdoms who gave diplomatic but not military support to the war on Troy.[45]

The mustering-point, Aulis, looks like an odd choice. We might have expected Agamemnon to have called the fleet to the Bay of Argos. But Aulis really was a port in the late bronze age, and its position towards the north-east meant that there was quite a short sailing distance to Troy.

The war over the Wilusan city – unnamed in the archives – was fought in the north-east of the Aegean, an area where the Mycenaeans had been taking slaves and where they had developed close trading links with one city in particular – Troy, and possibly even then called something like Troia. What remains unclear is the reason for the Mycenaean attack. Many suggestions have been made.

The collection of women as slaves and concubines was common enough at this period; the motive given by Homer is not too far from this: the (re)capture of a woman abducted by a Trojan prince – but it seems unlikely that an expeditionary force would have been mobilized for just *one* woman. Another possible motive is economic strategy. As long ago as 1912 Walter Leaf proposed that Troy was extremely desirable to the Greeks because the city commanded the mouth of the Hellespont and had become a nodal point in trading operations. Tolls on foreign traders were imposed, the hypothesis continues, and the Greeks were goaded into putting Troy under siege, strangling it by cutting it off from its trade.[46] Nilsson felt Leaf was imposing too modern an approach to bronze age people.[47] Nevertheless, given that the Mycenaeans were conducting a significant volume of long-distance trade via the Black Sea route, the Hellespont would have been a key location; maybe the Mycenaeans wanted to secure Troy in order to be sure of the freedom of the sea route past it. Another possibility is that the Greeks wanted to gain control of the Scamander valley.[48] A simpler explanation is that, having developed a conventional trading relationship with Troy, the Mycenaeans came to realize just how wealthy the city was and saw it as a target for plunder. Strategy or robbery? We can take our pick, as there is no firm evidence.

Certainly Troy VI, the Troy that fell to the Greeks in 1250 BC, Priam's Troy, would have been a prize worth taking. Sceptics have argued that Troy VI was too small to be the 'wide-spread Troy' described by Homer. The Troia Project of the 1990s has nevertheless proved the long-suspected existence of a bronze age city on the slopes to the south of the citadel. Manfred Korfmann, who led the project, shared Schliemann's view that more of Troy lay hidden. He and his team used a magnetometer survey to discover the city streets of the Roman period and traces of the bronze age city. Bronze age Troy, which was bounded by a defensive ditch 4m deep, turns out to have been thirteen times larger than previously thought, with a population of possibly five to ten thousand: easily big enough to have been a major central place. Troy VI, with its city stretching away on the south side of the citadel walls, would have been every bit as imposing as Mycenae. The citadel itself rose from the shore of the lagoon as if defending the town from

Plate 8.2 The south postern gate at Mycenae. Like Troy, Mycenae was built for siege warfare. This finely preserved tunnel through the thickness of the fortress wall was a sally-port.

sea-borne attack; approached from the sea, it would have been as impressive to Europeans in the bronze age as Manhattan was to European migrants in the 1930s.

Another view, that of Carl Blegen, is that the Homeric Troy was Troy VIIa, a patched, earthquake-damaged city that the absence of imported pottery shows was in decline. This weakened city lasted for only a generation before being violently destroyed by fire – and looted. Blegen believes that this event was the Homeric sack of Troy, which he dates to about 1240 BC. Blegen's Homeric Troy is not a glamorous place. The threat of siege drove many of the citizens into the citadel for refuge, and many small slum dwellings were crammed against the inside of the circuit walls. Scraps of human bones in the streets, a skull in a doorway, a man struck down in flight were evidence of the moment when the Mycenaeans broke through the defences of Priam's Troy.[49]

At about the same time as the Trojan War, and perhaps even during the same campaign, the people of the Seha River Land announced to the Hittite king that they no longer owed allegiance to him but to the Mycenaean king. The Mycenaean king seems to have arrived with an army, but then withdrew when he had word of Hattusilis's approach, leaving his Seha River

216

allies to face Hattusilis unsupported, which on the face of it was a shameful and dishonourable act. Hattusilis recorded that he ravaged the Land of the Seha River, deposed its king and installed in his place a loyal substitute. It was perhaps during an ignominious retreat from the Seha River Land that the Mycenaeans and their Anatolian allies sacked Thermi, the principal town on Lesbos. Here we have an instance of archaeological evidence of destruction supporting the Hittite story of Lesbos being attacked by the infamous Piyamaradus, and Homer's story of the sack of Lesbos by Achilles. There is another possible reading of events, though. 'Withdrew' on the Hittite tablet could be interpreted as 'relied on'. Although the tablet is badly damaged and incomplete, it could have meant only that the Mycenaean king relied on the Seha River People to create a diversion, a smoke-screen behind which he might take Troy, if not unnoticed then at least unmolested by the great army of Hattusilis. Another possibility is that the Seha River People heard of the approach of the Mycenaean expeditionary force, thought it had come to liberate them, were mistaken in the Mycenaeans' intentions and made what turned out to be a fatally premature declaration of loyalty.

What is almost certainly true is that behind the tales told in the *Iliad* and the *Kypria* (the epic that preceded the *Iliad*) were many Mycenaean raids, probably all of them smaller in scale than the spectacle presented by Homer.[50] The Trojan War of Homer is a conflation of events possibly spanning a couple of centuries, beginning about a hundred years before the supposed date of the Homeric siege.[51] The treatment meted out to Troy was inflicted on countless other towns along the Anatolian coast in the late bronze age.

A sword was found at Hattusa. On it is an inscription: 'As Tudhaliyas the Great King shattered the Assuwa country, he dedicated these swords to the storm-god, his lord.' The sword was evidently dedicated, with others, at Hattusas by Tudhaliyas II after his victory over Assuwa in 1430 BC. It was a sword captured from Assuwa; booty taken in battle was customarily dedicated to a protector-god. The sword is of a type that was made exclusively in Greece, and probably in Argolis at that, so an Assuwan warrior must, at some time before 1430 BC, have captured the sword from an invading Mycenaean warrior during a raid.[52] It is a sword that speaks eloquently of fighting between the Hittites and the unreliable kingdoms of western Anatolia – and of a military attack on western Anatolia by a Mycenaean army.

9

THE FALL OF
MYCENAE

At the close of the thirteenth century BC, barely two generations after the Trojan War, Mycenae fell. The precise circumstances under which the Mycenaean civilization came to an end are still shrouded in mystery. In the background were huge tensions that were sub-continental in scale. These underlying tensions were given ominously concrete expression a century earlier, with the Battle of Kadesh. This was a major confrontation that took place in Syria, where the armies of the two empires of Egypt and Hatti met head on. The outcome was inconclusive. Sixteen years later Ramesses II and Hattusilis III agreed a peace that included guarantees of mutual aid in case of attack by a third power. That third power might conceivably have been the Mycenaean confederation, or neighbours to the east. But the treaty was short-lived. In 1232 BC Merneptah repulsed an invasion of Egypt by Libyans and 'northerners from all lands'. In 1191 and 1188 Ramesses III defeated invaders from both land and sea; they came from the north-east to settle in the Nile Delta. At about this time Hattusa, the Hittite capital, was destroyed. Within the century between 1300 and 1200, the balance of power in the Near East had shifted irretrievably. The large-scale tensions experienced in Egypt, Hatti and the Levant were evidently felt by the Mycenaeans too; this was the time when the great fortification walls went up.[1]

Various mechanisms have been suggested, such as natural disaster, economic collapse, political implosion, revolution and invasion by barbarians.

One scenario is that a major earthquake in around 1200 BC caused the destruction at Mycenae and other centres. Great buildings collapsed at Tiryns; the survivors of the disaster built small temporary structures in the citadel, then constructed a well-planned new town outside. Pylos, the Menelaion, Zygouries, Midea and Eutresis were destroyed in 1200 BC and never rebuilt. Other centres like Mycenae and Tiryns were rebuilt and survived only to be destroyed later in the twelfth century. One – Athens – was never completely destroyed.

But an alternative possibility is that the Mycenaean centres were attacked by an enemy, one that has left little trace in the archaeological record beyond the destructions themselves. Around 1250 BC there was certainly trouble, and it may have been the beginning of the final phase. Outlying houses at Mycenae were attacked and burned, possibly prompting the massive strengthening of the fortification wall; arrangements were made to ensure a supply of water inside the citadel. Tiryns and Athens expanded their defences at this time. At Pylos, so far there is no evidence for a late fortification wall, but important goods and activities were brought in closer to the centre, and access to the temple-palace was restricted in an attempt to improve security. But the ruler at Pylos continued to maintain authority in long-established ways; the tablets show that ritual feasting continued right into the final year. But in around 1200 BC the temple at Pylos and the citadels at Mycenae and Tiryns were all destroyed in conflagrations.[2]

According to tradition, Pylos was short-lived and destroyed twice. No more than four kings reigned there from its founding to its fall. According to Diodorus, Nestor's father Neleus built the city, but later in his reign some unexplained disaster overtook the city.[3] This was remembered later as the destruction of Pylos by Heracles. Of the twelve sons of Neleus, only Nestor survived the attack, because he had been sent away, but Pylos was rebuilt on a grander scale than before, including a spacious palace for Nestor, who succeeded to the throne.[4] Then there was a war, in which Nestor fought, with the neighbouring kingdom of Elis. By the time of the Trojan War, Nestor was too old to lead his warriors into battle, so forty or fifty years seem to have separated the first destruction of Pylos from the Trojan War. The end of Pylos came in the second generation after Nestor: 'After the end of the war against Ilium, and the death of Nestor after his return home, the expedition of the Dorians and return of the Heraclidae two generations afterwards drove out the descendants of Neleus from Messenia.'[5] If these two generations were each twenty-five years long, the overall life-span for Pylos in Greek tradition comes to just one hundred years, which is what the archaeology also suggests – 1300–1200 BC.

Some commentators take the story of the return of the Heraclidae literally, and see in it an explanation for the parallel tradition of the Dorians. The Heraclidae, exiled to Attica, re-entered the Peloponnese not by the Corinthian Isthmus but by crossing the Gulf of Corinth and landing on the undefended north coast of Achaea. From there they advanced south into Arcadia and west into Elis, and from there attacked Pylos. The unprotected palace of Nestor was put to the torch. The Heraclid king who took Messenia as his share did not establish his court at Pylos but 'changed the royal residence to Stenyclarus'. Pylos was abandoned.

To a great extent, Pausanias' version of events fits the archaeological evidence, even though we have very little evidence for 'Heraclidae' or 'Dorians'. There is a hint at an invasion in the cemetery of inurned cremations found at Olympia; Slavs after all did penetrate the Peloponnese and settle in Elis.[6] Were the 'Dorians' perhaps Slavs?

Figure 9.1 Gold hilt of bronze sword from Grave Delta in Grave Circle B and made in about 1600 BC. The sophisticated and beautifully conceived pattern of spirals ends in a pair of lions' heads facing one another.

There are increasing doubts about the existence of the Dorians, who may have figured large in the minds of later Greek historians without necessarily having played any part in the fall of Mycenaean Greece. Those supporting the Dorian invasion used to attribute the introduction of iron-working and cremation to the Dorians, but both practices had begun before the fall of Mycenae.[7]

The tablets at Pylos give some clues to the nature of the final catastrophe there. Tablet Jn 829 tells of the surrender of temple-bronze for making spear-points, which smacks of an emergency. More dramatic is Tn 316, a scrappy, untidy and unfinished document belonging to the temple's final days. Pylos is written large, several times over on the left hand side, and there are lists of offerings and 'victims'. Gods and goddesses are listed, each receiving an offering of a gold vessel, which in itself cannot have been a regular ritual, and a human being. The gods are offered a man, the goddesses

220

a woman, probably offerings of human sacrifices. Early Greek legends often refer to human sacrifice, and there is the archaeological evidence of a similar propitiatory sacrifice at Anemospilia on Crete. The ceremonies were probably last-ditch attempts to avert disaster by calling on the intercession of Zeus and Hera and several other deities.[8]

Tablet An 657 outlines the deployment of coastguards, which suggests that attack was expected to come from the sea.[9] The temple-palace at Pylos was remarkably empty of portable objects when it was destroyed. Even the throne had been taken. Perhaps the building was systematically looted by a raiding party, who stripped it of its valuables before setting it on fire.

It is even possible to tell at what time of year Pylos fell. The end came when no sheep had been shorn, no grain harvested, no grapes pressed. It was early in the year. The tablets suggest that the year was counted from the winter solstice and the names of some of the months are known. Sphagianios was the month when the major festival at Sphagianes took place; classical months were similarly named after places. The heading of the list of final human sacrifices (Tn 316) is *po-ro-w-to-jo*, probably Plowistoios, 'the sailing month'. As navigation usually begins in the Mediterranean in March, Plowistoios is probably March, and that was probably the month when Pylos fell.[10]

The tablets list towns in the kingdom without mentioning that any were lost, which suggests that the destruction of Pylos was sudden. The immediacy and totality of the collapse of the kingdom may be partly explained in terms of the short history of Pylos' development – just one hundred years – and the strongly centralized bureaucracy with which it was governed. It was a much more strictly organized economy and society than the Minoan, allowing little self-reliance to the provincial settlements. The effect of destroying the nerve centre of an over-centralized polity is to cause its collapse; once Pylos was destroyed, the other settlements could offer no resistance.[11]

Who the attackers were is still a mystery. John Chadwick favoured the Sea Peoples. They were posing a major threat to the Nile Delta from 1225 BC onwards, were a major problem in the reign of Merenptah and Ramesses III and were repulsed by the armies of Ramesses III in 1191 BC. The Hittite Empire disintegrated at around this time as the High King lost control over his vassal states. A threat from the sea was clearly felt at Pylos, and there is evidence in the levy of temple-bronze for spear-points that imports of bronze may have been intercepted, that trading by sea had been restricted. Even so, there is no particular reason to implicate the Sea Peoples who attacked countries well to the east, Egypt included.[12] The identity of the Sea Peoples is in any case not known, so the problem remains unsolved.

Mycenaean centres that were well inland – Mycenae itself, for instance – were destroyed, and that has persuaded Lord William Taylour that they fell prey to internal troubles of some kind. Collapse may have followed in the wake of the Trojan War. Homer comments: 'Those events [of the Trojan War] were the beginning of the great wave of disaster that was rolling towards Trojans and Danaans alike.'[13] The *Odyssey* follows the fate of many of the survivors of the war. Menelaus and Nestor were fortunate in their homecoming, but the High King, Agamemnon, was murdered on his return, Odysseus wandered for ten years before reaching Ithaca, others were shipwrecked and forced to settle overseas. If Homer gives an approximation of what happened to the Mycenaean aristocracy, massive political, social and economic disruption must have ensued. For Mycenae, we are given a detailed scenario by the great dramatists of a later age, who had access to an ancient tradition. After Agamemnon's murder, those of his followers who survived doubtless caused Aegisthus trouble and it is easy to imagine Mycenae split by factions with conflicting loyalties. Eight years after the regicide, Agamemnon's son Orestes returned to kill both Aegisthus and Clytemnestra. The political and social tensions accompanying this kind of power struggle would have been weakening, and something of this general nature may well have led to Mycenae's fall.[14] The specific events leading to collapse at Midea and Tiryns must have been different, but possibly also followed on from the disruption caused by the Trojan adventure. Clytemnestra was not the only queen to be unfaithful during the war. Diomedes' wife Aegialia was unfaithful with Cometes. Idomeneus' wife Meda was unfaithful with Leucus. Odysseus' wife Penelope was besieged by suitors who wanted to usurp the throne of Ithaca.

Although the destruction by fire at one centre after another appears simultaneous in the archaeological record, it may have been spread across a decade or more, and resulted from different causes in different places. It is easy to imagine a political coup or revolt at a centre like Mycenae being copied at Midea, then Tiryns and other centres further afield. Mycenae, Tiryns, Midea were all burnt; Gla, Korakou, Zygouries, Prosymna, Berbati were abandoned or destroyed during this phase. The Dorians, for whom there is no archaeological evidence at this time, were perhaps not really Dorians at all, but the great Mycenaean underclass, rebelling against its masters.[15] The great fortresses would have been very difficult for a foreign invader to take, especially since the approach roads – at Mycenae certainly – were carefully watched. Taking these castles by surprise would have been impossible. But the local community, who would know every inch of the building, its sally-ports, its points of weakness, the footholds on the walls that they would have learnt when playing games as children, would be in a much stronger position to penetrate the fortifications, and probably without arousing suspicion. The scribes at Pylos went on recording as if nothing out of the ordinary was happening.

Climate change has been blamed for the collapse of the Mycenaean civilization; it has been argued that Attica flourished because it was wetter and Messenia declined because it became drier but this claim is not supported

Plate 9.1 The southern citadel wall at Mycenae.

by the evidence. Research suggests the opposite: that Messenia was twice as wet as Attica. A certain amount of circumstantial evidence was gathered in the 1970s to show that Europe, Asia Minor and Egypt were in climatic upheaval in 1200 BC; Hittites stricken by famine left the Anatolian Plateau for northern Syria, disastrous floods hit the Hungarian Plain as a result of heavy rain, and the snow-lines in Scandinavia and the Alps fell.[16] Another suggestion is that a shift in the climate favoured the balance of power in Europe between the civilized south and the barbarian north, but each hypothesis lacks solid supporting evidence.[17]

Another theory is that the 1200 BC disaster was caused by a major earthquake, and the destruction at Mycenae is consistent with this. There was a similar destruction at Tiryns. But Pylos, destroyed at the same time, is really too far from Mycenae – 100km – for them both to have been destroyed in the same earthquake. Perhaps the Argolid citadels of Mycenae, Midea, Tiryns, Asine and Argos were severely damaged by an earthquake and then the Laconian and Messenian centres were disrupted and destroyed by displaced Argives.[18]

The destructions and abandonments were concentrated in the Peloponnese. Attica was relatively unaffected; in fact in the half-century following 1200 BC, Attica flourished. One tradition, deeply rooted in Greek tradition, is that refugees from Pylos went to Attica.[19] Archaeology shows that people did arrive on the east coast of Attica after 1200 BC and set up a cluster of colonies: Brauron, Ligori, Kopreza and Perati. This matches the tradition of 'Neleids' living there, including the family of Peisistratus. The Neleid Melanthus is said to have stopped at Eleusis, where his family later held the priesthood. Later, these Eleusinian Pylians seem to have moved on to Salamis, where there is an important cemetery of cist-tombs on the coast facing Eleusis.[20] It is nevertheless dangerous to read too much into these folk tales, which may have been elaborated to give colour to a genealogy, or merely to entertain.

Can the legendary accounts illuminate? Homer tells of internecine quarrels. Pausanias tells of Agamemnon's son Hyperion, who was the last king of Megara; after Hyperion, the Megarans decided to do without kings.[21]

Pausanias records a later fall of Mycenae. In 468 BC, warriors from Argos attacked the people of Mycenae, who took refuge in their citadel. 'It was impossible for the Argives to storm the fort of the Mycenaeans since it was so very strong, being like Tiryns the work of the Cyclopes. Forced by necessity, however, the Mycenaeans surrendered their citadel because their food supply was finished.'[22] Perhaps some similar feud lay behind the late bronze age fall of Mycenae.[23]

After 1200 BC came a century of decline. The population decreased and dispersed, and the Peloponnese became seriously depopulated.[24] The huge eruption of the Icelandic volcano Hekla in 1159 BC caused major ecological and economic problems across north-west Europe, and its effects may have been felt as far south as Greece. The crisis, which lasted twenty years, may have been the final blow to a weakened civilization.[25] Some people emigrated to start new lives in Cyprus or the Levant, while many in Attica moved to Perati on the east coast. The Achaean coast of the Gulf of Corinth was settled on a significant scale at this time. After the sack of Pylos, many took refuge in the Ionian Islands, especially Cephallenia. Yet Mycenae continued to provide the inspiration for the new pottery styles, showing that it continued to be an influential centre of some kind and to some extent recovered from the disaster. There was some rebuilding within the citadel, in the ruins of the temple and across the western and south-western slopes, in three phases. The House of the High Priest was rebuilt and embellished with frescoes.[26] A building was raised on the temple-palace court, possibly as a replacement temple, and a comparable building was raised at the same time within the megaron at Tiryns.[27] But now the bonds of control were looser. There were no Linear B tablets now, no grandeur, no scribes, no master craftsmen, no tholos tombs. Chamber tombs disappeared and were replaced by simple cist burials in Argolis, Attica and Boeotia. By 1120 BC all the trappings of the Mycenaean civilization had disappeared; the Mycenaean period had finally petered out and the Dark Ages had begun.[28] After a few centuries, it was Argos that became the central place in Argolis, its status far outstripping that of Mycenae. The past of Argos was elaborately dressed to display this newly enhanced status. In the second century AD, when Pausanias visited Argos, he was shown the earth mound where the head of Medusa the Gorgon, a mythical contemporary of Perseus, was buried. Ariadne too was said to be buried at Argos.[29] Aeschylus was obliged by political correctness to set his *Agamemnon* in Argos, though it is clear that the place described is really Mycenae.

10

AND LIVE IN SONG FOR
GENERATIONS

THE MYCENAEAN PERSONALITY

We have known about the Mycenaean civilization through archaeology for only a century and a quarter. During that short time, several different images have emerged. The most enduring and indelible image is the one that predates the archaeological phase, the benchmark image we have been given by Homer. Homer has proved to be both a blessing and a curse to archaeology, sometimes supplying a validation for archaeological interpretation, but also misleading by incorporating anachronistic details from both before and after the heroic age – as well as including unknown quantities of pure fiction.

But even without Homer, if it is possible to set the epic vision aside, archaeology has pointed the way towards two very different pasts. There is a glossy, romantic Mycenaean civilization, as seen in the reconstructions painted by Piet de Jong. In this civilization the palace at Pylos becomes a gleaming, luminous, multi-coloured, Art Deco wonderland. Elaborately painted ceilings and beams are held aloft on tall and graceful fluted columns. The matt painted plaster floor is transformed by the artist into polished marble. Three courtiers chat with the youthful king as he relaxes elegantly on his throne. The overall image is cool and airy, full of light and grace.[1] The other Mycenaean civilization is dark, barbaric and primitive, dominated by ruthless egotistical warrior chiefs desperate to establish their dynasties by acquiring wealth and building grim oppressive citadels to frighten their enemies and cow their subjects. This is a Mycenae of greed and terror, Mycenae rich in gold.[2]

The two interpretations both contain elements of the bronze age reality, but are both partial. There was a war-like and aggressive aspect, but there was also fine architecture and artwork of extraordinary sophistication. There is an element of distortion for effect in the presentation. The airiness of Piet de Jong's Pylos palace, for example, has been achieved partly by flooding the chamber with light, when in reality there were no windows and only a small amount of reflected light could have got in through the light-well

226

or doorway, and partly by exaggerating the size of the chamber. The real room is 11m wide when, to judge from the height of the people, the room in de Jong's painting is half as wide again. The reflections on the floor make the columns seem loftier, but a matt-painted stucco floor can never have produced reflections in this way.

The two views are themselves, in part, a reflection of changes through time. The Early Mycenaean culture of the sixteenth and fifteenth centuries was different from the Late Mycenaean culture of the fourteenth and thirteenth centuries. The Early Mycenaean chiefs were obsessed with investing time and wealth in a celebration of death, and to an extent that is alien to native Greek antecedents. The style of the extravagantly rich shaft grave burials is so different from anything else in Middle Helladic Greece that it almost looks like an importation. In the Late Mycenaean culture, the mentality seems to change markedly – from the architecture of monumental graves to the architecture of temples and citadels, from warrior aristocrats to scribes and priestesses, from the aggrandizement of chiefs to the organization of a temple-palace economy, from extravagance to sobriety, from the world of the dead to the world of the living.[3] These shifts of emphasis resolve some of the apparent contrasts, including the often pointed out contrast between the moody and volatile warrior-aristocrats depicted in Homer and the coolly rational and systematic bureaucrats who ran the temple-palace economy.

On the other hand, this image of the later culture can mislead; while the scribes were calmly listing offerings on clay tablets, gangs of labourers were busy strengthening the fortifications of the great citadels. The Early Mycenaean society generated a competitive warrior-élite, a dynastic thrust that was doubtless one of the mainsprings of the Late Mycenaean society. The strongly military character of Late Mycenaean society and the development of the fortresses both sprang from that. This was a civilization built on quarrels, feuds, raids, wars. The Mycenaeans thrived on an atmosphere of armed and tense watchfulness. To an extent this was creative, in generating a spirit of competition and ambition. Homer shows this aspect of the Mycenaean world well, but he also shows the negative side of it: the difficulties in overcoming personal rivalries in order to achieve a common goal.[4] Agamemnon is depicted in Homer as a powerful High King with authority over a confederation of Achaean kingdoms, yet even he has great difficulty in organizing concerted action. The Linear B tablets make no reference to a High King at all, but imply instead that the Mycenaean states were autonomous. That division must have weakened them when joint action was needed – for defence.

Homer describes a society with an emphasis on clan structure, valour, pride in social position, glamorization of war, vainglorious boasting, brutal contempt for ordinary people, and the relegation of women to pretty possessions. Hector of Troy (who is also culturally a Mycenaean) says, 'Grant that this boy of mine may be, like me, pre-eminent in Troy; as strong and brave as me; a mighty king of Ilium'.[5] The political leaders in Homer are highly-strung, quick-tempered aristocrats, full of pride and rivalry; sometimes they behave more like spoilt brats in a boys' prep school than kings. Quarrels flare up all the time, between Agamemnon and Achilles, between Thersites and Odysseus, between Hector and Paris. The Achaean High King, Agamemnon, is as hot-blooded as any: 'The noble son of Atreus, imperial Agamemnon, leapt up in anger. His heart was seething with black passion and his eyes were like points of flame.'[6] This is not at all the society we see in the Linear B tablets dating from 1200 BC, and it may be that Homer is describing a society that is rather later – or earlier – than that of the tablets.

What is certain from the archaeology is that the Mycenaeans were electrified by the Minoan civilization, which they admired intensely and tried to emulate. The grandiose temple-palaces of Crete were not exactly copied on the Greek mainland, but similarly complex and expensive buildings – megastructures – were built at each urban centre, the biggest possibly not at Mycenae but at Thebes. The wall-paintings too were imitated, even to copies of bull-leaping frescoes.

WHAT WAS THE MYCENAEAN ACHIEVEMENT?

The distinctive Minoan-Mycenaean social and political structure was never to irradiate the rest of Europe. This may perhaps be because the complex economy and society developed in the Aegean had little relevance to the pre-urban communities of Europe. Perhaps the Mycenaean civilization was a little too far advanced in relation to the northern and central European communities to stimulate them to develop in the way that it had been stimulated by Minoan Crete, Hittite Anatolia and the great states and empires of the Near East; perhaps the gap was too wide. Mycenae had absorbed cultural ripples from Europe, and was one element in a complex web of interacting cells, yet it always remained on its edge, feeding on it without influencing it, except in a very indirect way, by stimulating commodity production in various remote places such as the copper mines of Ireland and Wales.[7]

Along with that failure came the collapse of the temple-palace society. During the centuries that followed, nowhere in Europe, Greece included, would have societies that were centred on great focal buildings, which is why interpreting the temple-palaces of Greece and Crete has posed so many problems. The 'Urnfield' Europe that followed was a very different Europe, with an emphasis on hill-forts, field systems, flat cemeteries, scrap hoards, votive offerings in rivers, and altogether less political order.[8] In Greece itself, life continued but at a culturally lower level; people returned to their agricultural base, to a more modest subsistence economy.[9] The repertoire of pottery styles shrank accordingly.[10]

The language of the Mycenaeans however did survive, as Greek, and from what we have seen some of their history and poetry survived too, in the tradition preserved in Homer. Elements of the Mycenaean religion and the myths and legends that surrounded it survived.[11] That is appropriate in that the Mycenaeans themselves had a distinct view of the past. Just as we value what has survived of them, they valued things that had survived from still more ancient times and attributed magical value to them. Five scarabs were found in the cabin of the Cape Gelidonia ship, which was wrecked in about 1200 BC on the southern coast of Anatolia. Some of the scarabs were then, at the time of the ancient shipwreck, as much as four hundred years old. A Syrian cylinder seal, possibly belonging to the captain, was made in the eighteenth century, and was therefore fully five hundred years old when the ship went down.

In common with other peoples of their time, the Mycenaeans were a sacrificial people. They regularly gave offerings of produce, gold and human sacrifices to appease the gods. They fed off existing neighbouring cultures, such as the Egyptian, Hittite and Minoan civilizations, selecting distinctive strands and copying and developing them in their own way. The Mycenaean culture was to a great extent a continuation of the regional Aegean culture. Like the great civilizations of ancient Egypt and Mesopotamia and Minoan Crete, the Mycenaean civilization was temple-centred. Like Egypt and Mesopotamia and Hatti, it had a grandiose élite, whose status was flaunted in extravagant and impressive building projects – the citadels and the tholos tombs.

The tablets imply a severely bureaucratic society, strongly centralized with a great deal of hierarchical control. That may not be the whole picture. The painted floor of the Pylos throne room, the most important room in the capital of a powerful Mycenaean state, contains a major mistake. It was intended to be a chessboard pattern, the squares filled with intricately differentiated marbled textures. The lines were probably drawn, starting at the north-west wall, by stretching string from pegs along the north-east and south-west walls. The hearth in the middle of the room interrupted this process after only four lines. On the far side of the hearth, the wrong pegs were joined and the result is parallelograms instead of squares.[12] In a rigidly autocratic society the workmen would have been punished (severely) and made to start again, but the mistake was apparently ignored, or at any rate indulged. This suggests a pleasantly relaxed society – one in which craftsmen were allowed to make occasional mistakes. Or is there something more telling still hidden in this incident? Is it that the bureaucratic process was so rigid that it did not contain the flexible procedures needed to deal with mistakes, disobedience or failures of competence? If so, we may be seeing one of the reasons why the civilization disintegrated. Either way, the unintended parallelograms were never repainted.

THE MYCENAEAN INHERITANCE

The oral transmission of the heroic story of the Trojan War was a slow fuse that would ignite the classical world once it came to be written down in the eighth century BC. The effect on Mycenae itself was immediate and spectacular. Just outside its walls, within decades of the writing down of the epic tale, the Agamemnoneion was built, the Sanctuary of Agamemnon. The Mycenaeans' perception of their own past was being altered.[13] From the arrival of the epic tale in written form, Greeks saw themselves differently – and behaved differently. It is a fine example of the power of the written word.

Alexander nursed a great admiration for Homer, and thought of himself as re-enacting scenes from the *Iliad*. He laid a wreath on the tomb of Achilles and called him a lucky man, in that he, Achilles, had Homer to proclaim his deeds and preserve his memory.[14] He donated his armour to the Temple of Athena at Troy. Alexander's brutal treatment of Betis, governor of Gaza, was modelled on the way Achilles punished his enemy by having him dragged behind a chariot. Alexander's obsession with Roxane was a conscious parallel with Achilles' infatuation with Briseis. Alexander's re-enactment of Homer was noticed by Plutarch. Homer has something to answer for in nurturing and encouraging this latter-day 'sacker of cities', who may have had that phrase ringing in his ears as he destroyed the magnificent city of Persepolis.

On a less theatrical plane, the Mycenaeans were also responsible for transmitting a range of arts and crafts. By first admiring and then imitating, the Mycenaeans passed various Minoan arts and crafts on to later generations. One example is the art of cloisonné enamel, a very particular jewellers' craft. Cloisonné involves using heat to fuse coloured glass into cells created by carving or wiring. The decoration on the Kourion sceptre is a fine example. There are also high-status sword and dagger hilts embellished in this lavish way.[15] It is easy to see why warriors were prepared to risk their lives to strip princely enemies of armour and weapons in the heat of battle: the prize was often a collection of objects of enormous beauty as well as value. The cloisonné technique may have been invented in the Aegean, or developed earlier in Egypt and imported from there. It was not used much and seems to have been forgotten. The technique was rediscovered by Byzantine goldsmiths two thousand years later.[16]

The Mycenaean civilization was more advanced than the cultures of the rest of Europe. So many of its attributes and achievements were borrowed, continued or held in high regard in later centuries that it is legitimate to regard the Mycenaean lands as a cradle of civilization. The heartland of the Mycenaean civilization consisted of the Peloponnese and the southern part of central Greece. Within that, much of the driving energy seems to have come from western Argolis, the Argive Plain and its surrounding foothills. Argolis might be added to the list of cradles of great Old World civilizations: the Indus valley, the Nile valley, Palestine, Mesopotamia and Crete.

According to the ancient Greeks, coins were invented in Argolis. The ability to convert any commodity or service into currency led to far greater flexibility in trade than barter. It made a great socio-economic leap forward possible. The place where coinage was invented, if it can be identified, would have a strong claim to being a cradle of civilization. According to Ephorus of Cyme, it was Phaidon, the early seventh-century tyrant of Argos, who struck the first Greek coins. These were the so-called 'tortoises' of Aegina. Phaidon struck these coins and dedicated to Hera the suddenly-obsolete iron spits that had previously been used as currency.[17] The coins were obviously more convenient to handle. There is even corroboration from archaeology for this remarkable story. One hundred and eighty iron spits were found in the ruins of the Argive Heraion in 1895, giving good reason to believe that Argolis was the birthplace of modern coinage.

The Mycenaeans were pioneers of modern engineering, launching large-scale and ambitious projects unmatched in Europe until the Roman period. The engineering projects included designing fortifications, building aqueducts such as the one bringing water into Pylos, building dams to divert rivers, and the huge scheme to reclaim Lake Copais. On a smaller scale, the Mycenaeans created terraces for agriculture, built level roads suitable for wheeled traffic, and designed bridges and culverts. Much of this work was a continuation of the Minoan preoccupation with hydraulic engineering.

They also made many architectural innovations. A simple one was the relieving triangle, a device for spreading the weight of a wall sideways and down onto door jambs. It was a significant halfway-house between the lintel and the arch. It was used on a flamboyant scale in the doorway to the Treasury of Atreus, where it was used to take the weight off a massive lintel, and in a less obtrusive way in the 'arches' of bridges and culverts, which had the same triangular form. Even the small windows piercing the rubble walls of houses and shrines were triangular, and lined with three stone slabs.

The Mycenaeans borrowed the downward-tapering Minoan pillar with its characteristic cushion capital, but refined and developed it. The typical Mycenaean pillar was taller, thinner, less tapering. These pillars were also used in rows to make colonnades, which created dazzling effects with alternating bars of light and shadow. The main courtyard of the temple at Tiryns had colonnades round three sides. This idea was later turned inside out to become a major exterior feature of Greek temples. The Parthenon is surrounded on all four sides by a spectacular colonnade, which became the main architectural effect. Colonnades were not a Mycenaean invention. There were colonnades in the temples at Luxor, Hattusa, Mallia and Phaistos. The Mycenaean use of the colonnade was nevertheless the probable means by which the architectural device became available to the archaic and classical architects of Greece.

The Parthenon was built without mortar. Like Mycenaean masonry, and Minoan masonry before that, the masonry of the classical Parthenon was held together by metal. Mycenaean ashlar masonry was carefully secured with vertical pins seated in square sockets or clamps. The classical masonry of the Parthenon was held together by horizontal H-shaped clamps, but the principle was similar.

Mycenaean architects seem to have invented attached half-columns, a decorative relief feature which became a major feature of Greek, Roman and Renaissance public architecture, though usually in flattened form. As far as I have been able to discover, the half-column makes its first appearance on the sculpted decoration for the relieving triangle above the huge doorway of the Treasury of Atreus. Later, the pilaster would be used by Michelangelo for St Peter's in Rome. The pilaster and attached half-column are a way of adding strong vertical lines within a façade, in addition to the edges of door and window apertures, and tying the top to the bottom at one unifying stroke. The device became a favourite with Michelangelo, enabling him to produce aesthetically strong wall designs.

Figure 10.1 Miniature ivory columns from the House of Shields, 3cm and 4.5cm tall. Probably made as fittings for furniture, they show how elaborate some of the full-sized columns were. They also display the fluting and gentle downward taper of the Mycenaean column.

Figure 10.2 The entrance to the Tomb of Clytemnestra, excavated by Sophie Schliemann. Mrs Schliemann stands in front of the partially cleared doorway. The huge relieving triangle would have been concealed by a decorative carved slab.

The Mycenaeans also adopted the fluted column, apparently from the Egyptians. Most Egyptian columns consisted of a series of curved bulges, but there were some with curved grooves that were made as early as 3000 BC at Saqqara. This unusual design, the 'Egyptian' fluted column, was in wide-spread use in Mycenaean Greece. The casts or imprints of full-sized fluted columns are found at some sites, and miniature ivory inlays showing both flutes and very elaborately carved capitals have survived. The last of the nine tholos tombs to be built at Mycenae was the Tomb of Clytemnestra. Its façade was decorated with attached half-columns of gypsum. These were carefully and beautifully carved with ornate capitals and vertical fluting.[18] This monument, which remained visible, may have been the means by which the fluted column was passed on to the architects of the first millennium, when it became a major feature of classical architecture, both Greek and Roman.

The Mycenaeans were the first to develop military architecture in Greece. Specially designed defensive architecture made its first appearance at Lerna in 2500 BC, with a strongly made defensive wall and miniature semi-circular bastions.[19] The same thing is seen in Euboea and at Kolonna on Aigina, so there was a locally generated tradition of defensive walling. It is not clear whether the fortification concept continued to develop independently; it may be that later on a fully fledged defensive architecture was borrowed from the Hittites; possibly the Mycenaean and Hittite traditions developed in parallel. The Hittite capital, Hattusa, had imposing fortification walls with bastions and massive gateways. To this already highly developed military architecture, the Mycenaeans added the single projecting bastion on the right hand side of the gateway – a distinctive innovation of their own. It was the beginning of a long tradition of urban fortification in Europe, as well as castle architecture, a tradition that reached its eventual culmination in structures like Caernarvon Castle in Wales and, closer to the heart of things, the Palamidi Fort at Nauplion.

As we saw in Chapter 6, the architectural concepts of house and shrine converged on the megaron, which could be used for either purpose, and then on the megastructure known as the palace. This convergence of ideas was followed through in the Athenian Acropolis. The ground plans of the Parthenon and the Archaic Temple of Artemis in Ephesus were further developments from the megaron design. The Parthenon was a temple to Athena

Plate 10.1 A modern bank in Nauplion – in Mycenaean style. It fits remarkably unobtrusively into a modern Mediterranean townscape, showing a continuity of architectural tradition.

– no one disputes that – but it was also described in a recent television documentary on the Acropolis as 'a *palace* fit for a goddess'. This is close to the Mycenaean phrase describing a temple to the goddess at Thebes: 'the *House* of Potnia.' This idea too was passed down through the Mycenaean civilization and was an inheritance from the earlier Minoan civilization.

The names of the gods and goddesses of the Mycenaeans lived on through many later generations. Hera, Artemis and Athena were Mycenaean goddesses long before they entered the classical pantheon. Both Homer and the evidence of the frescoes tell us that the Mycenaeans believed it was possible to meet and parley with the gods. People could encounter gods and have their destinies shaped by them. Much later, in about 550 BC, Peisistratus exploited this idea. He claimed he had had such an experience himself, so he had probably been steeped from childhood in Homeric tales.

The Mycenaean trading empire had its descendant in Pericles' Athenian trading empire, a fifth-century BC trading network extending from Britain in the west to India in the east. Like the Mycenaean empire before it, Periclean Athens was bellicose, always picking quarrels, always ready to go to war with rivals. Pericles persuaded the Athenians to go to war with Sparta, leading them into a bitter dragging conflict lasting a decade – not unlike the Trojan War 800 years before. The Mycenaeans left behind them a hard, militaristic tradition that would be held up by many later generations as a model for individual manliness and collective strength, the complement of the priestess-dominated civilization of the Minoans that the Mycenaeans displaced.

Above all, the Mycenaeans gave us the heroic ideal – the notion that it is nobler than anything else imaginable to risk everything for glory. The Homeric picture of the Mycenaean Greeks is a picture of a quarrelsome people, quick to anger, quick to resort to arms. It is a picture of a warrior élite to whom personal honour meant everything. The Homeric heroes were brave to the point of foolhardiness. They believed that the gods took sides, yet they fought on even when they knew the gods supported their enemies. In his fight to the death with Aeneas, Diomedes 'knew that Apollo himself had taken him [Aeneas] under his protection, but he cared nothing even for that great god, and persisted in his efforts to kill Aeneas'.[20] The gods impersonated mortals sometimes, which occasionally meant doing battle with the gods. This was hubris on a grand scale. The archaeology, as far as it goes, tells a similar story. The citadel walls speak of fierce feuding, and the architecture of the fortifications and tombs is swaggering and vainglorious.

Cleisthenes, brother of Peisistratus, was inspired by the Homeric and ultimately Mycenaean ideal of the hero ready to risk everything for glory. Cleisthenes organized the conspiracy to overthrow the tyrant Hippias, who was Peisistratus' son. Cleisthenes overthrew Hippias in 510 BC, but was then himself overthrown by Isagoras with the aid of Spartan allies. The

Plate 10.2 The citadel wall at Mycenae. This deliberately forbidding wall corner domin-
ates the approach to the Lion Gate (off picture to the right). The natural
rock outcrop in the foreground appears to have been deliberately smoothed
off to make it harder for attackers to climb.

Athenians were inspired by the Homeric ideals evidenced by the Olympic
Games, where anyone could compete and gain fame and glory; they overthrew Isagoras, recalled Cleisthenes and set up a democracy. Mycenaean
values enshrined in Homer conditioned both aristocrats and ordinary citizens
in Greece to behave in a particular way, conditioned them to pursue victory,
fame and glory at any cost. This found echoes in several later cultures,
including classical Greece and Rome and the major revival of aspects of
those cultures in the Renaissance. The grand reckless gestures of the great
Elizabethans, for example, owe much to the Mycenaean heroic tradition.
The Mycenaeans' great wish was to be remembered for their heroic deeds,
'and live in song for generations'.[21] It was Homer's epic poetry that made
their dream come true. The still-grand ruins of their tombs show that
Homer's heroic view was real. The warriors hoped to transcend death
through the memory of the living – by leaving an everlasting tomb, by
achieving fame through valour on the field of battle, and by dying beautifully in the flower of youth.[22] That Mycenaean concept of beauty in death
has fed cultures for many generations since, an almost irresistibly heart-
swelling – yet dangerous – idea.

They went with songs to the battle, they were young,
Straight of limb, true of eye, steady and aglow.
They were staunch to the end against odds uncounted,
They fell with their face to the foe.

They shall grow not old, as we that are left grow old:
Age shall not weary them, nor the years condemn,
At the going down of the sun and in the morning
We will remember them.[23]

Appendix A

ANATOLIAN CHRONOLOGY

SECOND HITTITE DYNASTY
(APPROXIMATE DATES)

Tudhaliyas I	1740–1710
Pu-Sarrumas	1710–1680
Labarnas	1680–1650
Hattusilis I	1650–1590
Mursilis I	1620–1590
Hantilis I	1650–1590
Zidantas I	1560–1550
Ammunas	1550–1530
Huzziyas I	1530–1525
Telipinus	1525–1500
Alluwamnas	1500–1490
Hantilis II	1490–1480
Zidantas II	1480–1470
Huzziyas II	1470–1460

THIRD HITTITE DYNASTY

Tudhaliyas II	1460–1440
Arnuwandas I	1440–1420
Hattusilis II	1420–1400
Tudhaliyas III	1400–1380
Suppiluliumas I	1380–1334
Arnuwandas II	1334–1333
Mursilis II	1333–1308
Muwatallis	1308–1285
Urhi-Teshub (Mursilis III)	1285–1278
Hattusilis III	1278–1250
Tudhaliyas IV	1250–1220
Arnuwandas III	1220–1200
Suppiluliumas II	1200–1180

Appendix B

THE KINGS OF MYCENAE

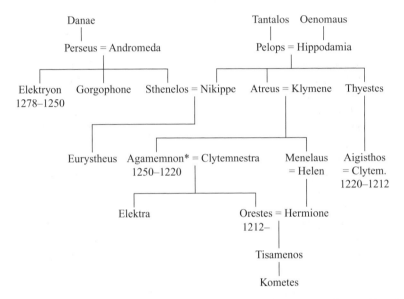

* Agamemnon was the son of Pleisthenes and the grandson of Atreus according to Hesiod, in which case the dates might have run Atreus (1278–1260), Pleisthenes (1260–1240), Agamemnon (1240–1220).

Appendix C

THE KINGS OF ORCHOMENOS

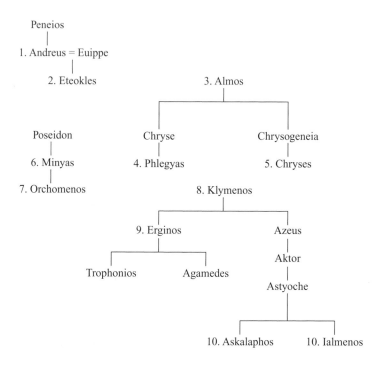

Askalaphos and Ialmenos jointly led the Orchomenos contingent to Troy, and were therefore contemporaries of Agamemnon. Thomson (1949, 188) comments that this regnal list represents an incoherent tradition. It may even so fairly represent a succession via four unrelated dynasties.

Appendix D

KING LIST FOR ARGOS

This traditional king list shows the (alleged) kings of Argos in chronological order, beginning with Argos himself.

Argos
Phorbas
Triopas
Iasus
Crotopus
Gelanor
Danaus (African immigrant and
    usurper; descendants were
    called Danaans)

Abas
Perseus
Megapenthes
Anaxagoras (after Anaxagoras,
    Argos was divided into
    three kingdoms)

THREE KINGDOMS OF ARGOS

Alector
Iphis
Sthenelus

Bias
Talaus
Adrastus
Aegialeus

Melampus
Antiphates
Oicles
Amphiaraus
Amphilochus

(After Amphilochus, the kingdom was reunified.)

REUNIFICATION OF ARGOS

Cylarabes
Orestes
Tisamenus
Temenus

Deiphontes
Cisus
Medon

Appendix E

THE EPIC CYCLE

The tradition of the Mycenaean expeditions to Anatolia and their aftermath was preserved in a sequence of poems together known as the Epic Cycle. It includes the *Kypria*, the *Iliad*, the *Aithiopis*, the *Little Iliad*, the *Ilioupersis* (the Sack of Ilios), the *Nostoi* (the Homecomings), the *Odyssey* and the *Telegoneia*. The *Iliad* and *Odyssey* have survived intact. The other poems have not, though we know their names and their contents because they were referred to in antiquity; fragments of some of them have survived as quotations.

The *Kypria* deals with the period immediately before the *Iliad* and gives additional information about the events running up to the attack on Troy. It may have been written in the eighth or seventh century BC, and there is a tradition that Kyprias of Halikarnossos was its author; the poem probably in any case contains material from a much older oral tradition. Although the *Kypria* itself has not survived, Proklos wrote a summary of it which has. Full texts of the *Iliad* and *Odyssey* are easily available (such as the Penguin translations by E. V. Rieu and Robert Fagles), but the Proklan summaries of the other poems are not, so it may be useful to quote some of them here.

THE PROKLAN SUMMARY OF THE *KYPRIA*

1 Zeus, with Themis, plans the Trojan War.
  While the gods are feasting at the wedding of Peleus, Eris stirs up a
    dispute among Athena, Hera and Aphrodite about their beauty.
  They are led by Hermes at the order of Zeus to Mount Ida for
    judgement by Alexandros.
  Alexandros, encouraged by the promise of marriage with Helen,
    decides in Aphrodite's favour.
5 Then on Aphrodite's advice he builds a fleet.
  Helenos prophesies to them concerning the future.
  Aphrodite commands Aineias to sail with Alexandros.
  Kassandra foretells future events.

After landing in the country of Lakedaimon Alexandros is welcomed
    as a xenos by the sons of Tyndaros,
10 and after that in Sparta by Menelaus;
    and Alexandros gives presents to Helen during a feast.
    Next Menelaus sails off to Crete, telling Helen to provide the guests
        with all their needs while he is away.
    Meanwhile Aphrodite brings Helen and Alexandros together.
    After their mating they load a mass of treasure on board and sail away
        by night.
15 Hera stirs up a storm against them,
    Landing at Sidon, Alexandros sacks the city.
    They sail to Troy, where Alexandros marries Helen.
    Meanwhile Kastor and Polydeukes are caught in the act
    of stealing the cattle of Idas and Lynkeus.
20 Kastor is slain by Idas, but Lynkeus and Idas are killed by
        Polydeukes.
    Zeus gives them [Kastor and Polydeukes] immortality on alternate
        days.
    Afterwards Iris reports to Menelaus what has been happening at
        home.
    He comes back and with his brother plans an expedition against Ilios,
    and then goes on to visit Nestor.
25 In a digression, Nestor describes to him how Epopeus was utterly
        destroyed after seducing the daughter of Lykourgos,
    and the tale of Oedipus,
    the madness of Herakles,
    and the story of Theseus and Ariadne.
    Then they journey over Hellas and assemble the leaders.
30 Odysseus pretends to be mad, since he is unwilling to join the
        expedition,
    but they find him out; at Palamedes' suggestion they kidnap his son
        Telemachus, forcing him to go.
    After that the leaders meet together at Aulis and sacrifice.
    The portent of the snake and the sparrows is revealed
    and Calchas foretells to them what the outcome will be.
35 Then they put to sea and land at Teuthrania and, taking it for Ilios,
        sack it.
    Telephos rushes out in defence and kills Thersandros, son of
        Polyneikes,
    and is wounded himself by Achilles.
    A storm falls on them as they sail away from Mysia and they are
        scattered.
    Achilles lands at Skyros and marries Deidameia, daughter of
        Lykomedes.

40 Telephos comes to Argos, prompted by an oracle,
and is healed by Achilles, so that he might become their guide on the
    voyage to Ilios.
The fleet gathers for a second time at Aulis.
While hunting, Agamemnon shoots a stag and boasts that he is better
    than Artemis.
So the goddess is angry and sends storms to hold them back from
    sailing.
45 Calchas explains the anger of the goddess and tells them to sacrifice
    Iphigeneia to Artemis.
They send for her as though she is to be a bride for Achilles
and prepare to sacrifice her.
But Artemis snatches her away and conveys her to Tauris
makes her immortal,
50 and sets a deer on the altar in place of the maiden.
Next they sail to Tenedos.
While they are feasting Philoctetes is bitten by a water snake
and is abandoned on Lemnos owing to the evil stench of the
    wound.
Achilles is given a late invitation
55 and quarrels with Agamemnon.
Then they go ashore at Ilios but the Trojans hem them in
and Protesilaos is killed by Hector.
Then Achilles drives them off and slays Kyknos son of Poseidon.
Next they take up their dead
60 and send an embassy to the Trojans to demand the return of Helen
    and the treasure.
But when the Trojans pay no heed they attack the city wall,
and next go out into the countryside and sack the cities round
    about.
Afterwards Achilles longs to see Helen,
and Aphrodite and Thetis arrange a meeting.
65 Next, when the Achaeans are eager to return home, Achilles checks
    them.
He drives off the cattle of Aineias
and lays waste Lyrnessos and Pedasos and many of the nearby
    cities,
and he kills Troilus.
Patroklos takes Lykaon to Lemnos and sells him into slavery.
70 Achilles takes Briseis as his prize out of the spoils, and Agamemnon
    Chryseis.
The death of Palamedes follows,
and the plan of Zeus to relieve the Trojans by withdrawing Achilles
    from

the alliance of the Achaeans,
and a catalogue of all those who fought together against the Trojans.

The *Iliad* follows.

THE PROKLAN SUMMARY OF
THE *AITHIOPIS*

1 The Amazon Penthesileia, daughter of Ares and a Thracian by birth,
    comes to Troy as a Trojan ally.
  Achilles kills her in the middle of her aristeia
  and the Trojans arrange her funeral.
  Thersites reviles and reproaches Achilles, saying that he loved
    Penthesileia, and is slain by Achilles.
5 A quarrel arises among the Achaeans about Thersites' murder.
  After this, Achilles sails to Lesbos, offers sacrifices to Apollo,
    Artemis and Leto,
  and is purified of the murder by Odysseus.
  Memnon, the son of Eos, who owns armour made by Hephaistos,
    comes to the aid of the Trojans.
  Thetis tells her son the outcome of events concerning Memnon.
10 In battle, Antilochus is killed by Memnon
  but Achilles kills Memnon.
  At this, Eos asks Zeus for immortality for Memnon, and it is
    granted.
  While routing Trojans and rushing into the citadel, Achilles is
    killed by Paris and Apollo.
  A heated battle begins over the corpse,
15 and Aias [Ajax] picks it up and carries it off to the ships,
  while Odysseus fights off the Trojans.
  Then they hold funeral rites for Antilochos
  and lay out the body of Achilles.
  Thetis comes with her sisters and the Muses and makes a lament
    for her son.
20 Then Thetis snatches him from the pyre
  and carries him over to the island of Leuke.
  But the Achaeans heap up his burial mound and hold funeral
    games;
  a quarrel breaks out between Odysseus and Aias over the armour of
    Achilles.

THE PROKLAN SUMMARY OF
THE *LITTLE ILIAD*

1 There is the judgement for the armour, and Odysseus wins,
    thanks to the machinations of Athena,
    but Aias goes mad, defiles the herds of the Achaeans and kills himself.
    After this, Odysseus goes on an ambush, capturing Helenos.
5 As a result of Helenos' prophecy about the city's conquest,
    Diomedes fetches Philoctetes from Lemnos.
    Makhaon heals Philoctetes.
    Philoctetes fights in single combat with Alexandros and kills him.
    The corpse is mutilated by Menelaus,
10 but the Trojans retrieve it and hold funeral rites.
    After this, Deiphobos marries Helen.
    Odysseus fetches Neoptolemos from Skyros;
    he gives him his father's armour
    and the ghost of Achilles appears to Neoptolemos.
15 Eurypylos, son of Telephos, comes to the aid of the Trojans as an ally.
    While he is having his aristeia, Neoptolemos kills him.
    Troy is under siege.
    Epeios builds the wooden horse, under Athena's direction.
    Odysseus, disguising himself [as a beggar], goes into Ilion as a spy.
20 Helen recognizes him.
    Jointly, they plan the capture of the city.
    Odysseus kills several Trojans and returns to the ships.
    After this, Odysseus and Diomedes carry the Palladion out of Ilion.
    The aristoi of the Achaeans climb into the wooden horse.
25 The rest set fire to their tents and sail away to Tenedos.
    The Trojans believe the siege is over.
    Pulling down part of the wall,
    they drag the wooden horse into the city,
    and feast if they had conquered the Achaeans.

THE PROKLAN SUMMARY OF
THE *ILIOUPERSIS*

1 Suspicious about the horse, the Trojans stand about wondering what
      to do.
    Some want to push it off a cliff,
    some want to burn it,
    and some say that it is hieros and want to dedicate it to Athena.
5 In the end the third group prevails.
    They give way to merry-making, feasting as if the war was over.

At this point two serpents appear and destroy Laokoon and one of his
    sons.

Aineias and his followers grow uneasy at this wonder and withdraw to
    mount Ida.

Sinon, who joined the Trojans as a spy, lights signal fires for the
    Achaeans.

10 who sail back from Tenedos,

and those inside the wooden horse fall upon their enemies.

They kill many and take the city by force.

Neoptolemos kills Priam, who has taken refuge at the altar of Zeus
    Herkeios.

Menelaus murders Deiphobos.

15 He finds Helen and takes her down to the ships.

Aias son of Oileus takes Cassandra by force, dragging her away from
    the xoanon of Athena.

Angry at this outrage, the Achaeans want to stone Aias to death,

but he takes refuge at the altar of Athena,

where he is safe from immediate danger.

20 The Achaeans put the city to the torch,

slaughtering Polyxena on the tomb of Achilles.

Odysseus kills Astyanax,

and Neoptolemos takes Andromache as his prize.

The rest of the spoils are shared out.

25 Demophon and Akamas find their mother Aithra and take her with
    them.

Then the Achaeans sail away,

while Athena plots their destruction at sea.

THE PROKLAN SUMMARY OF THE *NOSTOI*

1 Athena causes Agamemnon and Menelaus to quarrel about the voyage
    home.

Agamemnon stays on to appease the wrath of Athena.

Diomedes and Nestor set sail and return home safely.

Then Menelaus sets sail,

5 reaching Egypt with five ships, the rest being lost in a storm.

Those following Calchas, Leontes and Polypoites travel overland to
    Colophon, arranging a funeral there for Teiresias, who dies there.

The ghost of Achilles appears to those following Agamemnon as they
    are setting sail,

and it tries to stop them from continuing by prophesying future
    events.

Then the storm at the rocks called Kapherides is described,

10 and the destruction of Locrian Aias.
    Warned by Thetis, Neoptolemos makes his journey overland
    and, coming to Thrace, meets Odysseus at Maroneia,
    and then finishes the rest of his journey,
    after arranging a funeral for Phoinix, who dies along the way.
15 He himself arrives in the land of the Molossoi
    and is recognized by Peleus.
    Then comes the murder of Agamemnon by Aigisthos and
        Clytemnestra
    and the vengeance of Orestes
    and the safe return of Menelaus.

The *Odyssey* follows (the return of Odysseus)

The *Telegoneia* follows (the death of Odysseus)

NOTES

1 INTRODUCTION

1 Homer says that Odysseus came from Ithaca; Polis in Ithaca is the likeliest location for his harbour town. Wace and Stubbings 1962; Pentreath 1964, 155–60.
2 George Grote's 1846 *History of Greece* (London).
3 Pausanias Book II, 16, 5.
4 Schliemann 1868, 19.
5 Traill 1995, 49–50.
6 Traill 1995, 74.
7 Chadwick 1976, 182.
8 *Iliad* Book 10, lines 300–10.
9 The isolated mention of an iron arrowhead in the *Iliad* is an anachronism that must have been introduced in Homer's time. There are several implicit references to iron weapons in that swords are credited with doing things that bronze swords simply could not do. Achilles strikes a man on the neck, sending both head and helmet flying (*Iliad* 20, 482), and only a sword made of iron or steel could do this.
10 *Iliad* 23, 917–27.
11 Chadwick 1976, 185.
12 Chadwick 1976, 186.
13 Ozanne 1997, 27.
14 Feuer 1996.
15 Pausanias IX, 36, 3.

2 CITIES AND KINGDOMS

1 Michelet 1864.
2 Cunliffe 1998, 227.
3 *Odyssey* 15, 80.
4 Cunliffe 1998, 232.
5 Zangger 1998a, 5–6.
6 Strabo *Geography* 8. 4. 2.
7 Strabo *Geography* 8. 3. 7.
8 Chadwick 1976, 154.
9 Chadwick 1976, 37.
10 Palmer 1961, 83, 100, 101, 150–1; Chadwick 1976, 42–5; Bennet 1998, 117–23.

11 Bennet 1998, 122–3.
12 Palmer 1961, 78–9; Bennet 1998, 120.
13 *Iliad* 9, 179–83. Intriguingly, the towns are listed twice as 'facing the sea at the far edge of sandy Pylos'; in other words they are on the furthest edge of the Further Province, considered from the standpoint of the administrators at Pylos, the chief town of the kingdom.
14 Palmer 1961, 1977.
15 *Odyssey* 3, 210.
16 Jones 1967.
17 Cunliffe 1998, 225–6.
18 Cartledge 1979.
19 Huxley 1962; Simpson 1981; King 2002.
20 Harrison and Spencer 1998, 24.
21 Simpson 1965.
22 Chadwick 1976, 14.
23 French 2002, 25–6.
24 Diamant 1988, 153.
25 Davis 1986, 155.
26 Diamant 1988, 153–9.
27 Diodorus IV. 68.
28 Lehmann 1977, 230.
29 Palmer 1961, 211.
30 Palmer 1961, 214.
31 Davis 1998c, 56.
32 It is assumed that an initial smaller kingdom, the Hither Province, later expanded when the Further Province was added.
33 Davis 1998c, 58.
34 The fresco fragment is in Hora Museum.
35 Castleden 1991, 28.
36 Castleden 1991, 46, 136.
37 Castleden 1991, 27–8.
38 Blegen and Rawson 2001, 34.
39 Bennet 1998, 112.
40 Bennet 1998, 128–9; Loader 1998.
41 Mylonas 1983, 157.
42 Jansen 2002, 7.
43 Evans 1928, Vol. 2, 78.
44 Taylour 1983, 133–4.
45 Taylour 1983, 133–4.
46 Steffen and Lolling 1884.
47 Dickinson 1994, 162–3.
48 Loader 1998.
49 Taylour 1983, 106; Loader 1998; Jansen 2002, 21.
50 Simpson 1965; Jansen 2002, 21–2, 56.
51 Simpson 1965, 116–17; Jansen 2002, 10.
52 Jansen 2002, 10.
53 Jansen 2002, 12.
54 Jansen 2002, 17–18.
55 Jansen 2002, 15–16.
56 Jansen 2002, 122–3.
57 Castleden 1991, 77, 99.

58 *Odyssey* 4, 1–2.
59 *Odyssey* 3, 480–97.
60 *Odyssey* 3, 488–9.
61 *Odyssey* 15, 185–9.
62 *Odyssey* 15, 79–80.
63 Crouwel and Morel 1981. The design of the litter described here can be seen in a clay model. The Mycenaeans did not invent the litter; it was in use as early as 2000 BC.
64 Steffen and Lolling 1884, 5–7.
65 Jansen 2002.
66 Jansen 2002.
67 Schliemann 1880, 147.
68 Steffen and Lolling 1884.
69 The Larisa is a high conical peak, well-placed to act as the beacon for Argos and other settlements round the Bay of Argos. Some cyclopean blocks on the Larisa may be the remains of the Mycenaean watchtower (Simpson 1981, 24).
70 *Odyssey* 4, 524–5. By implication this watchtower is on or close to the Bay of Argos since, on hearing of Agamemnon's arrival, Aegisthus has time to set up an ambush in the palace at Mycenae before setting off to collect Agamemnon 'from the coast'.
71 Mylonas 1983, 156–7.
72 Dickinson 1994, 162–3.
73 By contrast, in the early bronze age, outlying areas like the Nemea valley and much of southern Argolis were temporarily *emptied* of people while major centres like Mycenae grew (Dickinson 1994, 59).
74 Papahatzis 1978, 112.
75 Mylonas 1983, 155.
76 Dickinson 1994, 78–9; French 2002, 64–5.
77 It was Christos Tsountas, not Schliemann, who excavated the 'palace' at Mycenae in 1885–87; his work was published in detail by Alan Wace.
78 French 2002, 47.
79 French 2002, 57.
80 This is the picture that is gradually emerging from those sites that have been excavated.
81 Tsountas found remnants of the bronze shoes.
82 The signs of fire on the hearth were noted by Mylonas 1983, 100.
83 See Mylonas 1983, 104 for the reasoning.
84 House I and House of the Columns.
85 *Odyssey* 7, 100–2. The text says 'golden youths', but they seem to be automata, robotic fittings of the same type as the gold and silver guard dogs which are described ten lines earlier as being on watch at the door; Homer therefore probably intends us to think of the youths too as gilded robots.
86 As Mylonas says (1983, 105), it is right to be cautious about parallels with Homer but unwise to ignore them.
87 *Odyssey* 7, 95–69.
88 Mylonas 1983, 106–7; French 2002, 58 supports Mylonas.
89 *Odyssey* 4, 297–302.
90 *Odyssey* 7, 336.
91 *Odyssey* 3, 339. The aithousa at Pylos would have echoed because it opened onto a fairly small court completely surrounded by walls.
92 Mylonas 1983, 106–8.

93 I suggest this, only.
94 Castleden 1990, 50.
95 French 2002, 62.
96 French 2002, 61.
97 Burn and Burn 1986, 65.
98 Mylonas 1966.
99 MacKendrick 1962, 19–20.
100 MacKendrick 1962, 21.
101 Burn and Burn 1986, 62–5; the secret passages were not discovered until 1962.
102 Simpson 1981, 24.
103 Burn and Burn 1986, 63; Athens Ministry of Culture.
104 Hellenic Ministry of Culture. Midea was excavated initially in 1907 by the German Archaeological Institute. Excavation was resumed in 1939 by the Swedish archaeologist Axel Persson, and there were more excavations in 1963 and from 1983 onwards under K. Demakopoulou and P. Astroem.
105 Taylour 1983, 161.
106 Taylour 1983, 121. It may be that the more moderate quantity of grave goods at Dendra is a more realistic reflection of what the aristocracy actually deposited. We have to bear in mind that it is possible that Schliemann surreptitiously added to his shaft grave finds at Mycenae.
107 Burn and Burn 1986, 93.
108 Taylour 1983, 106.
109 *Iliad* 21, 7.
110 Wace and Stubbings 1962, 398–421; Pentreath 1964, 155–60.
111 *Odyssey* 13, 363–4; referred to again in *Odyssey* 16, 232.
112 Grosvenor 1973.
113 Burn and Burn 1986, 74.
114 Much depends on whether we believe that the Mycenaeans were the Ahhiyawa. See Chapter 8 for discussion of this still-controversial issue. Wood 1985, 178.
115 Burn and Burn 1986, 75.
116 Loader 1998.
117 Iakovidis 1983, 102–7.
118 Iakovidis 1983, 102.
119 Loader 1998.
120 Burn and Burn 1986, 75–7. The drainage was not restored until modern times. Gla once more stands up as an island in a sea of crops – now cotton and rice.
121 Taylour 1983, 106; Loader 1998.
122 Wood 1985, 154.
123 Iakovidis 1983, 79–86.
124 Iakovidis 1983, 79.
125 Burn and Burn 1986, 164–5; Iakovidis 1983, 88–9.
126 Taylour 1983, 41.
127 Taylour 1983, 78.

3 THE PEOPLE

1 Dickinson 1994, 89.
2 French 2002, 474–5.
3 Mylonas 1983, 59.
4 French 2002, 34; Prag and Neave 1997, 117.

5 Prag and Neave 1997, 126.
6 Dickinson 1994, 88.
7 Anon 1999.
8 Ozanne 1997; Anon 1999.
9 Chadwick 1976, 68.
10 Prag and Neave 1997, 114–16.
11 *Iliad* 16, 127–8. The shield is 'gigantic' (*Iliad* 7, 307), 'a wall' (*Iliad* 8, 307; 11, 572), and big enough to hide an archer from head to toe. Pictures of the tower shield on gold rings show that it was strongly curved laterally, turning it into a portable half-tower that would have afforded some protection from the sides as well as in front.
12 Prag and Neave 1997, 123–4, quoting Angel, the excavator.
13 Prag and Neave 1997, 126–7.
14 Prag and Neave 1997, 134–5.
15 *Iliad* 2, 565–8.
16 Spindler 1994, 141–2.
17 Taylour 1983, 116–18; Cunliffe 1998, 298, 301.
18 Schofield and Parkinson 1994.
19 Taylour 1983, 118.
20 *Iliad* 18, 697; Shelmerdine 1998b, 109.
21 Chadwick 1976, 150–1.
22 *Iliad* 5, 842–7.
23 Taylour 1983, 115–18.
24 Wardle 1988.
25 Dickinson 1994, 89–90.
26 Taylour 1983, 115.
27 Mylonas 1983, 225.
28 Higgins 1981, 165.
29 Taylour 1983, 65.
30 Taylour 1983, 116; Higgins 1981, 169.
31 Dickinson 1994, 87.
32 Hood 1978, 188.
33 Hood 1978, 192.
34 Higgins 1981, 166.
35 *Iliad* 2, 118–28.
36 Higgins 1981, 167.
37 Hood 1978, 226–7.
38 Hood 1978, 224–5.
39 Dickinson 1994, 99; Higgins 1981, 138–9.
40 See Pylos tablet Er 312 (Chadwick 1976, 71).
41 At Sphagianes, the king was closely associated with the goddess Potnia.
42 Palmer 1961, 94–6.
43 In the days before television and photography, the sight of the king would have been a very rare event for ordinary people in most countries.
44 Chadwick 1976, 75.
45 Popham 1991.
46 Bass 1986; Shear 1998. The *Iliad* (6, 198–202) describes 'murderous signs scratched in a folded tablet, and many of them too, enough to kill a man'. In Homer's time there was already an awareness of the strange power of the written word. The Hittite king wrote letters to the King of Ahhiyawa; it is inconceivable that the King of Ahhiyawa did not reply (Lorimer 1950).

47 Edwards 1961, 270–1.
48 Edwards 1961, 270–1.
49 Chadwick 1976, 75.
50 Palmer 1961, 101.
51 Chadwick 1976, 73–4.
52 Palmer 1961, 105.
53 Willetts 1965, 59–60. The Gerontes are described by Strabo too (*Geography* 10. 480–4).
54 Taylour 1983, 132; Palmer 1961, 124.
55 *Odyssey* 1, 394–5.
56 *Odyssey* 8, 390–1.
57 Chadwick 1976, 70.
58 Chadwick 1976, 70–1.
59 Palmer 1961, 92.
60 *Iliad* 1, 43.
61 Dyczek 1994.
62 Chadwick 1976, 64.
63 Chadwick 1976, 66–7.
64 Palmer 1961, 100.
65 Palmer 1961, 141.
66 Chadwick 1976, 78–83.
67 Palmer 1961, 231; Wood 1985, 218–19 and endpaper.
68 Cunliffe 1998, 227.
69 Kilian 1988, 141.
70 Dickinson 1994, 306–7.
71 Chadwick 1976, 74.
72 Palmer 1961, 97–8.
73 Several sources including Kirk 1964.
74 Chadwick 1963.
75 Chadwick 1976, 42–3.
76 Ruiperz 1982.
77 Woodard 1986.
78 Chadwick 1987, 33.
79 Mylonas 1983, 31–61.
80 Although it is often said that there was an attempt to mummify one body, from Grave V, it is clear from Schliemann's account that it was merely a 'well preserved body' whose colour 'resembled very much that of an Egyptian mummy'. It was the chemist in Argos who made an attempt at embalming it for Schliemann, who later referred to it as 'nearly mummified'. The body was not embalmed in the bronze age (Prag and Neave 1997, 115–16).
81 Mylonas 1983, 59.
82 Cavanagh 1998.
83 Traill 1995, 168–70.
84 Traill 1995, 156, 173.
85 Prag and Neave 1997, 143–5.
86 Taylour 1983, 68.
87 Prag and Neave 1997, 111.
88 A parallel is Henry II's sponsorship of the 'discovery' of the grave of King Arthur at Glastonbury Abbey.
89 Mylonas (1983) treats Perseus as an historical figure, but stops short of proposing that one of the shaft graves might be his burial place.

90 Prag and Neave 1997, 111.
91 Prag and Neave 1997, 110.
92 Taylour 1983, 69.
93 Taylour 1983, 73.
94 Cavanagh and Lacton 1988; Frizzell and Santillo 1988.
95 Taylour 1983, 75.
96 French 2002, 40.
97 Taylour 1983, 79–80.
98 Ventris and Chadwick 1956, 348; Palmer 1961, 149–55.
99 Taylour 1983, 83–4.
100 Prag and Neave 1997, 110
101 Dickinson 1994, 208; Cunliffe 1998, 227.

4 EVERYDAY LIFE IN THE COUNTRYSIDE

1 Dyczek 1994.
2 Simpson 1981; Dyczek 1994.
3 Taylour 1983, 131–2.
4 Papadopoulos 1979.
5 Palmer 1961, 118–19.
6 Palmer 1961, 110.
7 Chadwick 1976, 107–8.
8 Dickinson 1994, 27–8.
9 Chadwick 1976, 110.
10 Cunliffe 1998, 230.
11 Iakovidis 1983.
12 Dickinson 1994, 46.
13 Chadwick 1976, 117.
14 Chadwick 1976, 121–2.
15 Taylour 1983, 121.
16 Chadwick 1976, 121–2.
17 Dickinson 1994, 46.
18 French 2002, 27.
19 Dyczek 1994.
20 Piteros *et al.* 1990; Dickinson 1994, 83.
21 Palmer 1961, 176.
22 *Iliad* 3; *Iliad* 6, 178–9.
23 Both Greeks and Trojans are described as 'stallion-breaking' (*Iliad* 3, 153, 158, 401; 4, 413). Tricca is described as 'stallion land' (*Iliad* 4, 232). Evidently horse-rearing was a very important activity in the Mycenaean world.
24 *Iliad* 5, 291–304.
25 Crouwel and Morel 1981.
26 Dietz 1991.
27 Chadwick 1976, 131; Mancz 1989, 210.
28 Dickinson 1994, 83.
29 Chadwick 1976, 132.
30 Chadwick 1976, 132–3.
31 Hunting from chariots is shown on the stela from Shaft Grave V; hunting on foot is shown on the dagger from Shaft Grave IV. Hunting dogs are mentioned in the tablets; men hunting with dogs are shown on murals at Tiryns.

32 *Odyssey* 17, 292–327.
33 Dickinson 1994, 27–8; Cunliffe 1998, 234.
34 Dickinson 1994, 90.

5 EVERYDAY LIFE IN THE TOWNS

1   Dickinson 1994, 93.
2   Dickinson 1994, 78.
3   Dickinson 1994, 78–80.
4   Taylour 1983, 85–6.
5   Taylour 1983, 101–2.
6   Chadwick 1976, 138–9.
7   Dickinson 1994, 144–5.
8   Taylour 1983, 47.
9   Mylonas 1983, 211.
10 Taylour 1983, 113–15.
11 Dickinson 1994, 143; Symeonoglou 1973.
12 Muhly 1996.
13 Palmer 1961, 152.
14 Chadwick 1976, 147–50.
15 Dickinson 1994, 99.
16 *Iliad* 4, 616; 5, 713–14; 6, 82–3; 17, 68; 17, 139–40; 22, 443.
17 Pausanias II, 17; *Iliad* 17, 1.
18 *Iliad* 7, 252–8.
19 *Iliad* 15, 742.
20 *Iliad* 5, 334.
21 Snodgrass 1999, 32.
22 Snodgrass 1999, 19–20.
23 Snodgrass 1999, 24, Plate 9.
24 Snodgrass 1999, 18–19, Plate 8; *Iliad* 10, 261–5.
25 Taylour 1983, 121–3.
26 Taylour 1983, 124–5; Dickinson 1994, 135.
27 Higgins 1981, 152.
28 Dickinson 1994, 101.
29 Mylonas 1983, 192.
30 Higgins 1981, 116–17, 122.
31 Taylour 1983, 125–6; Higgins 1981, 92–3.
32 Pausanias II, 16.
33 Taylour 1983, 125–7.
34 Dickinson 1994, 142.
35 Higgins 1981, 153.
36 Higgins 1981, 93.
37 Taylour 1983, 129.
38 Cunliffe 1998, 233.
39 Hood 1978, 77.
40 Higgins 1981, 94.
41 Hood 1978, 77.
42 Hood 1978, 77–8.
43 Dickinson 1994, 164–8.
44 Higgins 1981, 100.

45 Hood 1978, 79.
46 Hood 1978, 82–8.
47 Taylour 1983, 130–1.
48 Higgins 1981, 105–7.
49 Hood 1978, 40.
50 Higgins 1981, 107–8; Hood 1978, 40–1.
51 Hood 1978, 42.
52 Hood 1978, 42.
53 Higgins 1981, 110–12; Palmer 1961, 107.
54 Higgins 1981, 114; French 2002, 101–13.
55 Higgins 1981, 114–16.
56 Higgins 1981, 120–2.
57 Higgins 1981, 116.
58 Higgins 1981, 118.
59 French 2002, 107.
60 Younger 1998.
61 Younger 1998.
62 Shelmerdine 1998a; Blegen and Rawson 2001.
63 Shelmerdine 1998a, 84.

6 RELIGION

1 Taylour 1983, 43.
2 Taylour 1983, 43–4; Mylonas 1983, 181.
3 In this Dickinson supports Nilsson 1950.
4 Dickinson 1994, 286–93.
5 Dickinson 1994, 257.
6 Mylonas 1983, 181.
7 Kilian 1988, 148–9.
8 Dickinson 1994, 286–93.
9 Taylour 1983, 44–5.
10 Ozanne 1997, 176.
11 Ozanne 1997, 179.
12 *Iliad*, Book 7.
13 Chadwick 1976, 95 and 99; Palmer 119–31.
14 Palmer 1961, 82.
15 Palmer 1961, 128.
16 Palmer 1961, 124.
17 Dickinson 1994, 306.
18 Rutkowski 1986, 202–3; French 2002, 47.
19 Nilsson 1925, 468.
20 Rutkowski 1986, 192–3.
21 Taylour 1983, 47.
22 Rutkowski 1986, 193.
23 Rutkowski 1986, 180.
24 Dickinson 1994, 292.
25 Dickinson 1994, 279; Castleden 1990, 121; Castleden 1991, 170.
26 Taylour 1983, 49–53.
27 Rutkowski 1986, 178–9.
28 Rutkowski 1986, 174–5.

29 Taylour 1983, 49–61.
30 Dickinson 1994, 306.
31 Iakovidis 1983, 31.
32 Iakovidis 1983, 79–84.
33 Rutkowski 1986, 185–8.
34 Mylonas 1983, 190.
35 Castleden 1990, 79.
36 Mylonas 1983, 196–7.
37 *Odyssey* 1, 104–5.
38 Mylonas 1983, 198–9.
39 Mylonas 1983, 197–8.
40 Dickinson 1994, 280. Three Minoan images show this stance.
41 Rutkowski 1986, 209.
42 Mylonas 1983, 186. The clay larnax was from a chamber tomb at Tanagra in the area of Thebes.
43 Palmer 1961, 125–6.
44 Bendall 1999.
45 Shaw 1996.
46 Schuchhardt 1891, 119–20.
47 Mylonas 1983, 203.
48 Mylonas 1983, 201–2.
49 *Iliad* 3, 125–6 and 346–8; 7, 359–61.
50 *Odyssey* 3, 4–6.
51 Davis 1988, 52–5.
52 Aeschylus: *Agamemnon*. According to some traditions, at the last moment Artemis relented and substituted a deer for the sacrifice.
53 Anderson 1995.
54 Buck 1989.
55 Buck 1989.
56 Davis 1988, 54–6; Herodotus 2, 119.
57 Mylonas 1983, 200–1.
58 Mylonas 1983, 100.
59 Rutkowski 1986, 204.
60 Rutkowski 1986, 204–6.
61 Pausanias 8, 38, 7.
62 Mylonas 1983, 196.
63 Mylonas 1983, 187–8.
64 Rutkowski 1986, 207.
65 *Iliad* 6, 347–50.
66 Castleden 1990, 116.
67 *Iliad* 6, 307–8.
68 Mylonas 1983, 211. Interestingly, the image on this bezel has a row of triglyphs along the bottom, a decorative feature that was commonly run along the wall-foot or dado. The image was therefore probably copied intact from a lost fresco.
69 Bennet 1998, 112.
70 Ozanne 1997.
71 Gerard-Rousseau 1974, 164–5.
72 Rutkowski 1997, 209.
73 Castleden 1990.
74 It is surprising to find Fitton (2002, 123–5) even now agreeing with Evans' interpretation of the East Wing. The fresco on the wall of the Grand Staircase serving

the East Wing clearly shows a procession of men conducting a boy up the stairs to an initiation ritual, or possibly even to sacrifice (Castleden 1998). Nanno Marinatos has also skilfully demonstrated from the Theran evidence that the multi-door room (*polythyron*) was an architectural device for micro-controlling the visibility of semi-private religious ceremonies such as initiation rituals (Marinatos 1984). This evidence further increases the likelihood that the *polythyra* in the East Wing at Knossos were constructed for cult use.

75 Castleden 1990, 43–51.
76 Evans 1928, Vol. 1, 4; Castleden 1990, 70–3.
77 Spengler 1926; Faure 1973; Wunderlich 1975; Castleden 1990.
78 Followers of Evans, such as Sinclair Hood (1994), remain loyal to the palace idea, though (see discussion of Hood's counter-arguments in Castleden 1998, 141).
79 Castleden 1990, 75–87.
80 Castleden 1998, 101–9.
81 Fitton 2002, 133–5.
82 Castleden 1990, 84.
83 Castleden 1990, 92–5.
84 Dickinson 1994, 153–4.
85 Palyvou 2002.
86 The throne at Pylos is thought to have been wooden; only the shallow socket made for it in the stucco floor is left; the throne in the Throne Sanctuary at Knossos is made of stone – and so has survived intact.
87 MacKendrick 1962, 142–3.
88 Werner 1993.
89 MacKendrick 1962, 145–7.
90 Lang 1969.
91 As Rehak (1995) says, archaeology gives no support for the notion of an enthroned king.
92 Shelmerdine 1998a palace, 83–4.
93 Shelmerdine 1998a palace, 92.
94 Bennet 2001, 3; www.stream.blg.uc.edu/myc/bennet.
95 Chadwick 1976, 99.
96 Chadwick 1976, 34.
97 The pseudo-Egyptian style is seen in Muller 1930, 42.
98 Mylonas 1983, 99–100.
99 Mylonas 1983, 116 is unenthusiastic about the idea of a shrine, thinking that the Cult Centre disposes of the need for one.
100 Werner 1993, 129.
101 MacKendrick 1962, 145–7.
102 Mylonas 1983, 104.
103 Mylonas 1983, 212.
104 French 2002, 144.
105 French 2002, 145.
106 Thomson 1949, 280–2.
107 French 2002, 147.
108 Wood 1985, 81; Traill 1995, 240.
109 Pausanias VIII, 46, 3.
110 Harrison and Spencer 1998; Griebel and Nelson 1998.
111 Sammer 2001, 3.
112 Pausanias IV, 36, 1–2.
113 Castleden 1990, 47.

114 Castleden 1990, 108.
115 Pausanias IX, 37, 6.
116 Pausanias IX, 5, 2.
117 Pausanias IX, 5, 2; IX, 12, 3.
118 Pausanias IX, 16, 3.
119 Pausanias IX, 12, 3.
120 Symeonoglou 1985, 57–8.

7 A MYCENAEAN SEA-EMPIRE?

1 Cunliffe 1998, 268–72.
2 Barfield 1991.
3 Harding 1984.
4 Portugali and Knapp 1985.
5 Buchholz 1987.
6 *Iliad* 7, 5–6.
7 *Iliad* 2, 180.
8 *Odyssey* 23, 270.
9 Taylour 1983, 152.
10 Taylour 1983, 152.
11 Bennet 2001, 3; www.stream.blg.uc.edu/myc/bennet/.
12 Lolos 1998a, 31.
13 Palmer 1963, 130.
14 The Catalogue of Ships in the *Iliad* mentions that the Boeotian ships carried 120 men each, while the ships of Methone carried 50 each. In Homer's day, as in the bronze age, ships varied in size.
15 Zangger 1998b. The dates are based on well-dated sediment cores from the Osmanaga Lagoon.
16 Bennet: The Mycenaean Palaces: www.stream.blg.uc.edu/myc/bennet/.
17 Taylour 1983, 154.
18 Kilian 1988, 122–6; Dickinson 1994, 305–6.
19 French 2002, 48.
20 Castleden 1989, 130.
21 Castleden 1998, 121–5, 131–3.
22 Mee 1988, 301–5. By 1320 BC the great Minoan trading operation was over (Castleden 1998, 128).
23 Gale and Stos-Gale 1998, 382–3; Cunliffe 1998, 242–3.
24 Kilian 1988, 149–51.
25 Dickinson 1994, 304; Warren 1991.
26 Dickinson 1994, 304–6.
27 Cunliffe 1998, 227.
28 Castleden 1990, 33–4.
29 Mee 1988, 301–5.
30 *Iliad* 2, 126.
31 Kilian 1988, 149–51.
32 Cunliffe 1998, 238.
33 Cunliffe 1998, 242–3.
34 Mee 1988, 301–5.
35 Weickert 1957; Godecken 1988, 307–18.
36 Cunliffe 1998, 242.
37 Cline 1994.

8 THE TROJAN WAR

1 *Iliad* 18, 112–13.
2 Jones 1991 *Odyssey* Introduction, xxxvi.
3 Pausanias II, 23, 1.
4 Herodotus Book 2.
5 Lehmann 1977, 13–15.
6 Regnal list after Mcqueen (1986) and other recent sources. This is by no means definitive. In the last few decades the reign of Suppiluliumas I has been variously given as 1381–55, 1380–46, 1380–34, 1380–30, 1375–35 and 1370–30.
7 If Attarissiyas really was a Greek king, this early struggle for control over Cyprus between bronze age Greeks and Turks is an interesting foreshadowing of much later history.
8 Bennet 1999, 11–30.
9 Cline 1996.
10 Hansen 1997.
11 *Iliad* 2, 784–90. Achilles attacked Lyrnessos and seized Briseis there either before or after attacking nearby Thebes. This is a rare reference in the *Iliad* to the Teuthrania raid.
12 Sommer 1932, 275–94; Houwink ten Cate 1974, 149. The statues were presumably clay idols like the ones found in the Cult Centre at Mycenae, which were certainly portable enough to be ferried to central Anatolia.
13 Gurney 1990, 38–9.
14 Lehmann 1977, 233. The stammer is inferred from a documentary reference: 'The word in my mouth became small and issued somewhat haltingly from within me' (Lehmann 230).
15 Wood (1985, 182) suggests that he was a royal Arzawan.
16 Only possibly Lycia, which is generally assumed.
17 Hattusilis III according to Gurney (1990, 41) and (Wood 1985, 180).
18 Gurney 1990, 40–1, 43.
19 Wood 1985, 183–4.
20 Wood 1985, 185.
21 Wood 1985, 178.
22 Mcqueen 1986, 40. The hostility of the land of Arzawa is known from the tablets. King Unhazitis of Arzawa made war on Hatti in alliance with the Greeks; the Arzawan royal family had to flee to Greece when they were defeated (Wood 1985, 180).
23 Wood 1985, 179.
24 Wood 1985, 178–9.
25 Crossland and Birchall 1974, 159 in discussion.
26 Gurney 1990, 41.
27 Mcqueen 1986, 40.
28 Gurney 1990, 43.
29 Wood 1985, 179.
30 Mcqueen 1986, 39–40.
31 Cline 1996.
32 Gurney 1990, 44.
33 Lehmann 1977, 242, 255.
34 Lehmann 1977, 245–7.
35 Lehmann 1977, 248–9.
36 Wood 1985, 205.

37 E.g. Gurney 1990, 46–7.
38 Dickinson 1994, 253; Taylour 1983, 158.
39 Wood 1985, 177.
40 Bennet 1999, 11–30.
41 Dickinson 1994, 253.
42 But Aegyptios seems to have been a personal name in use among Mycenaeans, and maybe should not be interpreted too literally as 'the Egyptian'; today we would not assume that Miss Welsh came from Wales or that Clark Kent was Kentish.
43 Thucydides (*History of the Peloponnesian War* I, 9, 2) has Pelops father of Atreus originating in 'Asia'. Pindar (*Ol.* I, 24) speaks of 'Lydian Pelops'. Pausanias (V, 1, 7) mentions 'Pelops the Lydian who crossed over from Asia'.
44 Lang 1995.
45 Anderson 1995.
46 Leaf 1912.
47 Nilsson 1933, 26.
48 Wilamowitz-Mÿllendorf 1927.
49 MacKendrick 1962, 58.
50 Agamemnon launched an opening attack in error against Teuthrania, just to the south of Troy. Telephos the king of Mysia drove him and his army back to the ships, forcing a withdrawal. Michael Wood (1985, 22, 23, 206) cites the *Odyssey* 11, 519, but that passage reads, 'I could not tell you of all those he [Neoptelemus] killed in battle for the Argives, nor give you their names; but well I remember how the heroic Eurypylus son of Telephos fell to his sword, and how many of his Hittite men-at-arms were slaughtered at his side.' This may be about an abortive attack on Teuthrania, but Homer mentions fighting on the Trojan plain. Eurypylus, as prince of a land near Troy, might reasonably have been expected to be fighting as a Trojan ally, alongside the Trojans, at Troy itself. The Proklan summary of the *Kypria* refers to Telephos receiving a wound from Achilles, a detail not repeated in the *Odyssey*, which says that Eurypylus was wounded by Achilles and, rather oddly, taken back to Argos to be healed. The Teuthrania raid was evidently explicitly described in the *Kypria* (see Appendix E, the *Kypria*, lines 35–41).
51 The Trojan War of Homer is a conflation of events possibly spanning a couple of centuries, beginning about 100 years before the supposed date of the Homeric siege (Bryce 2002, 267).
52 Cline 1996. The sword is an Aegean Type B sword, a type concentrated at Mycenae.

9 THE FALL OF MYCENAE

1 The large-scale tensions experienced in Egypt, Hatti and the Levant were evidently felt by the Mycenaeans too; this was the time when the great fortification walls went up (Cartledge 1979).
2 Shelmerdine 1998a, 87–8.
3 Diodorus IV, 68. 6.
4 In the battle at Pylos, the gods themselves took part, just as they were to in the Trojan War. Hera, Hades and Poseidon supported Neleus; Heracles killed Neleus and wounded Hera in the right breast with a three-pronged arrow, causing her incurable pain. This may account for the later raising of a temple to Hera on the site.
5 Pausanias IV, 3.
6 Hood 1966; Hood 1974, 238–9.

7 Ozanne 1997, 241.
8 Chadwick 1976, 42–3.
9 Palmer 1962; Ventris and Chadwick Documents; Chadwick 1987.
10 Chadwick 1976, 189–92.
11 Tegyey 1974, 228–31.
12 Chadwick 1976, 192.
13 *Odyssey* 8, 82–3.
14 Mylonas 1983, 249.
15 Taylour 1983, 161; Crossland and Birchall 1974, 13.
16 Bryson, Lamb and Donley 1974.
17 Desborough 1964; Gimbutas 1974, 173.
18 Ozanne 1997, 242.
19 Herodotus V, 65, 146; Pausanias II, 18, 7; Strabo XIV, 633.
20 Sourvinou-Inwood 1974, 215–16.
21 Pausanias I, 43, 1.
22 Pausanias VII, 25, 5.
23 Mylonas 1966.
24 Crossland and Birchall 1974, 13.
25 Baillie 1989.
26 Mylonas 1983, 251.
27 French 2002, 136–7.
28 Taylour 1983, 161–3; Mylonas 1983, 252.
29 Pausanias II, 21, 6.

10 AND LIVE IN SONG FOR GENERATIONS

1 Blegen and Rawson 1966, 2001.
2 Mylonas 1983.
3 Diamant 1988, 153–8.
4 Edey 1975, 136.
5 *Iliad* 6, 568–70.
6 *Iliad* 1, 122.
7 Barfield 1991.
8 Cunliffe 1998, 243.
9 Chadwick 1976, 14.
10 Dickinson 1974, 127.
11 Cunliffe 1998, 303.
12 Blegen and Rawson 2001, 13.
13 Anderson 1995.
14 Arrian 1.12.1; Cohen 1995.
15 Mylonas 1983, 32. A bronze dagger dating to 1550 BC has a cloisonné-work hilt. It was found in Shaft Grave IV at Mycenae.
16 Hood 1978, 207.
17 Vecchi 2001, 49.
18 French 2002, 70.
19 Ozanne 1997, 24.
20 *Iliad* 5, 499–501.
21 *Odyssey* 3, 69.
22 Treherne 1977.
23 Laurence Binyon *1914: For the Fallen.*

BIBLIOGRAPHY

AJA = American Journal of Archaeology
Ant. = Antiquity
BSA = Annual of the British School at Athens
CA = Current Archaeology

Alden, M. 1981 *Bronze age population fluctuations in the Argolid from the evidence of Mycenaean tombs*. Göteborg: Paul Åströms Verlag.

Anderson, J. K. 1995 The Geometric Catalogue of Ships, in Carter, J. B. and Morris, S. P. (eds) 1995 *The ages of Homer*, 181–91.

Anon. 1990 *Troy, Mycenae, Tiryns, Orchomenos*. Athens: Greek Ministry of Culture.

—— 1999 *Minoans and Mycenaeans; flavours of their time*. Athens: Greek Ministry of Culture.

Astroem, P. 1983 *The Cuirass Tomb and other finds at Dendra, 2: Excavations in the Cemeteries, Lower Town and the Citadel*. Göteborg: Paul Åströms Verlag.

—— and Demakopoulou, K. 1996 Signs of an earthquake at Midea? *Fitch Laboratory Occasional Papers* 7, 37–40.

Baillie, M. 1989 Do Irish bog oaks date the Shang dynasty? *CA* 117, 310–13.

Balcer, J. 1974 The Mycenaean dam at Tiryns. *AJA* 78, 141–9.

Barfield, L. H. 1991 Wessex with and without Mycenae: new evidence from Switzerland. *Ant.* 65, 102–7.

Bass, G. F. 1967 *Cape Gelidonya: a bronze age shipwreck*. Philadelphia: Transactions of the American Philosophical Society, 57, part 8.

—— 1986 A bronze age shipwreck at Ulu Burun (Kaş): 1984 campaign. *AJA* 90, 269–96.

—— 1987 Splendours of the bronze age. *National Geographic Magazine* 172 (6), 693–732.

Baumbach, L. 1976 Linear B and Homer. *Akroterion* 21, 35–9.

—— 1979 The Mycenaean contribution to Greek religion. *SMEA* 20, 143–60.

Baumlein, W. 1839 Pelasgischer Glaube und Homer's Verhaeltniss zu demselben. *Zeitschrift fur die Althertumswissenschaft* 6, 1183.

Bendall, L. M. 1999 A time of offerings: dedications of perfumed oil at Pylos festivals, in Bennet, J. and Driessen, J. (eds) 1999 *A-na-qo-ta: studies presented to J. T. Killen*, 1–9.

Bennet, J. 1998 The Linear B archives and the kingdom of Nestor, in Davis, J. L. (ed.) 1998a *Sandy Pylos: an archaeological history from Nestor to Navarino*, 111–33.

——— 1999 Re-u-ko-to-ro za-we-te: Leuktron as a secondary capital in the Pylos region? in Bennet, J. and Driessen, J. (eds) 1999 *A-na-qo-ta: studies presented to J. T. Killen*, 11–30.

——— 2001 Agency and bureaucracy: thoughts on the nature and extent of administration in bronze age Pylos, in Voutsaki, S. and Killen, J. (eds) 2001 *Economy and politics in the Mycenaean palace states*, 25–35.

——— and Driessen, J. (eds) 1999 *A-na-qo-ta: studies presented to J. T. Killen*. Salamanca: Ediciones Universidad de Salamanca.

Bennett, E. L. 1959 The Mycenae Tablets II. *Trans American Philosophical Society* 48, 1–122.

Bintliff, J. (ed.) 1977 *Mycenaean geography*. Proceedings of Cambridge Colloquium, September 1976.

Blegen, C. W. 1921 *Korakou: a prehistoric settlement near Corinth*. Boston and New York: American School of Classical Studies at Athens.

——— 1928 *Zygouries: a prehistoric settlement in the valley of Cleonae*. Boston: American School of Classical Studies.

——— and Lang, M. 1958 The Palace of Nestor excavations of 1957. *AJA* 62, 175–91.

——— and Rawson, M. 1966 *The Palace of Nestor at Pylos in Western Messenia, Vol 1*. Princeton: Princeton University Press.

——— and ——— 2001 *A guide to the Palace of Nestor*. Athens: American School of Classical Studies.

Bloedow, E. F. 1988 The Trojan War and Late Helladic IIIC. *Prähistorische Zeitschrift* 63, 23–52.

Boardman, J. 1964 *The Greeks overseas*. Harmondsworth: Penguin.

Boer, W. den 1954 *Laconian studies*. Amsterdam: North-Holland Publishing Company.

Bouzek 1974 Bronze age Greece and the Balkans: problems of migrations, in Crossland, R. A. and Birchall, A. (eds) 1974 *Bronze age migrations in the Aegean. Archaeological and linguistic problems in Greek prehistory*, 169–77.

Branigan, K. 1989 Barra. *CA* 113, 182–3.

——— (ed.) 1998 *Cemetery and society in the Aegean bronze age*. Sheffield: Academic Press.

Broneer, O. 1939 A Mycenaean fountain on the Athenian Acropolis. *Hesperia* 8, 317–429.

Bryce, T. 1989 Ahhiyawans and Mycenaeans – an Anatolian viewpoint. *OJA* 8, 297–310.

——— 2002 *Life and society in the Hittite world*. Oxford: Oxford University Press.

Bryson, R. A., Lamb, H. H. and Donley, D. D. L. 1974 Drought and the decline of Mycenae. *Ant.* 48, 46–50.

Buchholz, H.-G. 1987 *Agäische Bronzezeit*. Darmstadt: Wissenschaftliche Buchgesellschaft.

Buck, R. J. 1989 Mycenaean human sacrifice. *Minos* 24, 131–7.

Bulle, H. 1907 *Orchomenos*. Munich: Verlag der Bayerischen Akademie der Wissenschaften.

Burford, A. 1960 Heavy transport in classical antiquity. *Economic History Review* 13, 1–18.

Burgess, C. 1989 Volcanoes, catastrophe and the global crisis of the late second millennium BC. *CA* 117, 325–9.

Burkert, W. 1985 *Greek religion*. Oxford: Blackwell.

Burn, A. R. and Burn, M. 1986 *The living past of Greece*. New York: Schocken.

Cameron, M. A. S. 1987 The 'palatial' thematic system in the Knossos murals: last notes on Knossos frescoes, in Hägg, R. and Marinatos, N. (eds) 1987 *The function of the Minoan palaces: Proceedings of the Fourth International Symposium at the Swedish Institute in Athens*, 10–16 July, 1984, 320–8.

Carpenter, R. 1966 *Discontinuity in Greek civilization.* Cambridge: Cambridge University Press.

Carratelli, P. G. 1954 La decifrazione dei testi micenei. *La Parola del Passato* 35, 113.

Carter, J. B. and Morris, S. P. (eds) 1995 *The ages of Homer.* Austin: University of Texas Press.

Cartledge, P. 1979 *Sparta and Lakonia: a regional history 1300–362 BC.* London: Routledge & Kegan Paul.

Caskey, J. L. and Blackburn, E. T. 1997 *Lerna in the Argolid.* Athens: American School of Classical Studies at Athens.

Castleden, R. 1990 *The Knossos Labyrinth: a new view of the 'Palace of Minos' at Knossos.* London: Routledge.

—— 1991 *Minoans: life in bronze age Crete.* London: Routledge.

—— 1998 *Atlantis destroyed.* London: Routledge.

Cavanagh, W. 1998 Innovation, conservation and variation in Mycenaean funerary ritual, in Branigan, K. (ed.) *Cemetery and society in the Aegean bronze age*, 103–14.

Cavanagh, W. G. and Laxton R. 1988 Problem solving and the architecture of tholos tombs, in French, E. B. and Wardle, K. A. (eds) 1986 *Problems in Greek prehistory*, 385–95.

Chadwick, J. 1963 The Mycenaean Tablets III. *Trans. American Philosophical Society* 52, 3–76.

—— 1976 *The Mycenaean world.* Cambridge: Cambridge University Press.

—— 1987 *Linear B and related scripts.* London: British Museum Publications.

—— and Baumbach, L. 1963 The Mycenaean vocabulary. *Glotta* 41, 157–271.

Cline, E. H. 1994 Sailing the wine-dark sea: international trade and the late bronze age Aegean. *BAR International Series*, 591.

—— 1996 Assuwa and the Achaeans: the 'Mycenaean' sword at Hattusas and its possible implications. *BSA* 91, 137–51.

Cohen, A. 1995 Alexander and Achilles – Macedonians and 'Mycenaeans', in Carter, J. B. and Morris, S. P. (eds) 1995 *The ages of Homer*, 483–505.

Cook, J. M. 1974 Bronze age sites in the Troad, in Crossland, R. A. and Birchall, A. (eds) 1974 *Bronze age migrations in the Aegean. Archaeological and linguistic problems in Greek prehistory*, 37–40.

Cornelius, F. 1955 Zur Ahhijawa-Problem. *Historia* 11, 112–13.

Crossland, R. A. and Birchall, A. (eds) 1974 *Bronze age migrations in the Aegean. Archaeological and linguistic problems in Greek prehistory.* Park Ridge, NJ: Noyes Press.

Crouwel, J. and Morel, J. 1983 *Chariots and other means of land transport in bronze age Greece.* Amsterdam: Allard Pierson Series.

Cunliffe, B. 1998 *Prehistoric Europe: an illustrated history.* Oxford and New York: Oxford University Press.

Davies, N. 1988 *Human sacrifice in history and today.* New York: Dorset Press.

Davis, E. N. 1986 The political use of art in the Aegean: the missing ruler. *AJA* 90, 216.

Davis, J. L. (ed.) 1998a *Sandy Pylos: an archaeological history from Nestor to Navarino.* Austin: University of Texas Press.

—— 1998b The discovery of the palace of Nestor, in Davis J. L. (ed.) *Sandy Pylos: an archaeological history from Nestor to Navarino*, 42–6.

—— 1998c The palace and its dependencies, in Davis, J. L. (ed.) *Sandy Pylos: an archaeological history from Nestor to Navarino*, 53–68.

de Fidio, P. (2001) Centralization and its limits in the Mycenaean palatial system, in Voutsaki, S. and Killen, J. (ed.) 2001 *Economy and politics in the Mycenaean palace states*, 15–24.

Demakopoulou, K. (ed.) 1988 *The Mycenaean world*. Athens: Greek Ministry of Culture.

—— 1995 Mycenaean citadels: recent excavations on the Acropolis of Midea in the Argolid. *Bulletin of the Institute of Classical Studies* 1995, 151–61.

—— and Divari-Valakou, N. 1993 A Linear B inscribed stirrup jar from Midea. *Minos* 27–8, 303–5.

Desborough, V. R. 1964 *The last Mycenaeans and their successors: an archaeological survey c. 1200–c. 1000 BC*. Oxford: Oxford University Press.

Diamant, S. 1988 Mycenaean origins: infiltration from the north?, in French, E. B. and Wardle, K. A. (eds) 1986 *Problems in Greek prehistory*, 153–9.

Dickinson, O. 1974 Drought and the decline of Mycenae: some comments. *Antiquity* 48, 228–30.

—— 1994 *The Aegean bronze age*. Cambridge: Cambridge University Press.

Dietz, S. 1991 *The Argolid at the transition to the Mycenaean age*. Copenhagen: National Museum of Denmark.

Driessen, J. 2002 The King must die, in Driessen, J., Schoep, I. and Laffineur, R. (eds) 2002 *Monuments of Minos: rethinking the Minoan palaces*, 3–14.

——, Schoep, I. and Laffineur, R. (eds) 2002 *Monuments of Minos: rethinking the Minoan palaces*. Liège: Université de Liège.

Dyczek, P. 1994 *Pylos in the bronze age: problems of culture and social life in Messenia*. Warsaw: Wydawnictwa Uniwersytetu Warsawskiego.

Edey, M. A. 1975 *Lost world of the Aegean*. New York: Time-Life International.

Edwards, I. E. S. 1985 *The Pyramids of Egypt*. Harmondsworth: Penguin Books.

Evans, A. 1928 *The Palace of Minos at Knossos*. London: Macmillan.

Fagles, R. (trans.) 1991 *Homer: The Iliad*. Harmondsworth: Penguin Books.

Faure, P. 1973 *La Vie quotidienne en Crete au temps de Minos*. Paris: Hachette.

Feuer, B. 1996 *Mycenaean civilization: a research guide*. New York: Garland Publishing.

Fitton, L. J. 2002 *Minoans*. London: British Museum Press.

Fitzgerald, R. (trans.) 1961 *Homer: The Odyssey*. London: Collins Harvill.

Forrer, E. O. 1924 Vorhomerische Griechen in den Keilschrifttexten von Boghaz-koi. *Mitteilungen der Deutschen Orientgesellschaft Literaturzeitung*, 113–18.

French, E. (ed.) 1979 *Excavations at Mycenae 1939–1955 by A. J. B. Wace and others*. London: British School of Archaeology at Athens and Thames & Hudson.

—— 2002 *Mycenae: Agamemnon's capital*. Stroud: Tempus.

—— and Wardle, K. A. 1986 *Problems in Greek prehistory*. Bristol: Bristol Classical Press.

Friedrich, J. 1929 Werden in den hethitischen Keilschrifttexten die Griechen erwahnt? *Kleinasiatische Forshungen* 1, 87–107.

Frizzell, B. S. and Santillo, R. 1988 The Mycenaean tholos – a false cupola?, in French, E. B. and Wardle, K. A. (eds) 1986 *Problems in Greek prehistory*, 443–4.

Frodin, O. and Persson, A. W. 1938 *Asine: results of the Swedish excavations 1922–30*. Stockholm: Generalsstabens Litografiska Forlag.

Furumark, A. 1954 Ägäische Texte in greischischer Sprache. *Eranos* 52, 51.

Garcia-Ramon, J. L. 1999 Mycenaean e-u-de-we-ro/Eu-dewelo-/'Having nice late afternoons', in Bennet, J. and Driessen, J. (eds) 1999 *A-na-qo-ta: studies presented to J. T. Killen*, 135–47.

Gerard-Rousseau, M. 1974 Connections in religion between the Mycenaean world and Anatolia, in Crossland, R. A. and Birchall, A. (eds) 1974 *Bronze age migrations in the Aegean. Archaeological and linguistic problems in Greek prehistory*, 164–7.

Gilmour, G. 1993 Aegean sanctuaries and the Levant in the late bronze age. *BSA* 88, 125–34.

Gimbutas, M. 1974 The destruction of Aegean and East Mediterranean urban civilization around 2300 BC, in Crossland, R. A. and Birchall, A. (eds) 1974 *Bronze age migrations in the Aegean. Archaeological and linguistic problems in Greek prehistory*, 129–39.

Goldman, H. 1931 *Excavations at Eutresis in Boeotia.* Cambridge, MA: Harvard University Press.

Graham, J. W. 1987 *The palaces of Crete.* Princeton: Princeton University Press.

Griebel, C. G. and Nelson, M. C. 1998 The Ano Englianos hilltop after the palace, in Davis, J. L. (ed.) 1998a *Sandy Pylos: an archaeological history from Nestor to Navarino*, 97–100.

Gurney, O. R. 1990 *The Hittites.* London: Penguin .

Guterbock, H. G. 1934 Neue Ahhijawa-Texte. *Zeitschrift fur Assyriologie*, 43, 321–7.

—— 1983 The Hittites and the Aegean World, Part 1, The Ahhiyawa Problem reconsidered. *American Journal of Archaeology* 87, 133–43.

Hägg, R. and Marinatos, N. (eds) 1987 *The function of the Minoan palaces: Proceedings of the Fourth International Symposium at the Swedish Institute in Athens*, 10–16 July, 1984, Stockholm.

Hamilakis, Y. 1996 A footnote on the archaeology of power: animal bones from a Mycenaean chamber tomb at Galatas, north-east Peloponnese. *BSA* 91, 153–66.

Hammond, N. G. L. 1974 Grave circles in Albania and Macedonia, in Crossland, R. A. and Birchall, A. (eds) 1974 *Bronze age migrations in the Aegean. Archaeological and linguistic problems in Greek prehistory*, 189–97.

Hansen, O. 1997 KUB XXIII 13: a possible contemporary bronze age source for the sack of Troy/Hisarlik. *BSA* 92, 165–7.

Harding, A. F. 1984 *The Mycenaeans and Europe.* London: Academic Press.

—— and Hughes-Brock, H. 1974 Amber in the Mycenaean world. *BSA* 68, 145–72.

Harrison, A. B. and Spencer, N. 1998 After the palace: the early 'history' of Messenia, in Davis, J. L. (ed.) 1998a *Sandy Pylos: an archaeological history from Nestor to Navarino*, 147–62.

Higgins, R. 1981 *Minoan and Mycenaean art.* London: Thames & Hudson.

Holland, L. B. 1924 The strong house of Erechtheus. *AJA* 28, 142–69.

Hood, S. 1966 An aspect of the Slav invasions of Greece in the early Byzantine period. *Sbornik Naradniho Muzea v Praze* 20, 165–71.

—— 1974 Northern penetration of Greece at the end of the Early Helladic period and contemporary Balkan chronology, in Crossland, R. A. and Birchall, A. (eds) 1974 *Bronze age migrations in the Aegean*, 59–71.

—— 1978 *The arts in prehistoric Greece.* Harmondsworth: Penguin Books.

—— 1995a The Minoan palace as residence of gods and men. *International Cretological Congress* A1, 393–407.

—— 1995b The bronze age context of Homer, in Carter, J. B. and Morris, S. P. (eds) 1995 *The ages of Homer*, 25–32.

Hooker, J. T. 1977 *Mycenaean Greece*. Park Ridge, NJ: Noyes Press.

—— 1979 *The origin of Linear B script. Suplementos a Minos 8*. Salamanca: Ediciones Universidad de Salamanca.

—— 1980 *Linear B: an introduction*. Bristol: Bristol Classical Press.

Hope-Simpson, R. 1966 The seven cities offered by Agamemnon to Achilles. *BSA* 61, 113–31.

—— 1981 *Mycenaean Greece*. Park Ridge, NJ: Noyes Press.

—— and Dickinson, O. 1979 *Gazetteer of Aegean civilization in the bronze age*. Goteborg: Paul Astroms Verlag.

Houwink ten Cate, H. J. 1974 Contact between the Aegean region and Anatolia in the second millennium BC, in Crossland, R. A. and Birchall, A. (eds) 1974 *Bronze age migrations in the Aegean. Archaeological and linguistic problems in Greek prehistory*, 141–61.

Huxley, G. L. 1962 *Early Sparta*. London: Faber.

Iakovidis, S. E. 1983 *Late Helladic citadels on mainland Greece*. Leiden: E. J. Brill.

Immerwahr, S. 1998 Death and the Tanagra larnakes, in Carter, J. B. and Morris, S. P. (eds) 1995 *The ages of Homer*, 109–21.

Jansen, A. G. 2002 *A study of the remains of Mycenaean roads and stations of bronze-age Greece*. Lewiston, NY: Edwin Mellen Press.

Jones, A. H. M. 1967 *Sparta*. Oxford: Basil Blackwell.

—— 1975 *Bronze age civilization: the Philistines and the Danites*. Washington: Public Affairs Press.

Jones, P. V. 1991 *Odyssey* (Introduction). London: Penguin Books.

Karageorghis, V. (ed.) 1991 *The civilizations of the Aegean and their diffusion in Cyprus and the Eastern Mediterranean, 2000–600 BC*. Larnaca: Pierides Foundation.

Kardara, C. 1971 The Isthmian Wall. *AAA* 4, 85–9.

Kase, E. 1973 Mycenaean roads in Phocis. *AJA* 77, 74–7.

Kilian, K. 1988 The emergence of wanax ideology in the Mycenaean palaces. *OJA* 7, 291–302.

Killen, J. T., Melena, J. L. and Olivier, J.-P. (eds) 1987 *Studies in Mycenaean and Classical Greek presented to John Chadwick*. Salamanca: Ediciones Universidad de Salamanca.

King, D. 2002 Helen of Troy's home found. *Minerva* 13, 5–6.

Kirk, G. S. (ed.) 1964 *The language and background of Homer*. Cambridge: Heffer & Sons.

Klein, N. L. 1997 Excavation of the Greek temples at Mycenae by the BSA. *BSA* 92, 247–322.

Klynne, A. 1998 Reconstructions of Knossos: artists' impressions, archaeological evidence and wishful thinking. *Journal of Mediterranean Archaeology* 11 (2), 206–29.

Lang, M. 1969 *The Palace of Nestor at Pylos in Western Messenia, Vol 2. The Frescoes*. Princeton: Princeton University Press.

—— 1995 War story into wrath story, in Carter, J. B. and Morris, S. P. (eds) 1995 *The ages of Homer*, 149–62.

Leaf, W. 1912 *Troy: a study in Homeric geography*. London: Macmillan.

—— 1915 *Homer and history*. London: Macmillan.

Lehmann, J. 1977 *The Hittites: People of a Thousand Gods*. London: Collins.

Littauer, M. 1972 The military use of the chariot in the Aegean in the late bronze age. *AJA* 76, 145–57.

Loader, N. C. 1998 *Building in cyclopean masonry, with special reference to the Mycenaean fortifications on mainland Greece*. Göteborg: Paul Åströms Verlag.

Lolos, Y. G. 1998a *The capital of Nestor and its environs.* Athens: Oionos.

—— 1998b Mycenaean burial at Pylos, in Davis, J. L. (ed.) 1998a *Sandy Pylos: an archaeological history from Nestor to Navarino,* 75–8.

Lord, L. 1941 Blockhouses in the Argolid. *Hesperia* 10, 93–112.

Lorimer, H. 1950 *Homer and the monuments.* London: Macmillan.

Luce, J. V. 1999 *Celebrating Homeric landscapes.* New Haven and London: Yale University Press.

MacKendrick, P. 1962 *The Greek stones speak.* London: Methuen.

McQueen, J. G. 1986 *The Hittites and their contemporaries in Asia Minor.* London: Thames & Hudson.

Mancz, E. A. 1989 An examination of changing patterns of animal husbandry of the Late Bronze and Dark Ages of Nichoria in the Southwestern Peloponnese. PhD thesis, Minnesota. Ann Arbor: University Microfilms International.

Mantzourani, E. K. and Theodorou, A. J. 1991 An attempt to delineate the sea-routes between Crete and Cyprus during the bronze age, in Karageorghis, V. (ed.) 1991 *The civilizations of the Aegean and their diffusion in Cyprus and the Eastern Mediterranean, 2000–600 BC,* 39–54.

Maravelia, A.-A. 2002 The tholos tombs at Mycenae. *Archaeoastronomy* 27, 63–6.

Marazzi, M. 1994 *La societa Micenea.* Rome: Bagatto Libri.

Marinatos, N. 1984 *Art and religion on Thera.* Athens: Mathioulakis.

Marinatos, S. 1936 Le temple géometrique de Dreros. *BCH* 60, 214–85.

Mee, C. 1988 A Mycenaean thalassocracy in the eastern Aegean?, in French, E. B. and Wardle, K. A. (eds) 1986 *Problems in Greek prehistory,* 301–5.

Michelet, J. 1864 *Histoire de France.* Paris: Hachette.

Moore, A. D. and Taylour, W. D. 1999 *Well-built Mycenae. Fascicule 10: The Temple Complex.* Oxford: Oxbow Books.

Morris, S. P. 1995 The sacrifice of Astyanax: Near Eastern contributions to the siege of Troy, in Carter, J. B. and Morris, S. P. (eds) 1995 *The ages of Homer,* 221–45.

Mountjoy, P. A. 1995 *Mycenaean Athens.* Goteborg: Paul Astroms Verlag.

—— 1997 The destruction of the palace at Pylos reconsidered. *BSA* 92, 109–38.

Muhly, P. 1996 Furniture from the shaft graves: the occurrence of wood in Aegean burials in the bronze age. *BSA* 91, 197–212.

Mylonas, G. E. 1966 *Mycenae and the Mycenaean age.* Princeton: Princeton University Press.

—— 1970 The lion in Mycenaean times. *Archaiologika Analekta ex Athinion* 3, 421–5.

—— 1983 *Mycenae rich in gold.* Athens: Ektotike Athenon.

Nilsson, C. M. 1925 *A history of Greek religion.* Oxford: Clarendon Press.

Nilsson, M. P. 1933 *Homer and Mycenae.* Philadelphia: University of Pennsylvania Press.

Ozanne, I. 1997 *Les Myceniens: pillards, paysans et poetes.* Paris: Armand Colin.

Padgett, J. M. 1995 A geometric bard, in Carter, J. B. and Morris, S. P. (eds) 1995 *The ages of Homer,* 389–405.

Page, D. L. 1959 *History and the Homeric Iliad.* Berkeley: University of California Press.

Palaima, T. 1987 Comments on Mycenaean literacy, in Killen, J. T., Melena, J. L. and Olivier, J.-P. (eds) 1987 *Studies in Mycenaean and Classical Greek presented to John Chadwick,* 499–510.

Palmer, L. R. 1961 *Mycenaeans and Minoans: Aegean prehistory in the light of the Linear B tablets.* London: Faber & Faber.

—— 1963 *The interpretation of Mycenaean Greek texts.* Oxford: Oxford University Press.

Palyvou, C. 2002 Central courts: the supremacy of the void, in Driessen, J., Schoep, I. and Laffineur, R. (eds) Monuments of Minos: rethinking the Minoan palaces. Proceedings of the international workshop, Crete of the hundred palaces?, Louvain, 14–15 December 2001. *Aegeum* 23.

Papadopoulos, T. J. 1979 *Mycenaean Achaea*. Göteborg: Paul Åströms Verlag.

Papahatzis, N. 1978 *Mycenae-Epidaurus, Tiryns-Nauplion*. Athens: Clio Editions.

Pausanias (Levi, P., trans.) 1971 *Guide to Greece*. London: Penguin.

Pendlebury, J. 1939 *The archaeology of Crete*. London: Methuen.

Pentreath, G. 1964 *Hellenic traveller: a guide to the ancient sites of Greece*. New York: Crowell.

Persson, A. W. 1942 *New tombs at Dendra near Midea*. Lund: C. Gleerup.

Piteros, C., Olivier, J.-P. and Melena, J. L. 1990 Les inscriptions en Linéaire B des nodules de Thebes (1982): la fouille, les documents, les possibilités d'interpretation. *Bulletin de Correspondance Hellénique* 114, 103–84.

Popham, M. R. 1991 Pylos: reflections on the date of its destruction and on its iron age. *Oxford Journal of Archaeology* 10, 315–24.

Portugali, Y. and Knapp, A. B. 1985 *Cyprus and the Aegean: a spatial analysis of interaction in the seventeenth to fourteenth centuries* BC *in prehistoric production and exchange: the Aegean and eastern Mediterranean*. Los Angeles: Institute of Archaeology, University of California.

Prag, J. and Neave, R. 1999 *Making faces*. London: British Museum Press.

Rehak, P. (ed.) 1995 The role of the ruler in the prehistoric Aegean. Proceedings of a panel discussion presented at the Annual Meeting of the Archaeological Institute of America, New Orleans, Louisiana, 28 December 1992. *Aegeum* 11.

Renfrew, C. 1998 Word of Minos: the Minoan contribution to Mycenaean Greek and the linguistic geography of the bronze age Aegean. *CAJ* 8, 239–64.

Reusch, H. 1956 *Die Zeichnerische rekonstrucktion des frauenfrieses im Bootischen Theben*. Berlin: Akademi-Verlag.

Rieu, E. V. (trans.) 1948 *Homer: The Odyssey*. Harmondsworth: Penguin Books.

—— (trans.) 1950 *Homer: The Iliad*. Harmondsworth: Penguin Books.

Ruiperz, M. S. 1982 Mycenaean dialects, in Harmatta, J. (ed.) 1982 *Proceedings of the Seventh Congress of the International Federation of Societies of Classical Studies*. Budapest: Akademiai Kiado, 2, 461–7

Rutkowski, B. 1986 *The cult places of the Aegean*. New Haven and London: Yale University Press.

—— 1987 Zur Bronzezeitlichen Religion und zu Bestaltungsbräuchen im Ägäischen Raum: Neues über vordorische Tempel und Kultbilder, in Buchholz, H.-G. (ed.) 1987 *Agäische Bronzezeit*, 407–25.

Sammer, J. 2001 Blegen at Pylos. Available at: www.varchive.org/nldag/pylos (accessed 1 February 2004).

Schliemann, H. 1868 *Itaque, le Peloponnèse, Troie. Recherches archæologiques*. Paris.

—— 1880 *Mycenae*. New York: Charles Scribner's Sons.

—— 1881 *Ilios, the city and the country of the Trojans*. New York: Charles Scribner's Sons.

—— 1886 *Tiryns: the prehistoric palace of the kings of Tiryns*. London: John Murray.

Schoep, I. 2002 The state of the Minoan palaces or the Minoan palace-state? in Driessen, J., Schoep, I. and Laffineur, R. (eds) 2002 *Monuments of Minos: rethinking the Minoan palaces*, 15–33.

Schofield, L. and Parkinson, R. B. 1994 Of helmets and heretics: a possible Egyptian representation of Mycenaean warriors on a papyrus from El-Amarna. *BSA* 89, 157–70.

Schuchhardt, C. 1891 *Schliemann's excavations: an archaeological and historical study.* London and New York: Macmillan.

Shaw, M. C. 1996 The bull-leaping fresco from below the Ramp House at Mycenae: a study in iconography and artistic transmission. *BSA* 91, 167–90.

Shear, I. M. 1998 Bellerophon tablets from the Mycenaean world? A tale of seven bronze hinges. *Journal of Hellenic Studies* 118, 187–9.

Shelmerdine, C. W. 1998a The palace and its operations, in Davis, J. L. (ed.) 1998a *Sandy Pylos: an archaeological history from Nestor to Navarino*, 81–96.

—— 1998b The perfumed oil industry, in Davis, J. L. (ed.) 1998a *Sandy Pylos: an archaeological history from Nestor to Navarino*, 101–9.

—— 1998c Umme and Nichoria, in Davis, J. L. (ed.) 1998a *Sandy Pylos: an archaeological history from Nestor to Navarino*, 139–44.

—— 2001 The evolution of administration at Pylos, in Voutsaki, S. and Killen, J. (ed.) 2001 *Economy and politics in the Mycenaean palace states*, 113–28.

—— and Palaima, T. G. (eds) 1984 *Pylos comes alive.* New York: Archaeological Institute of America.

Sherratt, S. 2001 Potemkin palaces and route-based economies, in Voutsaki, S. and Killen, J. (ed.) 2001 *Economy and politics in the Mycenaean palace states*, 214–38.

Shewan, A. 1931 Hittite names. *Classical Review* 45, 2–4.

Simpson, R. 1965 *A gazetteer of Mycenaean sites.* London: University of London Institute of Classical Studies.

—— 1981 *Mycenaean Greece.* Park Ridge, NJ: Noyes Press.

Snodgrass, A. M. 1971 *The dark age of Greece.* Edinburgh: Edinburgh University Press.

—— 1999 Arms and armor of the Greeks. Baltimore: Johns Hopkins University Press.

Sommer, F. 1932 Die Ahhijava-Urkunden. *Abhandlungen der Bayrischen Akademie der Wissenschaften. Neue Folge* 6.

—— 1934 Ahhijava-Frage und Sprachwissenschaft. *Abhandlungen der Bayrischen Akademie der Wissenschaften. Neue Folge* 9.

—— 1937 Ahhijava und kein Ende? *Indogermanische Forschungen* 55, 169–297.

Sourvinou-Inwood, C. 1974 Movements of populations in Attica at the end of the Mycenaean period, in Crossland, R. A. and Birchall, A. (eds) 1974 *Bronze age migrations in the Aegean. Archaeological and linguistic problems in Greek prehistory*, 215–25.

Spengler, O. 1926 *The decline of the West.* New York: Knopf.

Spindler, K. 1994 *The man in the ice.* London: Weidenfeld & Nicolson.

Steffen, H. and Lolling, H. 1884 *Karten von Mykenai.* Berlin: Dietrich Reimer.

Steiner, G. 1964 Die Ahhijawa-Frage heute. *Saeculum* 15, 365–92.

Symeonoglou, S. 1973 *Kadmeia I. Mycenaean finds from Thebes, Greece.* Göteborg: Åström.

—— 1985 *Topography of Thebes from the bronze age to modern times.* Princeton: Princeton University Press.

Taylour, W. 1983 *The Mycenaeans.* London: Thames & Hudson.

Tegyey, I. 1974 Messenia and the catastrophe at the end of Late Helladic IIIB, in Crossland, R. A. and Birchall, A. (eds) 1974 *Bronze age migrations in the Aegean. Archaeological and linguistic problems in Greek prehistory*, 227–32.

Thomson, G. 1949 *Studies in ancient Greek society: the prehistoric Aegean.* London: Lawrence & Wishart.

Traill, D. 1995 *Schliemann of Troy: treasure and deceit.* London: John Murray.

Treherne, P. 1977 Reclaiming heroism for the bronze age. *British Archaeology* 26, 7.

Tritsch, F. J. 1974 The 'Sackers of Cities' and the 'movement of populations', in Crossland, R. A. and Birchall, A. (eds) 1974 *Bronze age migrations in the Aegean. Archaeological and linguistic problems in Greek prehistory*, 233–9.

Tsountas, C. and Manatt, J. 1897 *The Mycenaean age*. Boston: Houghton Mifflin.

Vecchi, I. 2001 The earliest Etruscan cast currency and coinage. *Minerva* 12, 49.

Ventris, M. and Chadwick, J. 1973 *Documents in Mycenaean Greek*. Cambridge: Cambridge University Press.

Vermeule, E. 1972 *Greece in the bronze age*. Chicago: University of Chicago.

Voutsaki, S. and Killen, J. (ed.) 2001 *Economy and politics in the Mycenaean palace states*. Cambridge: Cambridge Philological Society.

Wace, A. 1932 Chamber tombs at Mycenae. *Archaeologia* 82.

—— and Stubbings, F. H. 1962 *A companion to Homer*. London: Macmillan.

Wardle, D. 1998 Does reconstruction help? A Mycenaean dress and the Dendra suit of armour, in French, E. B. and Wardle, K. A. (eds) 1986 *Problems in Greek prehistory*, 469–76.

Wardle, K. A. and Wardle, D. 1997 *Cities of legend: the Mycenaean world*. Bristol: Bristol Classical Press.

Warren, P. M. 1989 *The Aegean civilizations*. Oxford: Phaidon.

—— 1991 The Minoan civilisation of Crete and the volcano of Thera. *Journal of the Ancient Chronology Forum* 4, 29–39.

Werner, K. 1993 *The megaron during the Aegean and Anatolian bronze age*. Jonsered: Paul Åströms Verlag.

Whitelaw, T. 2001 Reading between the tablets: assessing Mycenaean palatial involvement in ceramic production and consumption, in Voutsaki, S. and Killen, J. (eds) 2001 *Economy and politics in the Mycenaean palace states*, 51–79.

Whittaker, H. 1997 *Mycenaean cult buildings*. Bergen: Norwegian Institute at Athens.

Wilamowitz-Moellendorff, U. 1927 *Die Heimkehr des Odysseus*. Berlin.

Willetts, R. F. 1965 *Ancient Crete: a social history from early times until the Roman occupation*. London: Routledge & Kegan Paul.

Wood, M. 1985 *In search of the Trojan War*. London: BBC.

Woodard, R. 1986 Dialectical differences at Knossos. *Kadmos* 25, 49–74.

Wright, H. E. 1968 Climatic change in Mycenaean Greece. *Ant.* 42, 123–6.

Wunderlich, H. 1975 *The secret of Crete*. London: Souvenir Press.

Younger, J. G. 1998 *Music in the Aegean bronze age*. Jonsered: Paul Åströms Verlag.

Zangger, E. 1998a The environmental setting, in Davis, J. L. (ed.) 1998a *Sandy Pylos: an archaeological history from Nestor to Navarino*, 1–13.

—— 1998b The port of Nestor, in Davis, J. L. (ed.) 1998a *Sandy Pylos: an archaeological history from Nestor to Navarino*, 69–74.

INDEX